JUDGING LYOTARD

Best known for his book *The Postmodern Condition*, Jean-François Lyotard is one of the leading figures in contemporary French philosophy. This is the first collection of articles to offer an estimation and critique of his work.

While the various chapters deal with different aspects of Lyotard's writings, they are all concerned with the question of judgement. The importance to Lyotard of judgement, and how it is itself to be judged, is a recurrent theme throughout the entire range of his work. It is perfectly evident in his continuing engagement with the work of Kant. Lyotard's own essay, '*Sensus communis*', which opens this volume, investigates through Kant the presuppositions of judgement. Other essays variously consider how in his writings Lyotard has rendered problematic existing forms of aesthetic, ethical, legal and political judgement.

Judging Lyotard is an important collection that will reintroduce Lyotard to English-speaking audiences. It is of particular interest to students of philosophy, critical theory and literary studies.

Andrew Benjamin is the general editor of the Warwick Studies in Philosophy and Literature. He is Senior Lecturer in Philosophy at the University of Warwick. His books include *Art, Mimesis and the Avant-Garde* and *Translation and the Nature of Philosophy*, which are also published by Routledge.

WARWICK STUDIES IN PHILOSOPHY AND LITERATURE
General Editor: Andrew Benjamin

It used to be a commonplace to insist on the elimination of the 'literary' dimension from philosophy. This was particularly true for a philosophical tradition inspired by the possibilities of formalization and by the success of the natural sciences. And yet even in the most rigorous instances of such philosophy we find demands for 'clarity', for 'tight' argument, and distinctions between 'strong' and 'weak' proofs which call out for a rhetorical reading. Equally, modern literary theory is increasingly looking to philosophy (and other theoretical disciplines) for its inspiration. After a wave of structuralist analysis, the growing influence of deconstructive and hermeneutic reading continues to bear witness to this. While philosophy and literature cannot be seen as subsidiaries of each other, even if philosophy is thought of as 'a kind of writing', much of the most exciting theoretical work being done today exploits their tensions and intertwinings.

The University of Warwick pioneered the undergraduate study of the theoretical coition of Philosophy and Literature, and its recently established Centre for Research in Philosophy and Literature has won wide acclaim for its adventurous and dynamic programme of conferences and research. With this series the work of the Centre is opened to a wider public. Each volume aims to bring the best scholarship to bear on topical themes in an atmosphere of intellectual excitement.

Books in the series include:

ABJECTION, MELANCHOLIA AND LOVE: The work of Julia Kristeva
Edited by John Fletcher and Andrew Benjamin

THE BIBLE AS RHETORIC: Studies in Biblical persuasion and credibility
Edited by Martin Warner

EXCEEDINGLY NIETZSCHE
Edited by David Farrell Krell and David Wood

NARRATIVE IN CULTURE
Edited by Christopher Nash

PHILOSOPHERS' POETS
Edited by David Wood

ON PAUL RICOEUR: Narrative and interpretation
Edited by David Wood

POST-STRUCTURALIST CLASSICS
Edited by Andrew Benjamin

THE PROBLEMS OF MODERNITY: Adorno and Benjamin
Edited by Andrew Benjamin

THE PROVOCATION OF LEVINAS
Edited by Robert Bernasconi and David Wood

WRITING THE FUTURE
Edited by David Wood

JUDGING LYOTARD

Edited by
Andrew Benjamin

London and New York

First published 1992
by Routledge
11 New Fetter Lane, London EC4P 4EE

Simultaneously published in the USA and Canada
by Routledge
a division of Routledge, Chapman and Hall, Inc.
29 West 35th Street, New York, NY 10001

Typeset in 10 on 12 point Baskerville by
Intype, London
Printed in Great Britain by
Biddles Ltd, Guildford

British Library Cataloguing in Publication Data
Judging Lyotard.
(Warwick studies in philosophy and literature)
I. Benjamin, Andrew. II. Series
194

Library of Congress Cataloging in Publication Data
Judging Lyotard/edited by Andrew Benjamin.
p.   cm. – (Warwick studies in philosophy and literature)
Includes bibliographical references and index.
1. Lyotard, Jean-François. I. Benjamin, Andrew E. II. Series.
B2430.L964J83   1992
194–dc20   91–30983
ISBN 0–415–05256–4   ISBN 0–415–05257–2 (pbk)

CONTENTS

CONTENTS

CONTRIBUTORS

ANNE BARRON is a Lecturer in Law at University College London. She is currently completing work on the relationship between legal discourse and the self.

RICHARD BEARDSWORTH is Assistant Professor of Philosophy and Literature at the American University of Paris. He is working on a study of the place of Hegel in the writings of Lyotard and Derrida.

GEOFFREY BENNINGTON is Senior Lecturer in French at the University of Sussex. His recent publications include *Lyotard Writing the Event* (1988) and *Dudding: Des noms de Rousseau* (1991). He is also a leading translator of the works of Jacques Derrida and Jean-François Lyotard.

PAUL CROWTHER is Lecturer in Art History at the University of St Andrews. His publications include *The Kantian Sublime* (1989).

DAVID INGRAM is Associate Professor in Philosophy at Loyola University of Chicago. His publications include *Habermas and the Dialectic of Reason* (1987) and *Critical Theory and Philosophy* (1991).

JOHN KEANE is Director of the Centre for the Study of Democracy and Professor of Politics at the University of Westminster. His publications include *Democracy and Civil Society* (1988) and *The Media and Democracy* (1991).

JEAN-FRANÇOIS LYOTARD teaches at the Collège International de Philosophie and the University of California, Irvine. His most recent publications include *Heidegger and 'the jews'* (1990) and *Leçons sur l'analytique du sublime* (1991).

CONTRIBUTORS

EMILIA STEUERMAN is Lecturer in Sociology at Brunel University. She has published in the area of social theory and is completing a book, *Modernity and Postmodernity*.

BILL READINGS is Associate Professor of Comparative Literature at the Université de Montréal. He has recently published *Introducing Lyotard: Art and Politics* (Routledge, 1991).

INTRODUCTION

Andrew Benjamin

These essays attempt to set out the stakes of judgement. They are to that extent already a judgement. However, with the work of Jean-François Lyotard the specificity of judgement – its sense and its dictate – is itself opened up to philosophical adjudication. It is thus that Lyotard's own text, '*Sensus communis*', continues his attempt to articulate his own philosophy via a systematic engagement with Kant. Here it takes the form of an investigation of the site and the presuppositions of judgement. The status of the community and the nature of judgement figure, in a different way, in the chapters to come.[1]

Part of the strategy of the papers collected here is to sanction the rehearsal of *différends*. The rehearsal involves their display. Time and again the confrontations and strategies marked out by the proper names, Lyotard, Habermas, Rawls or those implicated in the 'topics' (perhaps topoi) of postmodernism, liberalism, democracy, sublime, and *différend*, are presented and repeated. It goes without saying that these presentations resist neutrality. However, more is involved here than the absence of an assessment seeking its ground in an illusory objectivity. There are assessments. Judgement is taking place. The difference is that what is at stake here are the actual stakes of assessment themselves. It is thus that the political is given centrality. Identifying this point of convergence does not entail the effective presence of any essential sense of unanimity. The source of animation is to be located elsewhere. It is found in the problematic status of judgement itself.[2]

Anne Barron undertakes 'to explore the *différend* between Lyotard and Rawls'. The importance of this task is clear. At work within this particular confrontation is both the general question of subjectivity and the specific problem of the legal subject. Lyotard's own writings on justice do not need to emerge in the aporias of liberalism but in the concept of subject and thus of legislation they entail. The problem of power is thereby encountered. Richard Beardsworth offers a long and scrupulous reading of Lyotard's writings on judgement. His work shows an awareness that, inherent in its own activity, is the question of judgement itself. It is this awareness that provides his paper with its acuity. The limit that he identifies in Lyotard's conception of the political opens up the question of the extent to which a politics of judgement is possible.

John Keane is also concerned with the political. However, the argument he offers involves a reading of Lyotard which contends that the *The Postmodern Condition* can give rise to a philosophical allegiance – perhaps in spite of itself – to the project of 'the renewal and deepening of modernity's democratic potential'. A fundamental part of Keane's undertaking is a reinterpretation of this potential. It is thus that he is able to bring the two domains together. The importance of Keane's paper is that it offers a translation of *The Postmodern Condition* into the language of democratic theory. Emilia Steuerman offers a questioning reading of how and to what extent the concerns of Habermas and Lyotard differ. While part of the importance of her paper lies in its presentation of an extremely well-informed summation of this confrontation, it is her conclusion that is of central interest. In it she argues that, rather than there being a point of absolute dislocation between their undertakings, Lyotard can be read as offering a 'radicalization' of the project of modernity. What is at issue here is not compatibility but the possibility of a complementarity that would itself be the result of interpretation and judgement. It is a position similar to Steuerman's that informs Paul Crowther's rigorous interpretation of the philosophical stakes of *Les Immatériaux*, the exhibition organized by Lyotard and held at the Centre Georges Pompidou in 1985. Crowther has attempted to show that a critical reading of the way Lyotard distinguishes (or fails to distinguish) between the sublime and the avant-garde, both in relation to this exhibition and to some of his more general writing on art, can reveal how the aesthetic can be linked to the emancipatory. The aesthetic even in Lyotard's hands can, according to Crowther, come to complement the project of modernity.

David Ingram, in a detailed paper that engages with Hannah Arendt as well as Lyotard, is concerned with the use they both make of Kant. Ingram does not seek to challenge the recourse to

Kant as such but rather is concerned with the use made of it. In other words what is at issue here is the reading of Kant. In drawing on the work of Jean-Luc Nancy, Ingram gestures towards a far more Heideggerian Kant than does either Arendt or Lyotard. For Ingram it is as though Lyotard takes the fragmented as an end in itself. On the other hand, he wants to argue that even in the 'postmodern condition' the copresence of indeterminacy and determinacy still 'remain aspects of one and the same Being'.

The papers by Geoffrey Bennington and Bill Readings take the work of Lyotard outside its own explicit concern and into the domain of literature and film. It goes without saying that they are both acutely aware of the question of genre and thus of the place of a boundary or border raised by their specific undertakings. Bennington uses the occasion of Corneille's *Horace* to take up the specific case of the *différend*. After a meticulous reading of the function of the *différend* – a term announced within Corneille's own text – in the play's logic, Bennington concludes with a reworking of the question of judgement. Now, it is posed back to Lyotard in terms of the question of how is judgement to be judged? The dramatic problem that arises here is the extent to which this question can be answered within the terms that Lyotard himself has provided.

Bill Readings's focus is Herzog's film *Where the Green Ants Dream*. Readings is concerned with the representation as it comes to be played out in Herzog's film of justice and injustice to Aboriginals in contemporary Australia. Central to his undertaking are the presuppositions at stake in the problematic of representation. Indeed, Readings argues that the attempt to represent – limiting justice to 'a correspondence to models' – would involve an injustice. Justice becomes linked therefore to experimentation and thereby to the avant-garde. It is thus that his remarkable reading becomes an argument 'for a refiguration of the political'. Here, as in all the other papers, the political returns as and in the motif of judgement. The same will always have to be said of judgement.

Concluding these introductory notes by returning to Lyotard may seem to involve stepping beyond the confines of the contents of the chapters to come. If, however, Lyotard is taken as a name for a particular type of philosophical thinking, then it could always be argued that judging Lyotard returns to the philosophical problem announced in Heraclitus – namely thinking justice in relation to conflict. The return in this case would be the reiteration of the possibility of an ethics and a politics of heterology that resisted any delimitation by the Same. It is thus that it would bring with it the repetition of an-other philosophical task. While with Lyotard – the thinking marked out by the proper name – this is a task thought through Kant's writings, it also marks – by marking out – a philosophical adventure whose range remains to be fixed. Lyotard's work involves the centrality of a philosophical thinking that can itself be made part of a more generalized subversion of the Same. The name has become complex. It is thus that, because of the doubling of this mark, the name itself can never be self-referential. While it may change what is at stake, it can still be argued that this doubling demands judgement, hence judging Lyotard, therefore Judging Lyotard.

NOTES

1 A note on texts. The problematic status of translation and thus of translations has meant that where a given contributor has wanted, his or her translations have been maintained. In the case of *Le Différend* there should be no difficulties in moving from the French to the English because the book consists of numbered paragraphs and sections. In the case of other texts, where necessary dual references have, for the most part, been supplied. A number of these papers have been published before and therefore it is a pleasure to acknowledge the permission of the editors of *Paragraph, The Review of Metaphysics* and *New Formations* for permitting the republishing of the papers by Lyotard, Ingram and Steuerman.

2 Part of the interest that these papers hold is their use of the 'same' material; be this the 'same' line from one of Lyotard's texts or shared sources, e.g. Nancy's 'Lapsus Judicii'. Their reiteration throughout the papers raises the question not of their evaluation but of how they are to be evaluated. It is this point that needs to be generalized.

1

SENSUS COMMUNIS[1]

Jean-François Lyotard

These will be notes and remarks rather than an exposé: their community, in the sense of their reciprocal action which today we often
call system, will remain to be established. Although they're quite
'common' in the sense of trivial, this time. This preference is certainly imposed on me by lack of preparation but also by the subject.
The lack of preparation proceeds from the subject. No one will ever
be prepared for this *sensus*. Every community will forget and will
have forgotten this *sensus*. *Sensus communis* isn't *intellectio communis*,
gesunde Verstand, good sense, sound understanding, that of communication through the mediation of the concept. Even less is it *intellectio
communitatis*, the intelligence of the community. It's a question of a
community which is unintelligent still – but that *still* presents a
problem. Unintelligent, therefore, that's to say, proceeding without
intellect. And unintellected, too, that's to say one whose concept,
ex hypothesi, will always be missed. And if we are condemned to
think it, think of it, by means of a concept (this is required by
the exposé, the exposition, the Kantian *Exponieren*: 'to reduce a
representation of the imagination to concepts'[2] then the said 'community' of sense, and through sense alone, can be situated or put
in place negatively in the field of the *intellectio* by the exposé, in the
mode of critical thought when it deals with taste: pleasure but
without interest, universality but without concept, finality but without representation of an end, necessity but without argument. Lack
of preparation is the very fact of my subject, *sensus communis*, because
it demands it. It demands that the intellect be at a loss. That it
have got nothing ready. Without a show of readiness. Of which it's
incapable, because it is spontaneous activity, *Selbststätigkeit*. This
sensus and this *communis* appear to be ungraspable at their exposition.
The concept's other. So a good opportunity for metaphysics.

The understanding ought to stay disarmed, right up to its touch of this sense. Immunized against itself, to let itself be touched by, and to touch this *commun*. But its 'spontaneity', that activity whose principle is only in itself, its authoritarian munificence, the generosity of its office, of its *munus*, which is to synthesize by itself, off its own bat, cannot accept the sharing out of the munitions, the putting into common ownership of syntheses. The understanding will always find itself again in the community, it will refer the community back to its own power. It can only, at most, declare of its own accord that no, there *is* a synthesizing outside it, another way of synthesizing. But even in the apparent disavowal that the understanding makes of its activity, in the apparent modesty of this negative analytics (as one speaks of negative theology), its arrogance in distributing roles, in being master of communities can only continue to betray itself. Let's make no mistake about it: if thought, in so far as it is philosophical, consists in thinking by concepts, then with the *sensus communis*, philosophy touches on that thought which is not philosophical, touches on it precisely because it cannot handle it. And it's that that should be understood in *sensus*. It is by chance that the adverb *sensim*, which should mean 'so that it can be felt', mostly means 'imperceptibly'? A *sensus* imperceptible to the *intellectus*. A community imperceptible to the community or argumentable syntheses. With the question of this sense we are, in particular, at the confines of literature and philosophy, of art and philosophy. These confines were called *Aesthetics* in eighteenth-century Europe. It's a matter of tact or tangent, at least for philosophy. Philosophy has difficulty in making contact with the *sensus*. It wants, by vocation, by hypothesis, to keep itself intact from the *sensus*, or the *sensus* itself takes off at a tangent. But also it wants to think everything, to think according to its rules, intellection, and make no exception for the unintelligent and the untouchable.

So philosophy can only, as I can only in making this exposition, register that the concept, my concept, doesn't manage to touch the *sensus communis*. This sense is too near, or too far. More likely, this difficulty isn't even a matter of distance, of interval. This *sensus* isn't indeed situated in that space and time which the concept uses to know objects, in the space-time of knowledge. Nor in the space-time which sensibility in the first *Critique* gets ready (precisely) for knowledge by means of the schemata. For if there is a *sensus communis* it is made necessary by another necessity, another universality, and another finality than those which knowledge requires. So that even using these words gives rise to amphiboly. For the cognitive community (the scientific one in its most determinate modality), these words necessity, universality, finality, are names of categories which can be defined and exhibited, applicable in the space-time of experience. For the community of sense, and by sense, they designate those movements of the imagination (called by Kant reflection), which proceed obscurely (but this obscurity is called so by the understanding). Kant says: in comparison, through *Vergleichung*. It's this comparing that puts the intelligence in disarray, makes it unprepared in the face of the *sensus* which rounds it off, and that's what cannot be forestalled. It has to be said clearly: the *sensus* doesn't give rise to an experiencing, in the Kantian sense. The aesthetics of the beautiful isn't the aesthetics of truth. Taste teaches nothing about the object, it has no object, no referent. If there are forms in play in these two aesthetics, those of the first *Critique* are finalized towards knowledge, those of the third towards pure pleasure. And everything leads one to think that these last, more purely reflexive, more constitutive or productive, are diverted and tamed by the former. So it's *not* really impossible to forestall the *sensus communis*. The mind will always have got itself pre-pared (after the fact, naturally), will always be able to comment on it, take it with itself into the mental community, into its authority, and begin it again. And yet with this common sense it's indeed a question of something 'uncommon', out of the ordinary, of something singular according to intelligence.

> We often give to the judgment, if we are considering the result rather than the act of its reflection, the name of a sense, and we speak of a sense of truth, or of a sense of decorum, of justice, etc. And yet we know, or at least we ought to know, that these concepts cannot have their place in sense.
>
> (*KUK* §40, beginning; *CJ* p. 135)

Although in short we know that this sense isn't a sense at all. However, Kant adds, even to that common understanding, to that minimal intelligence presupposed in every man, to the least privileged intelligence, the most vulgar but the most distinctive of the human mind, must be rendered this 'mortifying [*krankende*] honour' of being called 'common sense'. Mortification: the understanding is demoted to a sense. Honour: this descent to the lowest is perhaps a new ascent to the well-springs of the capacity to judge, presupposed in every activity, intellectual even, and voluntary.

3

That may be what's at stake in the *Critique of the Aesthetical Judgement*. There would be judgement before the concept, and even before the schema, before that operation of synthesis, which is however very elementary, which brings together the pure diversity of sense-data (their matter) into unities which are apprehensible, reproducible, recognizable, and offers them as an experience to the grasp, to the *Ergreifen*, to the *Begreifen* of the categories of understanding. Some judgement, then, for Kant in the synthetic act which would not consist in determining regularities, as in the cognitive law, nor even in preparing them in sensible matter, by constructing spatio-temporal sequences which form objects in experience. A kind of non-denotative synthesis, not turned towards the object, and thus called strictly subjective, that is exclusively felt (there's the *sensus*, which is feeling). This sentimental synthesis, this judgement which is feeling, deserves to be attributed to a *sensus*, unlike good sense. For with this *sensus* we are sent back to the most humble, the most 'common' level of judgement, in a 'state of mind' which as yet owes nothing (nothing as yet, or already nothing) to knowledge and its intrigues.

And in the same way (turning now towards the other elder sister, the other great faculty, not the theoretical this time but the practical), there would be judging, synthesizing, independent of desire, whether it be empirical, as need or penchant, or transcendental, as pure will. That is to say, unlike every desire (I would add, although it's not Kantian: whether it is conscious or unconscious), a judgement not having 'knowledge' of its end. One could say: a blind judgement, quite blind, without even that 'clairvoyance' about what it hasn't got which is necessarily supposed by the psychoanalytical hypothesis of the 'fulfilling of desire' in the symptom, and by the accompanying hypothesis that the said symptom can be deciphered thanks to this aim (even if it were to be illusory) for fulfilment. A judging blind to every end, but for this very reason, not a symptom. Or, as Kant says, 'disinterested'. Without interest in liberty nor in pleasure in the usual sense. A state of mind that owes nothing as yet (nothing as yet or already no more) to the intrigues of willing, whatever it be. This feeling (since this *sensus* is sentimentality), when it is a question of tasting beauty, is precisely a feeling of pleasure, but a pleasure which doesn't come to fill up a lack not to fulfil any desire at all. A pleasure before any desire. This aesthetic pleasure is not the purpose of a purposiveness experienced (or not experienced) beforehand as desire. It has nothing whatsoever to do

4

with an end or purpose. It *is* finality, purposiveness itself, which had no end, no purpose in front of it and no lack behind it. So an instantaneous purposiveness, immediate, not even meditated by the diachronic form of the internal sense, nor by our way of remembering and anticipating. Certainly we (understanding, and reproductive imagination, memory) remember this instant and we will try to reiterate it. We will try to integrate it, to give it a place in our intrigues, our narratives, our explanations, all our arrangements of every kind. But it will have been independent of them. On the occasion of a form, which itself is only an occasion for feeling, the soul is seized by a small happiness, unlooked for, unprepared, slightly dynamizing. It is an animation of an *anima* there on the spot, which is not moving towards anything. It's as if the mind were discovering that it can do something other than will and understand. Be happy without ever having asked for it or conceived it. An instant which will seem very long, measured by the clock of intrigue, but which is not in the purlieus of its timekeeping; a flash made of delayings (you tarry near beauty), a form, a little synthesis of matters in space-time, made sense, *sensus*. A sense that has to be thought of as absolutely singular. The occasion is the case. And it would be this absolutely singular *sensus* which would be *communis*. So the finality, the purposiveness is end-less, purposeless, without a concept of its end. This is why the feeling of the beautiful has nothing to do with perfection, with this completion that *Volkommenheit* connotes.

Here, it is no longer the philosophy of intellect which can't touch this *sense*, it is our occupational willing, our philosophy of will, of the infinite will established in the west at least from Descartes and Hobbes down to Nietzsche and Freud, to make no mention of the political all-comers bearing very diverse names. What can a *communitas* be which isn't knitted into itself by a project? this philosophy whispers to us. Which has no Idea of what it wants to be and must be? Not having the Idea of its unity even as a horizon? These are false questions, directed by a line we haven't questioned: by the prejudice according to which what comes first is the diverse, chaos (matter, according to Kant himself and many others), and according to which a principle is needed to unify it even if only into elementary forms. A gravitation, an interaction, I don't know, which can make a One out of this multiplex. Desire, the will: this is one of the names of this principle of interaction and integration. And pleasure of happiness: this will be when the desired, the will having been achieved, the synthesis is made between what one is and what one wants or desires to be. Even if it is explained to us that that doesn't exist, that it's always missed, that this happiness of fulfilment is a trap – that changes nothing about the principle that community is the desire experienced by diversity.

And as we know, this picture tells a story. With the willing of the will, there is displayed a time, memory, and project, heritage and programme. A narrative.

But if there really is a *sensus communis*, then it is a pleasure which hasn't been, will not have been, obtained by desire or willing, which hasn't come to a conclusion, or belted together the two ends of an odyssey, not even for a moment. It will not have the character of a return, of a knot. And the *common* of this *sensus* will not have been a matter of project. This feeling creates no chronology, nor even a simple diachrony. It's not a question of an historical and social community which people of taste or artists, any more than people of science and will, form or want to form. It's not a question of 'culture', or pleasure shared in, through and for culture. And there is no progression promised to this pleasure of the beautiful, precisely because it isn't desired.

As you see, that makes a lot of 'no's and 'not's.

I quoted from paragraph 40 of the third *Critique*: 'We often give to the judgement, if we are considering the result rather than the act of its reflection, the name of a sense.' Sense and result. *Sensus* is reflection, the faculty of judging reflexively, but considered afterwards, and not when it's operating, it is a little like an instance of sensibility. Now at the end of the same paragraph:

> I say that . . . the aesthetical judgment rather than the intellectual may bear the name of a sense common to all (*eines gemeinschaftlichen Sinnes*), if we are willing to use the word 'sense' of an effect of mere reflection upon the mind, for then we understand by sense the feeling of pleasure.
>
> (*KUK* §40; *CJ* p. 138)

The faculty of judgement acts reflexively, according to Kantian vocabulary. The result of this operation (but probably it isn't an 'operation'), its effect on the mind, is the feeling of pleasure. The *sensus* is, then, like the seat of a capacity for pure reflection. A seat established afterwards. We know that Kant doesn't feel happy about assigning a place of residence to the intermediate faculty in the layered geography of the faculties – doubly layered (faculties of the soul, faculties of knowledge), each faculty being endowed with its a priori principle and with its domain or territory of reference – in this transcendental geography; the intermediate faculty: that is, the 'go-between' whose mission it is to make the link between intellection and desire, between theoretical understanding and practical reason. This capacity to negotiate is called, in the soul, the faculty of pleasure and pain, and in knowledge is called simply the faculty of judging.

Yet one judges everywhere, in every domain, and in all of them there is some *sensus* at work, a state of mind, even if it knows and wills. For the one that knows, Kant only explains things occasionally. There is, however, and this is transcendentally required, a feeling of pleasure, a euphoria associated with knowledge, that is, with the co-operation of sensibility and understanding required by knowledge, a subjective euphoria from the subsuming of an intuition under a concept, which guarantees objectivity. This is transcendentally required to such an extent that Kant has recourse to it in his deduction of the *sensus communis* in paragraph 21 of the third *Critique* (I shall come back to this). But this sentimental aspect of knowledge is kept rather clandestine. The transcendental *sensus* of ethical practice, on the contrary, has had considerable success, as we know, via the analysis of *Achtung*, of respect, in the second *Critique*. The fact remains that if we judge in ethics as we do in knowledge, the faculty of judging, the 'go-between' must be in action here as well as in aesthetics. But it is hidden, and stays so. The intermediary erases itself, slides away; the faculty of judging leaves the office of synthesis to its elder sisters.

Bringing together is the mission of the concept and/or of the reproductive imagination (the schema) in knowledge as such, and the mission of reason in moral practice. The preliminary work of feeling is operating more openly in the latter case, in the name of respect (and in the name of its counterpart, humiliation of the empirical individual's presumption and self-love). But it is kept at the level of 'motive', of *Triebfeder*, of the spring which projects an impure act of will, strung up in pathological motivations, towards the pure moral law. In this way, the faculty of judgement in its most humble form, feeling (here, pleasure and pain, for the feeling of obligation is mixed), is brought down, as in the case of the imaginative schema, to the rank of a mere sketch of a synthesis; is reduced by cricial analysis to the role of mere precursor and sign of the veritable a priori ethical synthesis, of the true condition for morality which is not obligation but law, the free synthesis of 'thine' action and of universal liberty, free, thanks to the free play of the 'as if', of the *so daß* between the prescription to 'act' and the universal principle of legislation valid for a community of reasonable and practical beings (also called 'persons').

So the *sensus* and the *commune* are necessarily separated in the case of knowledge and in the case of ethics. The cognitive community or the community of people of learning is, as Habermas would say, 'discursive'; or as K. O. Apel would put it, 'one of argument'. It is mediated by the agreement, required pragmatically, about the rules for establishing a true judgement. And the ethical community, if there is one, can only indeed be an ideal of practical reason, a suprasensible society formed from beings with free will; but even so, it too is mediated by the recognition of the suprasensible character of freedom, by the Idea (which is an Idea of reason, and not a concept of understanding) of a moral law which contains tautologically, so to say, the principle of this community in its determinateness. In any case, it isn't feeling, nor respect which makes up an ethical community, nor even which requires it. Obligation only requires community because the law, whose feeling obligation is, contains this community in its definition.

I mean that there is no moral *sensus communis*, but only a reason which is common in its practical ethical use. Or again, the seat of the common, when it is a question of being just, isn't in the feeling (even if the latter can forewarn us), but in an 'unfathomable' concept not found in experience: the Idea of freedom. Ethical community can't be immediate, it must be mediate, mediated by an Idea of reason. So that it is subject a priori (but that must be argued for, proved) to a progression which is the progression of susceptibility (*Empfänglichkeit*) to the Ideas of reason. This is the question of culture, of the culture of the will, that is of reason in its practical use. In the end, there is only a possibility of progress and progression if there is a concept, if the *ambitus* (the register) of what is conceived (through the understanding and through reason) becomes wider, and richer. Now it is constitutive of the concept that it develops in its scope (its quantity) or its tenor (its quality): it is impelled by maximization, says Kant. Haunted by the infinite. It is polarized by the principle of something suprasensible, whether cosmological or ethical. This is also why the feeling which can serve as a *signum* of the progress of humanity towards the best is not the immediate pleasure of the beautiful, and can't be (even if the beautiful is a passable *analogon* for the good), but is the feeling of the sublime, which far from being immediate and simple is divided in itself and needs the representaion of the Idea of freedom, and so the development of pure practical reason. History too has the infinite in it only through the concept.

But what might an aesthetical suprasensible be? The *sensus communis*, if we take *sensus* in the sense of feeling, cannot and must not be mediated by a concept. There, in aesthetics, the pure faculty of judgement, the capacity of bringing together the manifold without having the rule (concept) nor the law (Idea) of that bringing together – this is the definition of reflexivity – must operate without any additions, within the modesty of an immediate synthesis, the form, which makes the subjective synthesis, the feeling, immediately. In other words, reason in the broad sense, the theoretical faculty of *intellectio*, the practical faculty of *acta*, has no interest in it.

We have never finished with the true and the just, but the beautiful does not develop itself. The feeling which it is does not belong to process.

The paragraph in the first *Critique*, the Dialect of Cosmological Ideas, which points out three interests of reason, theoretical, practical and popular, needs analysing in detail. These interests can be contradictory. What is meant by popular? What we call political, at least in part: in the part of it concerning the 'public' or *Öffentlichkeit*. But aesthetics which is certainly concerned in this latter, isn't dependent on it, not at all, through its principle. For through its principle, on principle, aesthetics is not susceptible to any interest. Reason, be it popular, practical or theoretical, can find no advantage in it. Of course this is because the aesthetic feeling isn't mediated, whether by concepts or Ideas, and because it doesn't obey the impulse which drives the concept to extend the register of its domain of application. Because this feeling isn't in the service of any concept, isn't even subject to that kind of conceivable time that is the schema. In the pleasure of the beautiful, feeling is enough, absolutely enough. It announces nothing further. Is of no use to anything. A *go-between* in the process of coming and going, transmitting no message. *Being* the message. A pure movement which compares, which afterwards we put under house arrest in a seat called *sensus*. But this house arrest is itself only analogical. One that we project on an object when we call it beautiful. But the object is merely an occasion. It is still impossible to snap shut in a name

9

the capacity for reflection by and for itself, and the objectivity of beauty is still impossible to establish.

As for the *common* of this 'sense', the 'community' or communicability which qualifies it, that is certainly not to be observed in experience. It is certainly not what we call a 'public'. Not the society of art-lovers in museums, galleries, concerts, theatres, or who today look at reproductions of works (and, I may add, of landscapes) in their homes. The *sensus* must be protected from anthropologization. It is a capacity of mind. And yet . . ., only if the mind itself isn't taken aback, interrupted by pure aesthetic pleasure. Only if the anima or the animation procured by the beautiful doesn't put the mind in a state of suspense. Only if, to sum up, only if the mind isn't limited to the office and the exercise of intrigues.

So a secret *common*, that is, put aside, separated, secessioned, and as the expression goes in Latin *se-curus*, put out of reach of *cura*, of care, a common with no cares. *Sorgenfrei*, as Heidegger would not have written in 1927. Kant calls anima, soul, this mind free of care.

We know how Kant comes to detect this common in the analysis of taste. If pleasure is aesthetical, it is disinterested and without concept, but it also has to be universal in its quantity, unlike a particular preference, and it has to be necessary in its modality, unlike the pleasure which can be procured by an object in general (this pleasure is only possible, and the modality of its synthesis with the object will only be problematical), it has to be necessary also in opposition to the pleasure procured by an agreeable object (where the modality of the judgement made is assertoric: *de facto*, that pleases me).

If it were not to fulfil these conditions of necessity and universality, the first relative to the enunciation, the second to what is enunciated, a judgement of taste, the aesthetical feeling could never be isolated as such. And there would be no art because there would be no pure pleasure, independent of empirical or transcendental interests.

We are satisfied by an object which we find agreeable. But we don't require that this satisfaction be shared by everyone, nor posited as inescapable.

This said, neither the necessity of judging like this, nor the universality of the attribution of the predicate 'beautiful' to *this* rose, can be deduced. Kant says, about universality, that the singular judgement of taste is *enjoined (ansinnen)* on everyone; and about necessity, that it is not given apodictically, as the conclusion of a piece of reasoning, but as an *example*, alway singular, for a rule or norm of aesthetical feeling to which everyone should give their consent, but which always remains to be found; which is never found.

Before specifying, as far as an exposé can, the nature of this consent, enjoined and promised at the same time, just one observation: the analysis of quantity and that of modality, respectively the universality and the necessity of the feeling of the beautiful, converge towards a strange pole, 'surprising', says Kant, the *Einstimmung* or the *allgemeine Stimmung:* the beautiful must be declared in one single voice, in a chorus. This notion of *Stimme*, of voice, is introduced in paragraph 8, and is not developed. Should it be understood as what is voiced, or vocalized, what sounds 'before' any consonant, before any conceptual synthesis? It can also be understood as a unity of votes in an election, here that of a singular pleasure raised to the dignity of pure pleasure, of universal validity. What voice, what voices are concerned here? Whose are this or these voices? Those of empirical individuals? But what would these be doing in the transcendental determining of taste? I'm not saying that the Kantian text doesn't ask in passing for this anthropological reading. But the contrary recommendations – to stay inside strict critical analysis – are many and seem to me to exclude understanding and hearing these voices as if they were phenomena. It's not a matter of social consensus, and even less of one obtained by ballot. The beautiful doesn't get elected like Miss World.

But the preliminary observation that I wanted to make is the following: the analysis of the quantity (universal) and the analysis of the modality (necessity) of the aesthetic judgement proceed by means of the same mainspring, I would say the mainspring of the *other*, or to use the word with which Kant designates the operator of reflection, the mainspring of *comparison*, of *Vergleichung*. A sort of 'pragmatics' (excuse the word), for lack of something better, comes here to take over from the failing of the logical approach. For if the necessity is not apodictic, what then can it be? Exemplary, says Kant, and this makes us reflect on what an example is in transcendental logic. The state of the subject which is called taste, pleasure or beauty is a paradigm, a model for itself, at the same time that as a mere example it cannot turn itself into a model, fix itself as a thinkable Idea (to tell the truth, it can; there is an ideal of the beautiful; but the price paid is that an Idea of reason and an empirical concept are allowed to intervene in taste, and thus it loses its exemplary purity, its singularity).

And if universality isn't in the attribution of a predicate to the subject of the statement, that is to say to the object of knowledge, what can it be? Subjective, answers Kant. And that doesn't mean individual, that means: relative merely to the relationships of the faculties with each other in the subject. If there is a 'pragmatics', that is an examination of sense in terms of its destination (taste constitutes an example *for* the subject), then the senders and the receivers in action in this destination, in this *Bestimmung*, are the constitutive instances of the supposed 'subject'; imagination, understanding, at least. And the *Einstimmung*, that would be the chorus made up by these voices. A singular chorale, made piece by piece, one flower of vocal polyphony, another flower, then another, their suite not making a melodic intrigue, each one sufficing for itself in the internal comparison of voices, the suite only being constructed afterwards, to make a whole. The comparison doesn't take place from one chord to the next, but on each occasion between the sounds.

Here is where the true difficulty of understanding (and hearing) the *sensus communis* begins, once the anthropological temptation has been chased away. That it really is a question of this harmonic agreement for Kant, when he doesn't let himself be carried away by the anthropological reading of what he is trying to think, can find a proof in paragraph 21 of the third *Critique*, where the authorization to presuppose the *sensus communis* is extorted, one might say, from reason, by means of a demonstration whose amplitude is surprising, in that it goes back to the communicability of every piece of knowledge of an object and of the *sensatio* (of the *Stimmung*) which accompanies it, and even which precedes it 'in' the subject.

A demonstration constructed against Hume, on antiscepticism. If knowledge isn't an empty subjective game, then it must be communicable. But besides, and first of all, knowledge wouldn't be possible if the faculties in action to produce it didn't come into harmony (here is the *Stimmung*) one with another, 'on the inside' of the subject, so to say. This harmony must not be less communicable than knowledge itself, since it produces knowledge.

What does this harmony, this agreement consist in? In a proportion between the respective activity of the faculties which cooperate in knowledge. Now this proportion varies according to the objects of knowledge. (I imagine here a sort of transcendental

chemistry of the faculties' combinations: the proportion of imagination, of sensibility, of understanding, of reason isn't the same when
what is at stake is to establish a truth of experience, or a dialectical
argument, or a pedagogical rule or a moral principle. But we shall
see that it is a question of music rather than of chemistry. Of an
interior music. Or better: like an intimacy of sounds.) The subject
(but what subject – that's the point, as we shall see) is warned by
its state about this variable proportion, or rather the feeling is at
the same time this state and the signalling of this state. The *sensus*
is *index sui*. This is the voice, the *Stimme:* the subject gives voice to
itself 'before' it sees itself or conceives of itself.

(I shall not develop this point here, though it seems to me highly
important. It is always said that time, the internal sense, is the
auto-affection of the subject. But the pure sentimental *sensus* is an
auto-affection even more pure, a kind of transcendental coenes-
thesia, which 'precedes' all diachronization. The agreements, the
chords are only organized in a melodic line secondarily, through
the organization of rhythm into diachronic time. And there is not
even a harmonic rule or tempering to predetermine (inside themselves) their beauty or their singular exemplarity. The proportion
Kant speaks of is not harmonic, architectural, because it isn't the
object of a concept. It is a 'proportion' of timbres, of colourings, of
vocal lights.)

So what is given voice in taste is the division of the subject as a
division acc(h)orded for one moment, called together in convocation. The demonstration in paragraph 21 finishes like this, I gloss:
'it is necessary', it is quite necessary that, in the scale of all the
possible proportions among the faculties in action for a piece of
knowledge (always in the broader sense), there should be one that
is 'more appropriate'. Appropriate to what? Kant says: to the knowledge which is in question. It seems this is to give back an unexpected
and unwelcome privilege to the cognitive function, the referential
and determinant one (as if the concept came back into the description of the *sensus*). If, however, we give to the word 'knowledge' the
broad sense which it must have, and which it often has in Kant,
especially in this text, the 'appropriateness' of the said exemplary
proportion can only be applied to this proportion itself, in the state
in which the subject finds itself when such knowledge occurs, and
of which, Kant reminds us straightaway, only feeling warns the
supposed subject in 'animating' it, in waking it up. This feeling is
nothing other than this animation. Conclusion: it follows that this

agreement, I daren't say and one must not say, perfect, but beautiful, or about beauty, or in beauty, ex-cellent like the knowledge
which is its occasion, is a priori universally communicable. And as
the *sensus communis* is necessarily presupposed in the communicability of this agreement, since this *sensus* is only the name given
to the 'seat' (invented afterwards) where these proportions, including the excellent one, are woven, it is indeed reasonable to accept
the *sensus communis*.

I've said: the authorization to accredit a *sensus communis* is 'torn'
from reason by this demonstration. An uncertainty remains, or a
confusion about the identity of the terms put into common ownership by the *sensus*: is it a question of faculties, as I am claiming, or
of individuals? Written out in ordinary language, with all the risks
that implies, the conclusion means that, seen transcendentally,
every empirical individual is necessarily the possible seat of such a
euphony (rather than euphoria). And indeed, that isn't too difficult.
This is part and parcel of the general logic of the critique, in the
very notion of the a priori condition of possibility. Kant does not
say that the said euphony is necessary to every piece of knowledge.
He says that a proportion among faculties is necessary for every
piece of knowledge, and that it is necessary for one among all the
possible proportions to be pre-eminently euphonious. It happens or
doesn't happen empirically, and with anyone. But it must be able
to happen.

We could stop here, have done here, on this strictly transcendental basis for the *sensus communis*. But the matter is a bit more
complicated, or, which is the same thing, the demonstration in
paragraph 21 is rather too a priori; I could even say: a bit too much
out of the first *Critique*. What makes matters more complicated in
the third *Critique* is the way the appeal (let's call it the appeal) for
euphony is described: the summons, the *Ansinnen* and the wait, the
promise of euphony. More precisely, each individual internal (or
subjective) agreement, each judgement of beauty, each state of taste
appeals to the agreement of others, in its individuality. And it seems
here to be indeed a question of empirical individuals. Constitutively
so, it seems. This appeal constitutes that which makes aesthetic
pleasure into a pleasure distinct from every other pleasure. Every
other pleasure, including the case where they are at first glance
mixed in with the beautiful, is in the charge of an interest: an
inclination, a theoretical or practical interest. The appeal to the

other, contained in the beautiful, can itself give rise to a mistake about what is meant. And it did not fail to happen.

The appeal can be taken to be directed by an inclination to society. In paragraph 41, Kant protests against this confusion, which is almost the rule in English aesthetics until Burke, and which will be spread rapidly, after him, by Schiller, right up to the neo-Kantian and neo-neo-Kantian readings of the third *Critique:* it is said that taste prepares, or helps on, sociability. However, Kant writes, very clearly: 'This interest that indirectly attaches to the beautiful through our inclination to society, and consequently is empirical, is of no importance for us now' (*KUK* §41; *CJ* p. 140). And he goes so far in disconnecting the 'for the other' or the 'to the other' which are contained in the empirical *sensus* from any empirical nature that in the following paragraph he eliminates from pure taste everything connected with interest which could enter into it. Starting with the taste for human art, always suspected of 'vanity', of 'trickery', of procuring 'social joys' (*CJ* p. 142), and an impure content. A work is always the subject of a 'mediate interest' (*CJ* p. 142), turned towards its author's talent, an interest which has a priori nothing to do with the aesthetic feeling. On the contrary, the aesthetical pleasure which nature procures seems free from such mix-ups. But even there it will be necessary to purify the feeling that can be had from natural beauties, by extracting that element in pleasure which comes from what Kant calls the 'charms' which these beauties offer.

I shall not say anything here about these 'charms' except that what saves us from them, and sufficiently well, if Kant is to be believed, is the contemplation of 'beautiful *forms*' (*CJ* p. 141). Form is immediately felt, and it thus without any possible interest, since interest requires a finalized mediation. Form is without charm. What I won't say on this subject is that as a consequence, if disinterest is formal, then charm is material, that it is matter which exerts a charm on the mind, colour, timbre. (This division is worked out in paragraph 14: line against colour, harmony and composition against timbre. Kant resists with all his might an aesthetic of matter. At least when beauty is in question. For the sublime, it's another matter.) So again pleasure in landscape has to have expunged from it what attracts us to it, empirical individuals that we are.

This lawsuit brought against matter, even natural matter, sheds light on the constitutive function that going via the other has in the judgement of taste. The attraction for a red or for the timbre of the breeze in a poplar tree isn't communicable immediately a priori, it isn't universalizable without a concept. No more than liking spinach. Each of us can only demand (enjoin, expect) unanimity about forms. Why? Because in sensation form is that by which the imagination can put itself in agreement with the understanding. The understanding has no materiological competence. It is only the principle of rules. Form is a rule sketched out in material presence. Relying on form, we rely on the universality of the potential rules of the understanding. But didn't I say that the aesthetical forms of the third *Critique* are precisely not the schemas of the first, that they are freed from any cognitive destination?

Indeed the euphony of the two faculties will be the purer, the freer form is from concept, and thus independent of schematic structures. Because it's not right, either, that form should be subsumed directly under the concept, for that belongs to the constitution of objectivity; but it is necessary for taste that form, however dissonant it is in relation to the concept, however much a stranger, in its free production, from what the understanding can regulate, should none the less indicate (even in its dissonance) a possible task for the faculty of rules. And this is how form animates that faculty, one would like to say: how form provokes, excites the understanding. The dissonant agreement, the lack of harmony don't scare Kant, on the contrary.

Thus beautiful form doesn't just need to emancipate itself from matter, but also from the concept. The more distant (I would even say: improbable) is the resemblance of the form to the schema and with it to the concept, the more free is beauty, the purer is taste. And thus, the more communicable, since it is guaranteed against any cognitive interest. The imagination producing forms freed from matter and concept, but forms which still invoke possible rules, this invocation or evocation being the secret of the true convocation of the faculties the one by the other, as faculties which make up the subjective euphony. Now to make certain of this formal purification is the mission of the comparison with the other person's judgement.

But under the *sensus communis* we must include the idea of a sense *common to all (die Idee eines gemeinschaftlichen Sinnes)*, i.e. of a faculty of judgment which, in its reflection, takes account (*a priori*) of the mode of representation of all other men in thought, in order, as it were, to compare its judgment with the collective reason of humanity, and thus to escape the illusion arising from the private conditions that could be so easily taken for objective, which would injuriously affect the judgment.

(*KUK* §40; *CJ* p. 136)

And Kant adds, as if to aggravate the evidently anthropological character of this definition of the universalizing procedure, which to my great irritation seems completely to ruin the transcendental reading which I have just suggested: 'This is done by comparing our judgment with the . . . judgments of others.' After which, Kant continues on about the famous 'maxims of common sense', to think on one's own, to think by putting oneself in any other's place, always to think in agreement with oneself. Maxims of which the second, called the maxim of 'enlarged thought', is expressly assigned to the faculty of judgement.

The dossier seems heavy against my thesis or my hypothesis, according to which the common is transcendental, that it is an agreement, an uncertain polyphony, whose euphony isn't measurable, preparable, but which most assuredly can 'take place', as the phrase goes, on occasion, between faculties each endowed with their own timbre. The articles in this dossier suggest something quite different: the universality which is enjoined and promised in every judgement of taste is obtained by each human being when he compares his judgement with that of all the others. 'This is done', writes Kant, 'by comparing . . .'.

Let's look at it more closely. What is obtained, first of all. The idea of a common sense, and you know what a Kantian Idea is, it's a concept for which there is no corresponding intuition in experience. In paragraph 8, Kant writes; 'The universal voice [*die allgemeine Stimme*] is, therefore, only an idea' (*KUK* §8; *CJ* p. 51). The 'only' indeed says that there is no question of finding in experience a reality which corresponds to the Idea. Unless by succumbing to illusion, to transcendental appearance, against which all the Dialectic of the first *Critique* constructed the powerful defence mechanisms of the paralogisms, the antinomies, and the impossibilities of pure reason. But none of this will have stopped all well-meaning people, philosophers, politicians, theoreticians of art from joyously going in between this impermeability of the Idea to experience.

In the third *Critique*, the antinomy of taste is organized in the same way round the status as Idea of the *sensus communis*. Thesis: there is no concept in the judgement of taste. If there were one, it

17

would be possible to decide on the beautiful by means of a proof, by having recourse to the presentation of 'realities' in experience. Antithesis: concepts are involved in the judgement of taste, otherwise we would not even 'claim for our judgment the necessary assent of others' (*KUK* §56; *CJ* p. 184).

This seems to lead to the conclusion that the appeal to the *sensus communis* can be imputed to the part of the composition of taste which is the concern of the faculty of conception, that it draws its *communitas* from the necessity and the universality proper to the concept. And this also confirms the privilege accorded to form over matter in the purification of aesthetic pleasure. But the Antinomy also explains that this concept remains indeterminate and indeterminable; that is, without a possible intuitive proof in presentation, and that it is thus not a concept of understanding but a concept of reason, an Idea.

Is it a question of the Idea of *sensus communis* itself? No, the *sensus communis* as unanimity about the beautiful, unanimity required and promised in each singular aesthetic judgement, is the witness or the sign (and not the proof) 'lying in' (but this must be investigated) subjectivity, the witness or sign of an Idea which relates itself to this subjectivity and which legitimates this requirement and this promise. This Idea is that of the suprasensible, explains Kant in the Remarks which follow paragraph 59. An Idea of a 'suprasensible substrate of all his faculties [faculties of the subject]' (*CJ* p. 189), he writes. It is the Idea that it's in the nature of the subject (it is this 'nature' which is the suprasensible in question in aesthetics) for all his faculties to agree to make possible knowledge in general. Understand by knowledge: thought, and thus judgement, and the most elementary, the most miserable, of the modes of thought, reflection.

Principle of unification, or rather of unison, of the diverse voices of the faculties; principle which on the mind's side makes certain the possibility of knowing, that is of thinking; which makes certain that even the freest form in the imagination keeps an affinity with the power to understand. And even more: this principle of subjective unison is even more enlivened, the 'life' of the chorus of the faculties is even more intensified, when form seems to escape the intelligence. This suprasensible is brought into action in aesthetics as 'the general ground of the subjective purposiveness of nature for the judgment' (*KUK* §57; *CJ* p. 185). The idea is thus that of an 'interior' purposiveness, which isn't voluntary, nor conceived of, nor interested in any way, but which is natural to the mind, which is the nature of and in the mind. And this is why art at its basis belongs to nature, and why subjective nature is at bottom art.

I said: music, because music is the art of time, time is internal sense and the unison in question is interior to the subject. But this time, once again, is not the schema. And the synthesis which it makes isn't diachronic, melodic, according to a series announcing or preparing the ordinal series of numbers, the natural numbers as a series. The synthesis is, let me repeat, synchronic, an unmeasurable and unforestallable harmony, a harmony of the timbres of the faculties, on the occasion of a form.

I'll take the thread up again. First the *elaboration* of the problem: taste is a pleasure without mediation by intelligence or will; this pleasure is a judgement, one that is always singular; it requests, expects, demands, to be shared, it promises itself that; it hasn't conviction's means of argument, since itself it is unargued for; this is however why, although miserable and destitute, aesthetic pleasure distinguishes itself from the pleasures of interest; if we don't want to make art sink into knowledge or ethics, then the spontaneous demand for unanimity implied in every judgement of taste must be founded, the appeal to an aesthetic sense common to human beings must be founded.

So the *problem* is to be formulated thus: aesthetic pleasure being stripped of all universality, of knowing as of willing, we must find the principle which renders legitimate the claim to universality, a claim which is included a priori in this judgement which is yet always singular.

Now the *elaboration* of the *solution*: aesthetic pleasure is a feeling of pure internal euphony; the euphony can only be the 'internal' agreement between the two faculties, the two modes of functioning of the mind – its capacity to make something present, to posit it there; its capacity to bring something under rules, to take it with, to con-ceive it; this agreement is an a priori condition of all 'knowledge', not from the side of the 'knowable', but from the side of the 'knower'; if to present and to conceive were still absolutely heterogeneous operations, then not only would there not be any knowable experience, but there wouldn't even be a subject; there would be an operator of presentations and elsewhere an operator of connections; since such is not the case (since knowledge is possible), there must therefore be an a priori principle of unison of the two faculties, which guarantees the possibility of a subject of knowledge in general; this principle cannot be itself knowable in the strict sense, since knowledge presupposes a unified or unifiable subject according to this principle; there is therefore only an Idea of it, or, which comes to the same thing, the principle is a 'suprasensible substratum' and can be stated: there must be an affinity between the faculties for there to be knowledge in general.

At last the *solution* of the problem: if the euphony singularly felt in the pleasure of the beautiful of the judgement of taste brings with it right away the demand for universality, by appealing to a *sensus communis*, it is because this euphony is the immediate sign of the faculties' affinity, universally required; taste is the feeling of the 'natural' destination of the faculties to subjectivity; the principle of such a 'nature' being universally valid, the feeling of this destination must also be so; this is why aesthetic pleasure can legitimately claim to be universalizable by demanding the consent of everyone.

This pattern of argument (I have given it the form, dear to Kant, of the logical or mathematical problem, of the *Aufgabe*), this pattern of argument which is also a 'deduction' in the Kantian sense (to deduce is to establish the legitimacy of a 'claim', to establish that a synthesis is well founded when it claims truth or goodness or beauty), this pattern of argument calls for a large number of observations and questions. I shall formulate some of them. First a correction.

I've said that the *sensus communis* called forth by taste is the sign 'lying in' the subject of an Idea which relates to that subject. And that this 'lying in' should be further investigated. The metaphor isn't a good one. There is no cosiness, nor interiority, in the judgement of taste. In so far as it calls for itself to be shared, pleasure in the beautiful isn't an experiencing by an already constituted and unified subject. This *sensus* isn't the internal sense, the aesthetic feeling isn't the auto-affection of the subject. The knowledge of experience, in the first *Critique*, demands a supreme principle of unification, the *I think*, as the originary synthetic unity of apperception. If this is accorded Kant, it is quite easy to show that such a unity cannot grasp itself except in the form of the internal sense, which is time, for *I* is always behind on its knowledge; even when it tries to anticipate itself.

Compared to this deferred originarity of the *I*, the synthesis at work in aesthetical pleasure is at the same time more radical, less graspable, and wider in scope. For this synthesis is reflexive and not determining. In apperception, the *I* no doubt determines and redetermines itself ceaselessly from one moment to the other, but is still haunted by determination. In the pleasure in the beautiful, heterogeneous powers find themselves in unison. Because the implied judgement is reflexive, and not determining, the unity isn't presupposed, it is a state of 'comparison', a sudden equalling out of the faculties. This equalling out isn't a making equal, the two parties aren't a pair, they are still non-comparable. There is no common ground for 'presenting' something and for explaining it. The two parties defy each other. Between them there is defiance and mistrust, and therefore at the same time, confidence. I should like to say 'fiance', 'affiancing'. There is too much for the understanding to think in the forms, especially the very free ones, which imagination turns over to it; and the imagination is still threatened by that regulation which the faculty of concepts could always impose on forms, by the intellectual 'recuperation'; of forms. It is according to this competition of the two powers that, on occasion, sometimes, their possible concert can be heard. Then the proportion will have been right. But that proportion is still indefinable, it cannot be prepared or forestalled. The congruence in feeling of the faculties never comes about on the day of determination. When the understanding tries to take over this affiancing, it can only determine the schematism, only the form which is already determined and prepared for the concept. And it can only attribute this determinate synthesis to the determining faculty, that is to itself. In this effort of determination, the deduction of the synthesis of forms leads necessarily to legitimizing the synthesis by the *I think*, the synthetic apperception said to be originary. For this is the origin of all the determining and determinable syntheses.

But it isn't an origin for the reflexive syntheses. These happen without any *I think*. In a different light, in a different time. The critique of taste tries to make heard this bringing to light, this birth of a fiance between faculties. It finds its time and place in the light of reflection, violent and gentle like a rivalry. It cannot be questioned. It is analysis, the Analytic which deduces its legitimacy from the principle of a substratum of affinity. This substratum isn't a subject, not the subject, only an Idea which isn't implied in the concert, but in the analysis of the concert. If we try to keep at the level of the pleasure in the beautiful, when describing it, then we must not say that it is experienced by the subject, it is an uncertain and unstable sketch of the subject. A subjectivity hears itself from far off and intimately at the same time; in this frail and singular

21

unison, the subjectivity is being born, but it will never be born as such. Once born, the subject is only the *Ich denke*. And the aesthetical pleasure will always come along to disconcert it, to make it be at a loss through its own concert, and its reflexive relation to itself.

And since the pleasure which is the affiancing can't be inscribed in determination, even in the determination belonging to the temporal schema, this pleasure doesn't synthesize with itself during time, and consequently it forgets itself. It is immemorial. This is also why each pleasure in beauty is a birth. Why the community of faculties remains discrete, secret, separated from itself, not inscribing itself in synthesizable time. But this is not at all the same reason why the cognitive *I* misses itself in its effort to determine itself. There simply is no aesthetic transcendental *I*. At the most a pre-*I*, a pre-cogito, some sort of floating synthesis between the faculties, whose *I* isn't in charge, but 'nature'.

Consequently it cannot be said that the Idea of a 'natural' purposiveness of the subject for knowledge indicates itself by aesthetic pleasure 'lying in' the subject, for this sign of pure pleasure cannot be inscribed 'in' or 'on' a subject since the subject is not present either as a temporal support or as a synthesizing power. The community has no interior which needs protecting.

And lastly it should not be said either that the community will have an interior once the subject is born, that we will move from feeling to concepts, from art to philosophy, from *sensus communis* to *intellectus communis*, which is the *I think*. For this move doesn't exist. There is no transition here between reflection and determination, between the substratum of the faculties' affinity and the originary synthetic unity of apperception. Substance can't make itself into subject. It is essential to the subject to misrecognize itself as substance. Feeling isn't transcribed in the concept, it is suppressed, without 'relief' (*Aufhebung*). This sublation is the presumption of the concept. Knowledge demands that the imaginative syntheses should be subordinated to the understanding, subsumable under its rule. Knowledge puts an end to the rivalry. Forms are forced to keep step with the categories, in order to act as a test for them. Another proportion.

So much so that the community of faculties in the knowledge of the true is quite different from that which is in action in the feeling of the beautiful. The first is a hierarchized community, an architectonic one, the second is free, and rather out of breath. I shan't develop this point. One of its implications is that we can wait without undue worry for this 'death of art' prophetized by the philosophies of the concept. This does not mean that there is nothing to think about on this subject, especially when conceptual computable syntheses invade and occupy the field of art's materials and the domain of their forms. This I leave for discussion.

A second observation. The fact that the aesthetic community is transcendental doesn't dispense Kant from going back through anthropology in order to explain its nature. I'll come back to the text of paragraph 40:

> But under the *sensus communis* we must include the idea of a sense *common to all*, i.e. of a faculty of judgment which, in its reflection, takes account (*a priori*) of the mode of representation of all other men in thought,

to which Kant adds, as we have seen: 'This is done by comparing our judgment with the possible rather than actual judgments of others' (*KUK* §40; *CJ* p. 136). This operation of comparison apparently occurs over a collectivity of individuals. Interpreted like this, this operation induces a realist empirical anthropological definition of the said *sensus*. How many illusions or political crimes have been able to nourish themselves with this pretended immediate sharing of feelings?

However, looking more closely at the sentence, things are more hesitant. Kant has said 'possible rather than actual judgments', And he reaffirms the condition for universalization which he has already enounced 'by putting ourselves in the place of any other man . . .'. Now, in correct Kantian philosophy, the whole of the others, as a totality, isn't a category for which there can be a corresponding intuition in experience. It cannot be a question of an intuitable group. This whole is the object of an Idea.

The required comparison is an eidetic one. The task is to form a pure aesthetic judgement by 'imaginary variations', as Husserl would have said. The purposiveness of this mental 'technique' is to remove from the pleasure in the beautiful any empirical individual charm or emotion. And thus to make certain that what is left after this 'degreasing' is communicable. It will be communicable if it is well purified.

At the end of the same paragraph, Kant writes:

> We could even define taste as the faculty of judging of that

23

which makes *universally communicable*, without the mediation of a concept, our feeling in a given representation.

(KUK §40; *CJ* p. 138)

This definition is somewhat provoking ('we could *even* define'): the condition of the universal communicability of pleasure is enough to distinguish aesthetic pleasure from any other. It will be pure if it is really communicable. How to go on? The communicability is in proportion to the purity, transcendentally. Empirically the purity can be gauged by the communicability. Let's say: the communicability is the *ratio cognoscendi* of purity, and the latter is the *ratio essendi* of the former. The formula of the eidetic comparison which makes certain communicability can seem 'artificial', writes Kant, because it is 'expressed in abstract formulas' *(KUK* §40; *CJ* p. 136). Nothing in itself is more 'natural' than this abstraction. And indeed it's only a matter of letting oneself be guided by the principle of a substratum of affinity between the faculties, which is the suprasensible 'nature' of the subject, or rather of the pre-subject, in order to eliminate the dross of material interests and charms.

The *sensus communis* is still therefore a hypotyposis: it is a sensible analogon of the transcendental euphony of the faculties, which can only be the object of an Idea, and not of an intuition. This *sensus* isn't a sense, and the feeling which is supposed to affect it (as a sense can be affected) isn't common, but only in principle communicable. There is no assignable community of feeling, no affective consensus in fact. And if we claim to have recourse to one, or *a fortiori* to create one, we are victims of a transcendental illusion and we are encouraging impostures.

The essential is this: the feeling of the beautiful is the subject just being born, the first equalling-out of non-comparable powers. This feeling escapes being mastered by concept and will. It extends itself underneath and beyond their intrigues and their closure. This is what Kant understands by the 'natural substratum' which he places at its principle in his deduction. Thus it is a region of resistance to institutions and establishment, where is inscribed and hidden what happens 'before' we know what it is and before we want to make it into anything at all. This pleasure is an inscription without support, and without a code by which it can be read off. Miserable, if you like. It is the task of literatures and arts, the task of what is called writing, to reinscribe it according to its miserable state, without filling it full, and without getting rid of it.

NOTES

1 First published in *Paragraph* 11(1) (March 1988), pp. 1–23. Translated by Marian Hobson and Geoff Bennington.
2 Immanuel Kant, *Kritik der Urteilskraft*, paragraph 57, Anmerkung I: *Critique of Judgment*, translated with an Introduction by J. H. Bernard, New York and London, Hafner Publishing Co. 1966, p. 110. Hereafter abbreviated as *KUK* and *CJ*.

2

LYOTARD AND THE PROBLEM OF JUSTICE

Anne Barron

In *Philosophy and the Mirror of Nature*,[1] Richard Rorty characterizes
the history of the western metaphysical tradition as an extended
search for the foundations of knowledge and morality, underwritten
by the conviction that all conceptions of truth or justice are commensurable, that is, 'able to be brought under a set of rules which
will tell us how rational agreement can be reached on what would
settle the issue on every point where statements seem to conflict'.[2]
To forge a link between human rationality and the idea of a universal consensus and to insist, further, that through an appeal to
reason, truth – and hence the elimination of disagreement – might
be attained, is, as Rorty suggests, a familiar move within western
philosophy, particularly since the Enlightenment. Within Kantian
thought, this strategy assumes a specific form: the basis for consensus is located within a conception of the human person as rational
and autonomous. Human society may appear to be marked only
by conflict and cultural diversity; human history may seem to be
little more than a succession of discontinuous shifts and transformations. But underneath the apparently irreducible heterogeneity of
experience is a self that 'we' – in all epochs and in all corners of
the globe – share. As rational subjects 'we' are capable of reaching
agreement on the fundamental verities of existence.

As Rorty goes on to point out, to suggest that there is no such
common ground between human beings seems to endanger rationality itself.[3] In particular, it seems to recommend a form of politics
that would be nothing more than a war of all against all, and
therefore productive only of injustice. However, it is precisely this
association of justice with rational consensus that Jean-François
Lyotard sets out to deny. The aim of this paper is to explore the

différend between Lyotard, for whom 'there is no just society',[4] and John Rawls, author of *A Theory of Justice*.[5]

John Rawls's quest is for a regulative conception of justice, which can be acknowledged by all as 'a common point of view from which their claims may be adjudicated'.[6] Such a conception will find its origin in a public consensus, it will be capable of ordering and unifying the disparate moralities evident throughout the social body, and it will inspire universal recognition and respect. Yet any form of political justification appropriate to a modern society must acknowledge that there can be no popular agreement on one vision of the good, and that a plurality of opposing and incommensurable conceptions must be taken as given.[7] Rawls's work is an attempt to anchor and organize the dissensus, fragmentation and contingency characteristic of the modern social and political order. His question is, how is social unity to be understood in the face of the seemingly limitless diversity of contemporary human society? And granted that social unity is conceivable in some definite way, under what conditions is it actually possible?[8]

The answers supplied in *A Theory of Justice* are avowedly anti-teleological. The theory relies upon no particular specification of the good for society, a single dominant end in terms of which the actions of governments and institutions may be evaluated.[9] Rather, Rawls insists on the priority of the right over the good, and a conception of justice is a conception of right.[10] Social unity is not to be found in a finite set of shared values or aims – nor should it. Without unanimity on principles of right, however, it would be impossible to achieve a final ordering of conflicting claims, or to constrain in any way the range of desires and values properly entitled to satisfaction.[11]

The primacy of the right, as well as being a moral imperative, implies also that the principles of justice are derived independently of the values or conceptions of the good current in the society which they would regulate.[12] Rawls insists upon this, but at the same time he avoids claiming that the conception of justice he proposes is, or emanates from, a self-evident universal truth, or that its recognition is demanded by the essential nature or identity of persons.[13] It is based, not upon some transcendental point of view, but upon 'premises that we and others publicly recognise as true'.[14] Justice thus has its origin in truth, but truth is to be found in the coherence of the 'intuitive ideas'[15] embedded within (rather than suspended above) 'our' political culture.[16]

27

A Theory of Justice is to be understood, therefore, as 'political, not metaphysical'.[17] Nevertheless, it does rest upon a particular representation of humanity, which is to be taken as 'true' in so far as it is immanent to 'the political institutions of a constitutional democratic regime and the public traditions of their interpretation'.[18] At the core of the *Theory* is a description of the 'original position',[19] a distillation of the essence of society itself (a system of co-operation between free and equal persons) and the very source of justice (the fair terms of such co-operation).[20] The original position is a hypothetical state of nature, the parties to which inhabit a situation of complete equality and sameness. They are positioned behind a 'veil of ignorance',[21] and deprived of all knowledge of the particular facts that might set them in opposition: differences of race, class, sex and social status; of natural assets and abilities, and of values, aims and conceptions of the good. These details, in Rawls's view, are merely arbitrary: they have no place in a definition of moral personhood, and they are therefore irrelevant to the project of constructing a theory of justice. The original position is human society stripped to its moral core, shorn of its contingencies, complexity and conflict. Left behind is a conglomeration of moral persons, human beings who are indistinguishable from each other in their essential freedom and rationality, and whose task it is to define the fundamental terms of their association, to specify 'how they are to regulate their claims against one another and what is to be the foundation charter of their society'.[22]

Free and rational persons, however, are characterized above all else by a capacity for autonomous action, the ability to formulate and pursue a rational plan of life. It is this capacity, rather than the realization of any particular aim or goal, which is definitive of moral personality.[23] Yet the principles of justice are to regulate and constrain choice amongst conceptions of the good. How then can principles be devised, the observance of which would be consistent with human freedom? Rawls finds a solution to this dilemma in the theory of the social contract. A person acts autonomously when the principles governing his actions are chosen by him. These obligations, being self-imposed, are morally binding upon the subject who has subjected himself to them, because in giving effect to them, he affirms his true identity. Likewise, a society satisfying the principles of justice chosen jointly by free and rational persons in a situation of equality comes as close as a society can be to being a voluntary – and therefore a just – scheme. 'By acting from these principles persons are acting autonomously: they are acting from principles that they would acknowledge under conditions that best express their nature as free and equal rational beings.'[24]

The original position, although taking the form of a description, is not intended to conform to any identifiable reality. It is a lost origin. The society it represents is, unfortunately, absent: 'no society can . . . be a scheme of co-operation which men enter voluntarily in a literal sense; each person finds himself placed at birth in some particular position in some particular society, and the outcome of this position materially affects his life prospects.'[25] Its primary significance in the *Theory* is to serve as an uncontroversial common perspective on the social world, which anyone can adopt at any time simply by reasoning in accordance with the appropriate restrictions.[26] Once there, relieved of the contingencies that set us at odds, 'essential understandings',[27] and 'convergences of opinion'[28] at last appear possible and unproblematic.

This is significant, for it is of great importance to Rawls that the choice of a conception of justice in the original position be unanimous. The existence of consensus 'enables us to say of the preferred conception of justice that it represents a genuine reconciliation of interests'.[29] It also facilitates the design of social and political institutions in accordance with a determinate criterion. Hence, the original position is drawn in such a way that agreement is guaranteed: 'since the differences among the parties are unknown to them, and everyone is equally rational and similarly situated, each is convinced by the same arguments. . . . If anyone after due reflection prefers a conception of justice to another, then they all do . . .'[30]

Given Rawls's agenda, his insistence upon same basis for a universal consensus is inevitable. On the one hand, he claims an awesome adjudicatory capacity for his conception of justice. The principles of justice are to be given 'absolute precedence'[31] in the criticism and reform of political institutions; they are to regulate such institutions 'without question';[32] and they are to order and hierarchize the conflicting claims persons make upon one another, sorting the worthy from the unworthy. If this discursive policing is to be legitimate, it is essential that it be identifiable, potentially at least, from everyone's point of view. On the other hand, justice without consensus is in any event inconceivable to Rawls. 'Unless there existed a common perspective, the assumption of which narrowed differences of opinion, reasoning and argument would be pointless and we would have no rational grounds for believing in the soundness of our convictions.'[33]

To be rational is to be able to find agreement with other human beings.[34] The end of all social interaction – argument – is unanimity and the elimination of difference or, as Descombes suggests, to absorb the heterogeneous, to rationalize the incongruous; in short to translate the *other* into the language of the *same*.[35] The guarantor of this consensus is Truth: agreement becomes possible only when there exists a criterion according to which disagreement may be resolved. The description of the individual human subject at the centre of *A Theory of Justice* performs this function in Rawls's work. It is true because it is uncontroversial: it manages to capture the 'overlapping consensus'[36] presupposed at a deep level by contemporary political institutions as to what the essential attributes of humanity really are. And because it is true, it will inform and constrain the conception of justice which is built upon it. Moral personality is the 'fundamental aspect of the self',[37] and the nature of the self as a moral (i.e. free and equal) person is the same for all.[38] What is definitive of moral personality is the capacity to choose, not the objects of choice, and this capacity is located in a self which must, therefore, be 'prior to the ends which are affirmed by it'.[39] The Rawlsian subject is thus an antecendently individuated subject,[40] whose boundaries are fixed prior to experience, and whose unity is 'founded on the higher order desire to follow . . . the principles of rational choice'.[41] Diversity is an *effect* of this fundamental sameness: it is the capacity of each autonomous subject to formulate plans of life which leads each of us to adopt different ends and purposes – and this, indeed, is the problem for a society characterized by a relative shortage of natural and other resources. In conditions of moderate scarcity, mutually disinterested persons will tend to put forward conflicting claims to the division of social advantages.[42] Hence the need for principles which will guide the process of adjudicating between and 'ordering' these claims. The true principles of justice for a society the basic unit of which is the moral person are to be found in a true conception of what it is to be a moral person: the prescriptive is to be derived from a description of the self.

> [T]o express one's nature as a being of a particular kind is to act on the principles that would be chosen if this nature were the decisive determining element. Of course, the choice of the

parties in the original position is subject to the restrictions of that situation. But when we knowingly act on the principles of justice in the ordinary course of events, we deliberately assume the limitations of the original position. One reason for doing this . . . is to give expression to one's nature.[43]

One is a subject in so far as one is autonomous; one is autonomous to the extent that one is capable of being the author of one's own laws. Justice is subjection/subjectification according to the criterion of autonomy: only those principles which could have been chosen by all the wills simultaneously can qualify as the true principles of justice.

The legitimacy of Rawls's conception of justice, then, is guaranteed by the figure of the subject who is also legislator. The roles of addressee and author of the law are interchangeable. Each is the same as the other in its possession of that universal essence – the capacity for rational choice – and consensus as to the meaning of justice can be established by appealing to this fact of sameness: just prescriptions are those which emanate from the rational, autonomous subject that is each of us. For Jean-François Lyotard, this liberal vision harbours a nostalgic yearning after a certain ideal of communication, whereby 'an author can write while putting himself at the same time in the position of reader, being able to substitute himself for his own reader, and to judge and sort out what he has accomplished from the point of view of the reader that he also is'.[44] Lyotard's concern is to suggest how justice is to be understood in a situation where social interaction cannot be experienced as the easy exchange of meanings between equal partners, where the position of the other remains always irreducibly other, incapable of being assumed by the one who speaks, and where the one who speaks in turn occupies many different places at once. This is postmodernity: 'the date does not matter.'[45]

Lyotard begins with a description. Postmodernity is characterized by the dispersion of the social into a multiplicity of incommensurable 'language games'. 'The picture that one can draw from this observation is precisely that of an absence of unity, an absence of totality. All of this does not make up a body. On the contrary.'[46] Postmodern society is 'pagan': it is without a metadiscourse in terms of which the universe of language games – or 'phrases'[47] – can be ordered and hierarchized. It is therefore without a set of stable criteria which would guide the process of judging, whether

31

in the pursuit of knowledge, the evaluation of art, or the conduct of politics. 'There is no metalanguage . . . the famous theoretical discourse that is supposed to ground political and ethical decisions.'[48] Liberalism seeks a source of unity and a regulating ideal in the category of the autonomous subject, an entity which can place itself in a position (the original position?) *outside* an endlessly vibrating 'patchwork'[49] of discourses, and there assume a perspective from which the whole chaotic field of phrases might be apprehended and dominated. In this realm, the self, freed from the risk of exposure and destabilization, can find its identity – and can become like other selves. Paganism, on the other hand, takes as its premise the impossibility of autonomy or equivalence, and instead takes as given the dissolution of the self within a complex fabric of social relations. '[H]uman beings are never the authors of what they tell, that is, of what they do.'[50] Discourse can never be mastered by the subject, for language games 'position the person who enters the game'.[51] Language precedes and makes possible the speech of the individual subject, by situating the speaker within a pragmatic context: 'we are always in the hands of some narrative or other: someone has always already said something to us, and we have already been spoken.'[52] The social bond is therefore composed, not of the exchanges of free-standing, self-possessed individuals, but of the 'moves' within a multiplicity of language games, which, because innumerable, unstable and interlocking, produce a plurality of identities: 'they are games that make us into their players, and we know therefore that we are ourselves several beings (by "beings" is meant here proper names that are positioned on the slots of the pragmatics of each of these games).'[53]

In some of his more recent work, Rawls himself has attempted to work through the implications for his own conception of justice of this notion of the de-mastering and fragmentation of the subject. Whilst not seeking to deny that a conception of the self as autonomous and unified underlies *A Theory of Justice*, Rawls has been concerned to emphasize the political nature of his conception. That is,

> persons can accept this conception of themselves as citizens and use it when discussing questions of political justice, without being committed in other parts of their life to comprehensive moral ideals often associated with liberalism, for example, the ideals of autonomy and individualism.[54]

The political, in other words, must be distinguished from the personal; the public from the private. In his/her 'nonpublic' dimension, the individual may well be consumed and defined by experience, lacking a sense of self beyond the roles contingently inhabited and the ends pursued. The individual may perceive that behind particular convictions and attachments there is nothing at all, no stable identity which gives unity to a life experienced as a succession of random episodes. But this behind-the-scenes dispersal of the modern subject is not to be permitted to influence the design of laws and political institutions. The instability of the self is merely an effect of the plurality of conceptions of the good current in contemporary society; this plurality is productive of conflict not only between, but within, persons. The citizen, however, is entitled to claim a 'public' identity which is 'independent from and not identified with any particular conception of the good or scheme of final ends',[55] and which therefore is not affected by changes over time in his or her conception of the good.

> For example, when citizens convert from one religion to another, or no longer affirm an established faith, they do not cease to be, for questions of political justice, the same persons they were before. There is no loss of what may be called their public identity, their identity as a matter of basic law.[56]

Thus the subject of the law is an abstract subject, not a living individual, embedded in a complex history which produces a continual reconstitution of personal identity; rather, a fiction, a subject without a name,[57] a no-body. As such, and only as such, the person can be governed by laws which are 'universal in application'.[58] Confronted with the discontinuity and heterogeneity of lived experience, Rawls retreats to a realm of abstraction. Only here can the social web – 'a multitude of encounters between interlocutors caught up in different pragmatics'[59] – become a social totality, unified by reference to the stable identity of the 'citizens' that compose it.

Within this vision, the idea of justice is associated with that of consensus and with the active subordination of plurality to a set of universal principles. For Lyotard, on the contrary, 'to place oneself in the position of enunciator of the universal prescription is obviously infatuation itself and absolute injustice'.[60] Consensus 'does violence to the heterogeneity of language games';[61] a pagan world which is suspicious of metanarratives needs 'an idea and practice of justice that is not linked to that of consensus'.[62] A postmodern justice would demand the recognition that language games are multiple and incommensurable, but would avoid the complacent relativism of the position that within the boundaries of each game, anything goes: what is just within a community at a given moment is that upon which there is agreement. This apparently tolerant position can only lead to the end of politics, the celebration, again, of consensus and 'the manufacture of a subject that is authorised to say "we" '.[63] Thus paganism must make use, paradoxically, of a regulator, an Idea which could safeguard the 'agonistic aspect of society'[64] by affirming the capacity of the imagination to experiment with the rules of the language games that situate us, and thereby shake them loose from the dead weight of convention.

> The point is not that one keeps the games, but that, in each of the existing games, one effects new moves, one opens up the possibility of new efficacies in the games with their present rules. And in addition, one changes the rules: one can play a given game with other rules, and when one changes the rules, one has changed the game, for a game is defined by its rules.[65]

Kant introduces as a regulator the Idea of a totality: humanity must form a whole. Postmodernity, however, must invoke an Idea of society as a non-totalizable universe of diverse language games, an Idea which has not already been made present but which 'remains to be attained; it is ahead of us'.[66] There must be not only a multiplicity of justices, but a justice of multiplicity.[67]

'How can a regulatory use of this Idea of the political take place?'[68] This is the question raised repeatedly in Lyotard's work. What he proposes is an unremitting struggle against the terror perpetrated by those discourses which claim to have said the last word on the true meaning of justice, and which actively seek to impose that interpretation on the entirety of social relations. '[I]t is our business not to supply reality but to invent allusions to the conceivable which cannot be presented.'[69] To regulate the political by reference to a justice of multiplicity would be to open up the closed categories of thought that govern social and political life to the 'violence'[70] of endless experimentation, and in this way to make possible the expression of injustices which are otherwise borne in silence.

It is in *Le Différend*[71] that this notion of activating and bearing witness to conflict is put forward as a political strategy. As David Carroll points out,

Le Différend has as its critical-political goal the uncovering of *différends* where they have been repressed or supposedly resolved; it argues for the necessity of listening to the idiom not given its day in court, to the silence imposed on the victims of oppression and injustice. It attacks all mechanisms of repression, all courts, institutions, systems of thought that perpetuate the injustice of universal judgment and thus do not recognise the silence imposed on their victims.[72]

At issue here is not the question of how differences are to be resolved, but of whether they can be 'phrased'. Lyotard is concerned to suggest a strategy of 'revenge' against the law – that is, any system of prescriptions which purports to regulate conflict with a view to finalizing it. On its way to the 'right answer', law inevitably excludes and marginalizes statements which cannot be accommodated within its own tightly drawn parameters, and subordinates every claim concerning the meaning of justice to its own meta-language. Thus every case of justice according to law carries within it the potential for a *différend*: '[a] case of differend between two parties takes place when the "regulation" of the conflict which opposes them is done in the idiom of one of the parties, while the injustice suffered by the other is not signified in that idiom.'[73] The dispute between labour and capital, for instance, is just such a *différend*.[74] Neither positive law nor the law of the market can conceive of the relationship between the worker and his/her labour in terms other than those of possession or surrender by an abstract subject of a commodity: the worker's identity as labour-power cannot be asserted within either idiom. In law, the owner of a commodity has the right to demand payment of an agreed consideration from its purchaser, but the extraction of surplus value is an injury which cannot be expressed in terms of legal rights. 'He who lodges a complaint is heard, but he who is a victim, and who is perhaps the same, is reduced to silence.'[75]

Rawlsian liberalism also acknowledges that grievances may arise for which there is no 'language' in existing positive law. Further, the stated aim of *A Theory of Justice* is to provide a set of guidelines for the criticism and reform of political institutions, including law: the theory therefore advocates that such institutions be constantly open to revision, that is, to the admission of new claims. For Rawls, however, this process always carries the promise of finality. In order for it to be assessed whether *damnum* is to be permitted to become *injuria*, these claims must in turn be judged by reference to a determinate criterion, and submitted to a 'tribunal'[76] which is supreme. Thus Rawls's disciple, Ronald Dworkin, has suggested that *A Theory of Justice* implicitly makes an appeal to a form of natural law.[77] Since the theory affirms the value of individual choice, it must be taken as treating the protection of individual human rights as fundamental to the just organization of society. In Dworkin's view, there is one basic natural right presupposed by the overall argument of the book – basic, in the sense that all other rights are justified by and derived from it, and natural in the sense that it is not the product of deliberate legislation or explicit social custom. This is the right of all to equality of concern and respect in the design and administration of political institutions. To the extent that positive law does not respect this natural right, it is unjust and ought to be amended.

Lyotard, however, is emphatic in his rejection of this position.

> It is wrong to call 'rights of man' that which is invoked by vengeance against the law. *Man* is surely not the name which fits this instance of appeal, nor *right* the name of the authority which this instance available itself of.[78]

The discourse of rights is proper to the abstract judicial subject: rights are borne by each human being as a moral person, irrespective of social position – in other words, by Rawls's self-identical 'citizen'. Moreover, 'right' is that which is prior to the good, the universal which precedes and presides over all contingent particulars. To translate all claims into the language of rights is already to have performed an act of reduction, and to have affirmed the authority of this discourse to contain all other phrases. Whereas for Lyotard, the challenge is precisely to 'activate the differences',[79] to produce an endless proliferation, rather than a selective refinement, of language games, and, within them, of visions of the just.

The strategy proposed, then, is one of perpetual struggle to voice ideas, opinions or injustices systematically excluded from the universe of phrases: a continuous incitement of speech. But to valorize struggle and the power of expression is, it seems, immediately to refer to a subject of resistance – an enunciating capability, 'the one who speaks'.[80] This in turn not only invokes the very notions of agency and intentionality that it is the concern of postmodernist thought to discredit, but also opens up a crucial dilemma for any form of radical politics: the dissolution of the subject seems to render it impossible to give any content to a strategy of social transformation in terms of subjective experience. On the other hand, it is clear that 'the death of the Subject' is not the same as the end of subjecthood, if the latter is understood as the attainment of a position within discourse. Fragmentation leads to the proliferation of many new forms of subjectivity rather than the simple elimination of human identity as such. For Lyotard, resistance consists in the assertion by these subjectivities – often devalued by the dominant political culture – of the fact that they exist. 'Every one of us belongs to several minorities, and what is very important, none of them prevails. It is only then that we can say that society is just.'[81]

However, here there arises a problem of a different order. As Foucault, amongst others, has remarked, to be a subject is, necessarily, to be subjected:

> There are two meanings to the word *subject*: subject to someone else by control and dependence, and tied to one's identity by a conscience or self-knowledge. Both meanings suggest a form of power which subjugates and makes subject to.[82]

The subject is a function of discourse, but for Foucault, discourse is generated by power: it possesses its own internal regime of power/ knowledge relations. Power is productive rather than merely prohibitive – the individual 'is not the *vis-à-vis* of power; it is . . . one of its prime effects'[83] – and operates through the interaction of disciplinary technologies of the body and confessional technologies of the self.[84] Processes of objectification and subjectification here presuppose each other. The subject who is induced to speak the truth about himself will already have been analysed, manipulated and finally normalized: disciplined.

But if self-conscious identity is a product merely of elaborate mechanisms of domination, then it could hardly serve as a base from which to launch a strategy of resistance to power. There can be no privileged site of struggle, either, for effects of power circulate within every discourse, whether dominant or not, and leave their trace in every human action. The celebration of subjectivity in any form seems to play directly into the hands of power. This is the position of Baudrillard, for whom subject resistance is a response carefully orchestrated by 'the system':

> The liberating practices correspond to *one* of the aspects of the system, to the constant ultimatum we are given to constitute ourselves as pure objects; but they do not correspond at all

to the other demand to constitute ourselves as subjects, to liberate, to express ourselves at any price, to vote, to produce, to decide, to speak, to participate, to play the game – a blackmail and an ultimatum just as serious as the other, probably more serious today.[85]

For Baudrillard, the more subversive tactic would be that of 'hyper-conformity':

> To a system whose argument is oppressive and repressive, the strategic resistance is to demand the liberating rights of the subject. But this seems rather to reflect an earlier phase of the system, and even if we are still confronted with it, it is no longer a strategic territory: the present argument of the system is to maximize speech, to maximize the production of meaning, of participation. And so the strategic resistance is that of refusal of meaning and the refusal of speech – or of the hyperconformist simulation of the very mechanisms of the system, which is another form of refusal by over-acceptance. It is the actual strategy of the masses. This strategy does not exclude the other, but it is the winning one today, because it is the most adapted to the present phase of the system.[86]

Lyotard would refuse both the idea of a system and the possibility of a 'winning' strategy. Power relations are multifarious and unstable, less a face-to-face confrontation producing a final victor than an endless antagonism: the relationship between discourses 'does not obey a pragmatics of border to border, between two properly defined blocks or two armies, or two verbal sets, confronting each other. On the contrary, it is a place of ceaseless negotiations and ruses'.[87] 'Context control', if it occurs, is always contingent and fragile. Like Foucault,[88] Lyotard would acknowledge that stable mechanisms may often replace the free play of antagonistic reactions: institutional constraints may impose limits on language games and thus restrict the inventiveness of the players in making their moves. But,

> [w]e know today that the limits the institution imposes on potential language 'moves' are never established once and for all (even if they have been formally defined). Rather, the limits are themselves the stakes and provisional results of language strategies, within the institution and without.[89]

For Lyotard, the only available option is to match wits, or 'ruse', with the fate one has been given, to make experimental moves *within* the language games that situate us (for there is no outside), and in this way to generate new effects throughout the social network. This is not to speak of an essential freedom, or of a form of initiative that belongs to the individual. The possibility of a countermove is presupposed by the existence of a game, and it is not a matter of 'conquering the narrative, that is, of putting oneself forward as the utterer, and imprinting one's name on it'.[90] However, the nature of the countermove is always indeterminate. Situated as we are at the 'nodal points'[91] of many communication circuits, we are bombarded and displaced by many conflicting messages, and it is precisely this positioning within a fragmented universe that enables a whole field of possible responses, inventions and new combinations of phrases to open up. To contemplate what remains to be done is to experience an ineradicable tension between pleasure and pain: the pleasure that comes from always being able to conceive of possibilities beyond what already exists, and the pain accompanying the realization that whatever exists never quite attains the horizon of the conceivable. Ultimately, whether we are energized or paralysed by this sentiment depends on where we choose to place the emphasis.

NOTES

1 Richard Rorty, *Philosophy and the Mirror of Nature*, Oxford, Blackwell 1980.
2 ibid., p. 316.
3 ibid., p. 317.
4 Jean-François Lyotard, *Just Gaming*, Manchester, Manchester University Press 1985, p. 25.
5 John Rawls, *A Theory of Justice*, Cambridge, Mass., Harvard University Press 1971.
6 ibid., p. 5.
7 John Rawls, 'Justice as fairness: political not metaphysical', *Philosophy and Public Affairs* 14(3) (Summer 1985), pp. 219–51, at p. 229.
8 ibid., p. 249.
9 Rawls (1971), op. cit., p. 560.
10 ibid., pp. 446–52.
11 ibid., p. 448.
12 Michael Sandel, *Liberalism and the Limits of Justice*, Cambridge, Cambridge University Press 1982, p. 2.
13 Rawls (1985), op. cit., p. 219; (1971), op. cit., p. 21.
14 Rawls (1985), op. cit., p. 229.

15 ibid.
16 ibid., p. 228.
17 ibid., p. 219.
18 ibid., p. 225.
19 Rawls (1971), op. cit., pp. 17–22; chapter 3.
20 Rawls (1985), op. cit., pp. 234–5.
21 Rawls (1971), op. cit., pp. 136–42.
22 ibid., p. 11.
23 ibid., pp. 509, 561.
24 ibid., p. 515.
25 ibid., p. 13.
26 ibid., pp. 138–9.
27 ibid., p. 517.
28 ibid.
29 ibid., p. 142.
30 ibid., p. 139.
31 ibid., p. 565.
32 ibid.
33 ibid., pp. 517–18.
34 Rorty (1980), op. cit., p. 316.
35 Vincent Descombes, *Modern French Philosophy*, Cambridge, Cambridge University Press 1980.
36 Rawls (1985), op. cit., p. 225.
37 Rawls (1971), op. cit., p. 563.
38 ibid., p. 565.
39 ibid., p. 560.
40 Sandel (1982), op. cit., pp. 19–21.
41 Rawls (1971), op. cit., p. 561.
42 ibid., p. 128.
43 ibid., pp. 252–3.
44 Lyotard (1985), op. cit., p. 9.
45 ibid., p. 15.
46 ibid., p. 94.
47 In *Le Différend* (Paris, Minuit 1984), Lyotard abandons Wittgenstein's terminology of the language game in favour of that of the phrase, because

'language games' implied players that made use of language like a toolbox, thus repeating the constant arrogance of Western anthropocentrism. 'Phrases' came to say that the so-called players were on the contrary situated by phrases in the universes those phrases present, 'before' any intention.
    ('Interview', *Diacritics* 14(3) (Fall 1984), pp. 16–21, at p. 17)

48 Lyotard (1985), op. cit., p. 48.
49 ibid., p. 94.
50 ibid., p. 36.
51 ibid., p. 98.
52 Jean-François Lyotard, *Instructions païennes*, Paris, Galilée 1977, p. 47.
53 Lyotard (1985), op. cit., p. 51.

54 Rawls (1985), op. cit., p. 245.
55 ibid., p. 132.
56 ibid.
57 Rawls (1971), op. cit., pp. 131–2.
58 ibid., p. 132.
59 Lyotard (1985), op. cit., p. 73.
60 ibid., p. 99.
61 Jean-François Lyotard, *The Postmodern Condition: A Report on Knowledge*, Manchester, Manchester University Press 1984, p. xxv. (Hereafter Lyotard 1984a.)
62 ibid., p. 66.
63 Lyotard (1985), op. cit., p. 81.
64 Lyotard (1984a), op. cit., p. 16.
65 Lyotard (1985), op. cit., p. 62.
66 ibid., p. 83.
67 ibid., p. 100.
68 ibid., p. 94.
69 Lyotard (1984a), op. cit., p. 81.
70 Lyotard (1985), op. cit., p. 100.
71 Jean-François Lyotard, *Le Différend*, Paris, Minuit 1984. (Hereafter Lyotard 1984b.)
72 David Carroll, 'Rephrasing the political with Kant and Lyotard: from aesthetic to political judgements', *Diacritics* 14(3) (Fall 1984), pp. 74–88 at p. 78.
73 Lyotard (1984b), op. cit., §12.
74 ibid.
75 ibid., §13.
76 ibid., §44.
77 Ronald Dworkin, *Taking Rights Seriously*, London, Duckworth 1977, pp. 150–83.
78 Lyotard (1984b), op. cit., §44.
79 Lyotard (1984a), op cit., p. 82.
80 Lyotard (1985), op. cit., p. 33.
81 ibid., p. 95.
82 Michel Foucault, 'The subject and power', afterword in *Michel Foucault: Beyond Structuralism and Hermeneutics* (second edn), ed. Herbert L. Dreyfus and Paul Robinow, Chicago, University of Chicago Press 1983, p. 212.
83 Michel Foucault, *Power/Knowledge: Selected Interviews and Other Writings 1972–77*, ed. Colin Gordon, New York, Pantheon 1980, p. 98.
84 Michel Foucault, *Discipline and Punish*, Harmondsworth, Penguin 1977; Michel Foucault, *The History of Sexuality*, Harmondsworth, Penguin 1978.
85 Jean Baudrillard, 'The masses: the implosion of the social in the media', *New Library History* 16(3), pp. 577–89, at p. 588.
86 ibid.
87 Lyotard (1985), op. cit., p. 41.
88 Foucault (1983), op. cit., pp. 224–6.

89 Lyotard (1984a), op. cit., p. 17.
90 Lyotard (1985), op. cit., p. 41.
91 Lyotard (1984a), op. cit., p. 15.

3

ON THE CRITICAL 'POST': LYOTARD'S AGITATED JUDGEMENT

Richard Beardsworth

I

Lyotard has been predominantly considered in England and America as the philosopher of 'postmodernity', or even of 'postmodernism'. The editors of a recent book entitled *Postmodernism and Society* state characteristically in this regard that '[f]or Lyotard . . . postmodernity is seen as a post-metaphysical, post-industrial, pluralist, pragmatic and restless set of partially differentiated social orders'.[1] Implicit in this account of Lyotard's work – and most evidently *The Postmodern Condition* – is the assumption that Lyotard is attempting to define a socio-historical category, what comes *after* modernity, the 'post' of postmodernity.[2] Much of *The Postmodern Condition* could be seen to lend itself to this reading: not only because of its stated analysis of 'knowledge' in the 'post-industrial' age, but also because of the explicit axis of its account of 'delegitimation', together with its stress on 'little' narratives after the demise of the 'grand' narratives of the Enlightenment and post-Enlightenment (seen respectively to order knowledge according to the practical finality of humanity or to organize it within the speculative and dialectical development of *Geist* and the proletariat). This story of 'the postmodern condition' is now well known and accompanies, whether sympathetically or unsympathetically, much contemporary socio-cultural analysis and literary theory in their attention to questions of subjectivity and difference.

The other work of Lyotard which has attracted attention, and which together with *The Postmodern Condition* forms the major reference point to the Anglo-American reception of Lyotard, is *Just Gaming*.[3] The two works have indeed been put together. *The Postmodern Condition* ended with an argument for dissensus and

43

multiplicity after the model of the contemporary physical sciences' search for instabilities and in resistance both to the rules of capitalism, finalized according to the end of 'performativity', and to the communicational theory of Habermas with its stress on transcendental intersubjectivity and normative consensus. *Just Gaming*, an earlier work although it was translated into English later than *La Condition postmoderne*, seemed to be an attempt to think the 'paralogical' idea of legitimation with which *The Postmodern Condition* ended but which it did not elaborate upon in the more strict terms of justice. *Just Gaming* has come to be seen, therefore, as a 'postmodern' treatise on ethics, a sort of discipline supplementing the 'post-metaphysics' and 'physics' of *The Postmodern Condition*. Lyotard has not fared well in this partial systemization of his work since the late 1970s. Let me give a quick example. At one point in the dialogue which makes up *Just Gaming*, Lyotard is concerned, following in part Kant and Lévinas, with the undeducible or non-derivable character of prescriptives. Within an argument (that we shall return to) which attempts to separate out what he calls, after Wittgenstein, the 'language games' of prescriptive statements from those of cognitive statements, he remarks to his interlocutor:

> If you asked me why I am on that side [the question is one of a hypothetical attack on an American computer in Heidelberg used to programme the bombing of Hanoi], I think that I would answer that I do not have an answer to the question 'why?' and that this is of the order of . . . transcendence. That is, here I feel a prescription to oppose a given thing, and I think that it is a just one. This is where I feel that I am indeed playing the game of the just!
>
> (*JG* p. 69)

To judge in this way 'without criteria' and not to derive one's judgement from a theoretical model of justice – to accept à la Kant the transcendence of the moral law signalled in the 'feeling' of obligation – has, predictably, drawn the indignation and verve of many a 'post-Kantian', specifically those within Hegelian, Marxist or rationalist traditions of thinking justice. In his recent work *The Ideology of the Aesthetic*, Eagleton, for example, comments on Lyotard's argument in the following terms: 'Thus suspended in vacant space, the prescriptive or political is left to the mercies of intuitionism, decisionism, consequentialism, sophistry and casuistry.'[4] Eagleton's own argument deals with *Just Gaming* in the context of

Lyotard's interest in the aesthetic (that of *L'Economie libidinale* and his more recent work on the 'sublime') and maintains rapidly that the 'postmodernist' and 'post-structuralist' fascination with art and literature as a metaphor and substitute for, or supplement to, politics points to its utter lack of credentials in the political domain, if not to its latent fascistic 'aestheticisation of politics'. The alternative political case to Lyotard is seen to be Habermas. A similar, although more nuanced, kind of argument is made by Peter Dews's *Logic of Disintegration: Post-Structuralist Thought and the Claims of Critical Theory*.[5] Here, the knell of 'postmodernism' is sounded and, with it, its 'philosopher', Lyotard.

The above remarks refer to two accounts of Lyotard's work, both made under the aegis of postmodernity and/or postmodernism. Whether one endorses this work or not, one can see that the approach and terms of the debate are none the less couched in terms of a historical category and in terms of a 'pragmatics' of experimentation given the 'modern' failure to legitimate either theory or practice. Now, Lyotard has been, to put it kindly, rather simplified through this 'postmodern(-ist) consumption of him.

In the following pages, and in order to complicate the terms of this appropriation, I wish to pursue Lyotard's stress on, and account of, *judgement* with and since *Just Gaming*.[6] I will be looking first at two arguments in Lyotard's article 'Answering the question: What is the postmodern?', to be found as an afterword to the major text in *The Postmodern Condition*.[7] I will then return to *Just Gaming* and its elaboration of the game of the just and a general justice of multiplicity. Finally, I will turn to Lyotard's further refinement of this latter argument in an article written shortly after *Just Gaming* and entitled 'Introduction à une étude du politique selon Kant', reproduced in parts in both *The Differend* and *L'Enthousiasme: la critique kantienne de l'histoire*.[8] By tracing this specific itinerary, in particular Lyotard's relation to Kant's philosophy, we will both broaden and deepen the 'context' in which Lyotard wishes to use the term 'postmodern' and we will gain a certain purchase on the question of judgement which he poses concerning the general theme of 'delegitimation' as well as on one or two problems that his explicit account of judgement meets. In addressing these latter problems, the prefix 'post' will be given, finally, a certain inflection which, perhaps, goes beyond what Lyotard has himself attributed to the term 'postmodernity'.

II

At the beginning of 'Answering the question: What is the post-modern?' Lyotard confronts Habermas's rebuff of 'French' thinking in 'Modernity: a project unfinished', in which he, among others, is stamped with the label of 'neo-conservatism'.[9] The confrontation is centred around a certain use of Kantian philosophy and the means of resistance to a world dominated by technology or splintered, as Habermas would put it, by 'instrumental reason'. Lyotard considers Habermas's use of Kant, specifically the latter's understanding of a 'transcendental public' and of aesthetic judgement as a bridge between freedom and necessity, as one regulated by the norm of 'the unity of experience'.

> Habermas considers that the remedy for the splintering of culture and its separation from life can only come from 'changing the status of aesthetic experience when it is no longer primarily expressed in judgements of taste', but when it is 'used to explore a living historical situation', that is, when 'it is put in relation with problems of existence'. What Habermas requires from the arts and the experiences they provide is . . . to bridge the gap between cognitive, ethical and political discourses, thus opening the way to a unity of experience.
>
> (*PMC* p. 72)

Lyotard is referring, here, to Habermas's argument in *Theory of Communicative Action* that 'aesthetic expressive discourses' anticipate, in shaping what is pleasing to individuals, the ideal community of transparent communication by their accommodation of 'a generalised other' through the normative procedures of language. For Habermas, these procedures are inherently rational and thereby serve as media for all other forms of action – be they instrumental, strategic, practical or theoretical.[10] It is by these procedures that one can debate, for example, what pleases in an orientation to mutual understanding. More importantly in our context, Habermas thereby bridges what Kant in the introduction to the *Critique of Judgement* calls the 'yawning abyss' between theory and practice by the fundamental norms of rational speech that are presupposed in all discourse given the necessity of an a priori linguistic inter-subjectivity for discourse to be possible at all.[11] He thus generalizes, as Lyotard stated above, Kant's judgement of taste (as the latter expounds it in paragraph 40 of the *Critique of Judgement*), perceiving in the aesthetic judgement the transcendental grounds of a communicative politics which can shore up the failures of the philosophies of the subject.

For Lyotard, this argument commits – what will become an insistent methodological arm in his work of the 1980s against communication theory, Marxism and positivism – a series of transcendental illusions in the Kantian sense.[12] Let me expand upon Lyotard's criticisms of Habermas in the article by profiting also from certain statements made in *The Differend* which work against both a communicational approach to language and the philosophicopolitical weight which Habermas wishes it to carry. The argument assumes (i) that one can define the nature of language when language as such forms, at best, a whole (or an Idea in the Kantian sense) that cannot be cognitively validated (cf. *D* §5, §§92/5, §§106/7, §180, §188 and §229); (ii) that the 'social relation' (transcendental intersubjectivity and the ideal speech situation which accompanies it) can be deduced; which presupposes both theoretically and methodologically a consensus that has first to be judged as either particular to a specific domain of experience or not; (iii) that the norm of the unity of experience, or the rational consensus anticipated through the various, heterogeneous domains of rationality, is indeed the 'ultimate end' of these domains, presupposing, again, that the world can be thought primarily according to the consensual end particular to the cognitive sciences; and, consequently, (iv) that the bridge between the practical and the theoretical can be crossed by the intersubjective norms implicit in aesthetic experience rather than – as Kant would wish and Lyotard has tirelessly reminded us – being thought *analogically* through the procedures of what Kant calls in the *Critique of Judgement* 'reflective judgement'. I will come to this last point in more detail later. Lyotard would, therefore, beg to differ with Habermas's remedies, indeed with the very notion of a remedy (hence his move to the 'Analytic of the sublime' in the *Critique of Judgement* in the article and elsewhere, and, as we shall see, his excessive stress on 'dissensus'), and would argue that Habermas's desire to articulate difference through the hegemony of cognitive judgement is unjust to the many strands of the social fabric which resist translation into a common structure of language.

My purpose in alluding to (and expanding upon) this confrontation between Lyotard and Habermas has been to stress how *alert* the former wishes to be when crossing between and over the domains of, for example, cognition, ethics, politics and art. If one is as equally concerned as a Habermas at the so-called 'autonomization' of these spheres in modern culture and advanced capitalism (if not their progressive reduction to the technical rules of 'exchange' and 'performativity'), this does not mean that one should prolong the philosophical or socio-cultural attempt to unify their relations with each other by tying them back, in resistance to the amoralism of advanced capitalism, to a cognitivist account of communicative ethics (the refinement of the 'project' of 'modernity'). For Lyotard this not only smacks of a nostalgic, ultimately nihilist and totalistic conception of culture (a Lyotard who has been rather too quickly celebrated or denounced); as I suggested above, it fails, immediately, to do *justice* to the heterogeneous spheres that make up the social fabric. It is this general notion of justice which interests Lyotard.

Concomitantly, and perhaps more importantly to begin with, Habermas presupposes that philosophy *knows* already what its own rules of procedure should be. And yet, this is precisely what is in question for Lyotard. Philosophy, if it is a particular 'sphere' of activity (or what he will call in *The Differend* a 'genre'), *is looking for its rule*. As Lyotard was to put in the preface to *The Differend* (a preface whose claims would need to be carefully untied in relation to the book's third and sixth chapters, 'Presentation' and 'Genre, Norm'):

> Unlike a theoretician, the [author] does not presuppose the rules of his own discourse, but only that this discourse too must obey rules. The mode of the book is philosophical, and not theoretical (or anything else) to the extent that its stakes are in discovering its rules rather than in supposing their knowledge as a principle.
>
> (*D* p. xiv)

This is why, for Lyotard, philosophy is *critical* (in the Kantian sense) and why it is concerned with *judgement*. Philosophy judges; it neither prescribes nor theorizes, because it does not know its rule, a rule or set of rules by which it could offer or promise either a 'system' of itself or a 'doctrine' derivative of the system.[13] Philosophy's sentences 'are articulated in such a way as to show that this articulation is not a matter of course and that the rule for their articulation remains to be found' (*D* §180, trans. modified, and cf. §98 and §228). Put differently, the necessity of judgement is absolute because there is no absolute judge (necessity). Philosophy is a constant witness to the implications of this paradox throughout the social fabric and feels the need to 'invent' judgements given the necessary contingency of all judgements. We will also come back to this claim in more detail later. It not only serves as a way to read Lyotard's styles of philosophizing, it paradoxically places philosophy in the world at the very moment it is unable to offer the world *an* ethics, *a* politics, *an* aesthetics, *a* philosophy of history, etc., as well as the way in which the latter should link up with each other. And, if philosophy is to respect its stakes in this sense, then the philosopher is, after Kant, working under the feeling of an agitation 'of an uncertain watchman who is always on guard as to cases or rules – a sentinel'.[14] We can, perhaps, begin to understand one of the 'posts' of 'postmodernity' in this sense.

Now let me turn to the second argument of 'What is the post-modern?' which interests me. It is, in fact, close in its implications to what has been said above and will allow us to question through Lyotard's attention to judgement both the socio-historical and 'aesthetic' appropriation of his 'postmodernism'. Lyotard elaborates what he considers to be the stake in modern and, particularly, twentieth-century writing and art: that it presents that there is something of the order of the unpresentable ('présenter qu'il y a de l'imprésentable').[15] The terms are again Kantian and draw specifically on the 'Analytic of the sublime' in the third *Critique*. In this tortuous subsection of the *Critique of Judgement*, Kant distinguishes between a judgement of taste and what I will call its *limit*, which he defines as 'a feeling of the sublime'. In a judgement of taste, the object occasioning the feeling of pleasure in the subject is judged to be beautiful and the judgement itself is accorded an imputed universality. If I state that *x* is beautiful, I impute the same judgement to everyone else. It is this imputation which allows Kant to grant the aesthetic feeling an a priori status analogous to that of 'respect' in the second *Critique*. It also allows him to read such a judgement as a 'reflective' accord between the faculties of understanding and imagination which *promises* (and nothing more, as Habermas would claim) a community of agreement. As the solution to the antinomy of aesthetic judgement will elaborate, the agreement between the two faculties allows for the disinterested universality of the judgement, but it does not allow one to state what the beautiful is, thereby subsuming the 'case' under a 'classical' code of rules which determines in advance our agreement about what is beautiful or not. Nevertheless, what is crucial to the judgement of taste is that the object has *form*. It is the feeling of the sublime that signals the loss of this form and pulls the feeling of pleasure appropriate to a judgement of taste into a *tension* between pleasure and pain. Kant draws the distinction in the following terms:

> The beautiful in nature is a question of the form of the object, and this consists in limitation, whereas the sublime is to be found in an object even devoid of form, so far as it immediately involves, or else by its presence provokes, a representation of *limitlessness*, yet with a super-added thought of its totality. . . the beautiful is directly attended with a feeling of the further-ance of life, and is thus compatible with charms and a playful imagination. On the other hand, the feeling of the sublime is a pleasure that only arises indirectly, being brought about by the feeling of a momentary check to the vital forces followed at once by a discharge all the more powerful, . . . the sublime does not so much involve positive pleasure as admiration or respect, i.e. merits the name of a negative pleasure. . . . that which, without our indulging in any refinements of thought, but, simply in our apprehension of it, excites the feeling of the sublime, may appear, indeed, in point of form to contravene the ends of our power of judgement, to be ill-adapted to our faculty of presentation, and to be, as it were, an outrage on the imagination, and yet it is judged all the more sublime on that account. . . . how can that which is apprehended as inherently contra-final be noted with an expression of approval? All that we can say is that the object lends itself to the presentation of a sublimity discoverable in the mind. For the sublime, in the strict sense of the word, cannot be con-tained in any sensuous form, but rather concerns ideas of reason, which, although no adequate presentation of them is possible, may be excited and called into the mind by that very inadequacy itself which does admit of sensuous presentation.
>
> (*CJ* §23)

Lyotard glosses:

> We have the Idea of the world (the totality of what is), but we do not have the capacity to show an example of it . . . We can conceive the infinitely great, the infinitely powerful, but every presentation [through the imagination, the faculty of presentation] of an object destined to 'make visible' this absolute greatness or power appears to us painfully inade-

quate. Those are Ideas of which no presentation is possible. Therefore they impart no knowledge of reality (experience); they also prevent the free union of the faculties which gives rise to the sentiment of the beautiful . . . They can be said to be unpresentable.

(*PMC* p. 79)

With this Kantian schema, the stake, as Lyotard sees it, of modern art has been to 'make visible' that there is something which cannot be made visible, accepting, thereby, the dis-unity of the subject, signalled in the sublime disposition, which is split between its ability to use its reason, its understanding and its imagination. Hence Lyotard's prolonged interest in avant-garde and non-figurative painting, considered to be concerned with constantly testing the rules of presentation which constitute 'reality' and with presenting negatively (through, for example, abstraction) something like the Ideas of the infinite which Kant accords to our purely conceptual faculty of reason. Modern art is, then, concerned with remaining faithful to the split espied by Kant between what we conceive and what is 'real', refining and experimenting on the frameworks which allow for (the illusion) of presentation (Euclidean space, the frame, the canvas, the museum, etc.). It is in this sense that the article 'What is the postmodern?' can be seen to be combating, in turn, the 'nostalgic', or fundamentally 'realist' desire for a stabilizable instance of discourse implicit in the calls for a return to meaning, to a 'responsible' artistic community (addresser), to a public (addressee) or to an objectifiable reality (verifiable referent) – a struggle which is pursued in *The Differend* on many registers, note-ably in its work on the referential status of reality and in the distinction it wishes to make between what is cognitively valid and what are 'signs' (or, feelings) which demanded a different set of rules and language to find expression and thus a different rule of validation.

But there are, for Lyotard, very schematically, two ways of approaching this dis-unity signalled in the feeling of the sublime; two ways, that is, of presenting the 'that there is something of the order of the unpresentable'. He takes such examples as Chirico and Proust on the one hand and Duchamp and Joyce on the other, and conceptually maintains the difference to be the following:

[M]odern aesthetics is an aesthetic of the sublime, though a nostalgic one. It allows the unpresentable to be invoked only as the missing contents; but the form, because of its recognizable consistency, continues to offer to the reader or viewer matter for solace and pleasure. Yet these sentiments do not constitute the real sublime sentiment, which is an intrinsic combination of pleasure and pain: the pleasure that reason should exceed all presentation [our capacity to conceive Ideas], the pain that imagination or sensibility should not be equal to the concept. . . . The postmodern would be that which, in the modern, invokes the unpresentable in presentation itself; that which denies itself the solace of good forms, the consensus of a taste which would make it possible to share collectively the nostalgia for the unattainable; that which searches for new presentations, not in order to enjoy them but in order to make one feel more that there is something of the order of the unpresentable [*pour mieux faire sentir qu'il y a de l'imprésentable*].

(*PMC* p. 81, trans. slightly modified)

Now, despite the division between these two ways of invoking the unpresentable, it is clear that what comes 'after' modern art is already 'in the modern'. The 'post' of 'postmodernity' does not imply a temporal succession. The distinction could be considered here as a question of *tone* and *style* predicated on the refusal to shore up the loss of the unity of the subject by offering a reconciling form to cover over the pre-existing distinction between 'form' and 'content', placed here in terms of the imagination and reason. This immediately suggests that the 'post' is *necessarily* a question of experimentation, one through which art no longer follows the classical aesthetic rules of the beautiful (of *form*, of what pleases), but asks itself constantly, through its practice and its relation to tradition, what the rules of art are. This is why there can be no *aesthetic* of the sublime, although Lyotard does not make the point absolutely clear in this article. For the very notions of what the aesthetic and its object are are placed in question by 'avant-garde' art. It is along these lines that we should also read a previous comment: 'A work can become modern only if it is first postmodern. Postmodernism thus understood is not modernism at its end but in the nascent state, and this state is constant [*récurrent*]' (*PMC* p. 79).

The above places in question both a socio-historical approach to Lyotard's understanding of the postmodern and an Eagleton-type approach to his interest in art. Not only, for example, would a Montaigne be 'postmodern'; 'postmodern' art questions the very ends of the aesthetic as a category or realm. This is why I have stressed the particular phrase 'présenter qu'il y a de l'imprésentable'. Contrary to common belief, Lyotard is, again, not proposing an aesthetic *of* the sublime. For this would be the attempt *to present the unpresentable*; an endeavour which, following a Kantian argument, Lyotard would judge severely as 'unjust' and which he sees, in his work from *Just Gaming* onwards, as organizing modern politics' desire to present in the world Ideas (a republic, labour force, communism, etc.) which cannot be validated according to the rules of cognitive proof. Rather, he is proposing, within the conceptual oppositions of language bequeathed to him, a *negative* 'aesthetic' which alludes to what falls outside the realm of presentation through a 'negative' presentation. This last point would eventually encourage us to suggest that a hidden target of this article is, more interestingly than Habermas, Heidegger's reflections on art during the 1930s and the stress that Heidegger places on the beautiful, form and futural self-fashioning as he forges a set of relationships between fundamental ontology, art and the *polis* through the 'common root of the transcendental imagination'.[16]

Thus, Lyotard's philosophy of the 'postmodern' is indeed an argument for 'experimentation' and 'multiplicity', but only *given that* the 'bridges' between the 'subject''s faculties and spheres of activity (reason, understanding, imagination, sensibility) are not evident and that the rules for crossing them are not given (either transcendentally or empirically). The lack of a rule is not just a present historical phenomenon (or its philosophical diagnosis), it is the reflective activity of thought or production as such in its 'nascent state' and this would in fact apply to *all* thinking and art whatever the manoeuvre then is to cover up the 'initial' indeterminacy. If one pushed Lyotard's analysis here – and also related his work to that of Derrida – such manoeuvres would be in the history of philosophy, for example, and despite their crucial differences, the positing of God, Being, the Subject, *Geist*, the proletariat, cognitive rationality, etc. and would *constitute* the 'history' of philosophy in the equally 'recurrent' inability to evacuate the indeterminacies which the initial lack of a rule leaves behind *in* the attempt to evacuate it. A re-reading of *The Postmodern Condition*'s account of 'grand' narratives would be merited in this light since there is some evidence to suggest in Lyotard's account that these narratives of legitimation do not work in the first place and that the 'post' of 'modernity' is both a recognition of this and an attempt to play upon it. To say this is to link up, partly, with what Lyotard argues at the end of the article and to relate it to the previous comments on philosophy's judicious disposition. I quote again:

> A postmodern artist or writer is in the position of a philosopher: the texts he writes, the work he produces are not in principle governed by preestablished rules, and they cannot be judged according to a determinant judgement, by applying familiar categories to the text or the work. Those rules or categories are what the work of art itself is looking for. The artist and the writer, then, are working without rules in order to formulate the rules of *what will have been*. Hence the fact that work and text have the characters of an *event*; hence also, they always come too late for their author, or, what amounts to the same thing, their being put into work, their realization (*mise en œuvre*) always begins too soon. *Post modern* would have to be understood according to the paradox of the future (*post*) anterior (*modo*).
>
> (*PMC* p. 81)

If one does not have a pre-established rule by which to judge, then, for Lyotard, one is exercising what Kant calls 'reflective judgement', the search for a rule to judge particulars. The distinction made in the *Critique of Judgement* between determinant and reflective judgement is the following: 'If the universal (the rule, principle, or law) is given, then the judgement which subsumes the particular under it is *determinant*. . . . If, however, only the particular is given and the universal has to be found for it, then the judgement is simply *reflective*' (*CJ* p. 18). The analogy that Lyotard is making between writing, art and philosophy is one predicated on the paradoxical temporality of the future anterior. Only once (or, *après coup*) one has produced the work, will the set of rules by which it can be judged be possible. (Whether this paradox can be thought exclusively in terms of reflective judgement will be the concern of the last part of this chapter.) This is the reason why a work which is not consciously classical (in the sense elaborated above) or modern (in the sense of maintaining a classical consistency of form) has the character of an *event*. Lyotard is, accordingly, attempting to think invention and experimentation in terms of this future anterior rather than exclusively, as in the tradition of aesthetics, in terms of *form*, or, as in the hermeneutical tradition of interpretation, in terms of agreement. The 'postmodern' writer does not *know* whom he is addressing or, ultimately, what indeed he is saying because the rules organizing his address are not present. They will have been. The 'post' of 'postmodernity' is not only neither a socio-historical category nor a fanciful, 'poststructuralist' play on the 'signifier'; it is also not a concept which can be thought of in terms of linear time. In this sense it is probably not a *concept* at all, subsuming under itself the unity and stability of a referent (a 'postmodern' case). Rather, the term should be seen as itself an *experiment* which is trying to witness reflectively the difficulty of 'presenting' *events*.[17] It could, indeed, be argued that Lyotard's more recent attention in *The Differend* (especially the chapter 'Presentation') to what could be called a general ontology of 'sentence-events', where what is radically 'unpresentable' is the 'presentation' itself of whatever is presented (the 'that there is a sentence'), does nothing but confirm (and radicalize) this kind of interpretation of the article.

The above comments on 'Answer to the question: What is the postmodern?' have certainly left a lot of questions unanswered, specifically concerning the terms in which one is to articulate the multiplicity which Lyotard wishes to be a kind of (meta-)principle of judgement. I have simply wished to stress a certain orientation within the article: its stress on heterogeneity given the lack of a rule to cross over the 'bridges' between cognition, politics, ethics and art, its concern to consider philosophy as radically subjected to this indeterminacy, its implicit wish to consider this state of being 'without rules' as eminently involving questions of justice and the status of the final analogy between the reflective practice of art (including literature) and that of philosophy, based on their concern with the paradox of the 'future anterior'.

These themes all testify to Lyotard's agitation with 'theory' which he sees as an example of 'determinant judgement' and to his own agitation concerning his judgements upon the indeterminate rule of reflective judgement. This is why, as I said above, it would be best to see Lyotard's work as a series of experimental *essais* (more pagan than pious), aimed at producing effects or coups in a given situation which will engender in turn other coups. Writing is considered in this perspective as an 'art' (in the sense of the analogy explicated above) of invention and transformation rather than as a discourse of or on truth. One such coup (or rather, 'counter-coup' – I won't pursue the distinction here) has been the postmodernist appropriation of him: Lyotard was, after all, the one to exploit the term 'postmodern', intervening in an area predominantly populated by literary and architectural judgements that would have themselves, necessarily, an effect on the reception of his own use of the term. But there can be other, more interestingly agitated, coups among which are Lyotard's later writings which will have had a retrospective effect on how one might read his earlier work.

III

Before we turn explicitly to one of these more recent writings, let us now look more closely at *Just Gaming*. As I briefly mentioned earlier on, the stake of this work is twofold. First, it wishes to separate, in critical fashion, the rules pertaining to cognition and description from those of prescription in order to witness the singularity of both prescriptives in particular and ethics in general. Lyotard translates these spheres or domains into the Wittgensteinian language of 'language-games' since he is suspicious of the humanism informing the (Kantian) language of a subject representing to itself through its faculties the difference between these spheres and thus advocating, if only analogically, a promised finalization of their differences. We will have to readdress this radicalization of Kant. Second, *Just Gaming* wishes, partly on the basis of this critical act of separation, to elaborate a more general Idea (in the Kantian sense) of justice which would testify to, elaborate and ultimately regulate the incommensurabilities not only between questions of cognition and those of the particular 'game' of prescription, but those between the various and multiple games that make up the social 'patchwork' – an indefinite task which Lyotard will come to think under the Idea of an 'archipelago'. The links with the concerns of 'What is the postmodern?' are clear; here, however, Lyotard is directly concerned with thinking the relations between judgement, justice and multiplicity.

In the first part of the argument, Lyotard maintains that to ground justice upon a description (whether it be, in Kantian terms, cognitive or dialectical) is to assume the priority of description over prescription and that the descriptive games are an adequate description of the totality of language. The political 'terror' which it can lead to (nothing more nor less than a totalistic conception of language) is predicated on the enforcement of prescriptions validated by a description of reality which it is the purpose of those prescriptions to bring about. The specificity of a prescription is thereby lost by being plugged into a theoretical ordering on a (meta-)

descriptive level. This is where and how *Just Gaming* draws its energy from the belief in the equivalence of totality and terror and how it conceptualizes what it sees to be the 'metaphysical' prejudgement which would wish that matters of ethics and politics can be derived according to ontological or theoretical principles. The *dispositifs* of Platonic, Marxist and 'modern' (self-legislating autonomy) models or developments of justice are all considered to commit the transcendental illusion of conflating prescriptives with descriptives in this way, despite the important differences Lyotard sees in the different articulations of this illusion (*JG* pp. 19–59).

Now, more trivially, if one wishes, one may well link a prescriptive ('Open the door!') with a descriptive ('The last sentence is a prescriptive') but such a linking (or *enchaînement* as *The Differend* will say) does not annul the executory force specific to the language game of prescription. Whether one obeys the order or not is another matter. At the level of refinement which Lyotard is concerned with here, there is an incommensurability between these two language games (or three, if one now separates out the dialectical from the cognitive). This incommensurability is then investigated by Lyotard in terms of the 'pragmatic' destination of the instances which make up what will be called later the 'universe' of each type of sentence (*D* §25 *et al.*). In the prescriptive, the stakes are not those of truth or falsehood and this is reflected both by the 'virtual' nature of the referent (to be actualized) and by the position of the addresser and addressee of the sentence. In an order the addressee is obligated (again whether he or she obeys or not); in a descriptive both the addresser and addressee are concerned with the status of the referent (its truth or intellectual interest) and are necessarily (even if only potentially) in exchangeable positions. Thus to place prescriptions in the domain of truth and falsehood by trying either to legitimate or deduce their authoritative force is to wish that in the game of prescription the subject of knowledge – situated on the exchangeable poles of addresser and addressee in a cognitive or descriptive sentence – can still be privileged, that is intrude upon the asymmetrical relation between the poles of addresser and addressee in a prescriptive. This may well be our desire; but critical judgement does not exercise itself, as we saw earlier, in pleasure alone and will be alert to the temptation to elide this difference when considering matters of justice.

The difference is radicalized when it comes to ethical obligation. For, here, the addresser pole or instance of the universe of the prescriptive is 'transcendent' and the addressee receives the order as an 'empty obligation' (*JG* p. 52). Translating the work of Lévinas into his own terms, Lyotard alludes to the Judaic commandment 'Be just!' as well as to the non-deducible character of the moral law and to the feeling of duty or respect which is an effect (or addressee) of the law in Kant's *Principles of a Metaphysics of Morals* and the *Critique of Practical Reason*.[18] It is along these lines that Lyotard continues to remove the possible hegemony of knowledge over ethics from the rules of the latter. But, as he remarks in *The Differend*, it is difficult, once this separation takes place, to think of ethics as a 'language game' (or genre) (*D* §171). For what rules does it have? The critical purchase which the empty obligation seems to provide is an exclusively negative critique of attempts to fill it in. This would undoubtedly do a lot of work, despite Eagleton's earlier claims to casuistry and intuitionism. One can imagine a sort of rabbinic figure (fully aware that he could not make others listen to him) dancing, agitatedly, on the parameters of society, duly warning the latter's politicians of the dangers of trying either to describe or present justice as if it were a state of affairs which could be known. Kant partly plays this role in his historico-political writings in making a distinction between the Idea of a republican civil order and the attempt to produce it as if it was a phenomenon (see, for example, 'Answer to the question: What is enlightenment?', 'On the common saying: "This may be true in theory, but it does not apply in practice"' and 'The contest of faculties').[19]

But neither Kant nor Lyotard remain with the 'empty' obligation, as it could be argued Lévinas does given his suspicions of ontological discourse. For Kant, if we take an (unmotivated) interest in the moral law, it is also because the law must be effected. If the law does nothing but whisper to us its empty voice, its demand is nevertheless *that* it be effected. Its dictum, as Lyotard has recently put it in an article entitled 'L'Intérêt du sublime', is its whisper.[20] For Kant, the law also implies what 'should' be a 'good' performance. As is well known, this is described in the *Critique of Practical Reason* as a law which has 'the form of law', that is, a law which is universalizable and which Kant then determines as applicable to particular wills *as if* it was a universalizable law of nature (*CPrR* p. 35). Lyotard follows Kant very closely here for reasons which will become clear. As the former has argued since *Just Gaming* and beyond *The Differend*, Kant makes the transcendental distinction between ethics and knowledge to then unmake it, but only analogically. If he re-invites a relation between the two realms of undeducible freedom and the deducible laws of nature through the formulations of the categorical imperative, this invitation or 'bridge' is a sort of fiction. For example, the second and third formulations of the imperative in the *Principles of the Metaphysics of Morals* – 'Act as if the maxim of your action were to become through your will a universal law of nature' and 'Every rational being must act as if he by his maxims were at all times a legislative member in the universal realm of ends' – do not command the addressee of the moral law to act so as to *produce* a community of 'rational beings', but solely to act *as if* the maxims of his or her action was to be a law of this community. (This distinction will inform all of Kant's political writings, specifically his adversion to revolutionary politics and the important demarcation he makes in the 'Perpetual peace' essay between a 'political moralist' and a 'moral politician' – themes that Lyotard has elaborated upon in *The Differend* and *L'Enthousiasme: la critique kantienne de l'histoire*.[21]) If Lyotard, in company with Lévinas, has reservations with the way in which Kant has here allowed a certain universalist rationalism to cover over the initial (and recurrent) obligation of the moral law (Kant is in this sense certainly too much of an Enlightener for Lyotard), he is equally aware that Kant has placed an analogical fiction at the heart of ethical conduct which bridges the incommensurability between ethics and knowledge only on the condition, paradoxically, that one has not 'crossed' the bridge. The distinctions between the 'language games' of ethics, knowledge and politics are thereby simultaneously maintained, just as an effective critique of politics and a way to think ethical action in the world are opened up.

Kant formalizes this move by making a distinction between judging *regulatively* and judging *constitutively*. We are here in fairly familiar territory since to judge regulatively is to judge reflectively *according* to an Idea of reason. Indeed, as we shall see, 'reflective judgement' in the ethical orientation of Kant's philosophy is *always* regulative in the sense that it is guided by an Idea – a point which 'What is the postmodern?' either did not wish to elaborate upon or had gone beyond (a question which I'll leave unanswered for the moment). The Kantian judge has no determinant rules by which to judge an ethical action or maxim since the moral law is undeducible. However, he can think the Idea of freedom not as a *condition* of action but as a regulative 'horizon' outside but in analogy with the rules of nature in the 'real' (*JG* p. 90). This reading of Kant is then radicalized by Lyotard, in turn, given Kant's Enlightenment step to finalize the differences between the respective realms under the teleological Idea of an objectively purposeful nature. I will address this step in a moment given, precisely, the difficulty of Lyotard's next task to displace Kant's Idea of unitary finality, having accepted the crucial Kantian distinction between regulative and constitutive judgement. This will finally take us back to the reflective orientation of philosophy and the paradoxical temporality of the 'future anterior' informing it, what I called the 'post' of 'postmodernity'.

What, then, is the Lyotardian move to a generalized 'ethics' above and beyond the specificity of the prescriptive? We have seen both from the article 'What is the postmodern?' and the first major argument of *Just Gaming* that the concern of justice is both to judge and hold to the specificity of the prescriptive and judge and hold to the specificities of each language game in resistance to the domination of the social bond by one language game (most often the rules of description, but also the rules particular to capital or to teleology (in the Kantian sense) or, indeed, to narrative (as in *The Postmodern Condition*)). The above concern is therefore not going to produce *an* ethics, since this would simply finalize language games according to one particular game: a danger implicit even in Lévinas's philosophy given his wish to root ontological (and aesthetic) discourse upon the an-archical ethical opening to the other (however rootless this opening is). Lyotard's response in *Just Gaming* is something of a fiat that pulls against the methodological implications of his interest in Kantian analogical orientation discussed above (the unmaking of the distinction between ethics and knowledge). For he simply reverses the unitary finality which he associates with Kant's Idea of justice (the 'as if' of universal legislation) into that of a multiplicity. This is the move which has earned Lyotard the reputation of being a kind of Rortyesque pragmatic pluralist, if not relativist, one by which critics have found it, of course, appropriate to place Lyotard under the banner of 'postmodernism'.

> [T]he question we now face is that of a plurality, the idea of a justice that . . . would be that of a plurality, and it would be a plurality of language-games . . . Every one of us belongs to several minorities [territories of language] . . . and not one of them prevails. It is only then that we can say that the society is just.
>
> (*JG* p. 95)

The justice of the social bond would obtain as long as the rules of validation of one game did not encroach upon another. Thus the Idea of justice becomes, in a somewhat convenient linguistic turn, 'the multiplicity of justices' (rules) of each game and 'the justice of their multiplicity' (*JG* p. 100). And 'just' judgement intervenes 'inasmuch as those games are impure' and are not being played 'by their specific rules' (encroachment or the transcendental illusion). Lyotard is certainly able in this formulation (a sort of 'postmodern' categorical imperative if one wishes) to safeguard the specificity of the prescriptive and work towards a generalized 'ethics'. However, as some critics have noted, the 'just' playing of the game of language games is done at the risk of converting the agonistic principle of this game of language games into a closed system of heterogeneous determinations and finite rules dominated by the metaprescriptive 'Be plural!' (cf. *JG* p. 100).[22] The refusal to allow the language games to determine each other thus undermines the ideas of conflict, combat, surveillance and dispersion which it was supposed to establish and by which judgement guided itself to begin with (in for example the *separation* of matters of ethics from those of knowledge). To put it differently, since the heterogeneous games can only be 'just' (in the generalized sense of being proper to their rules) in so far, for example, as the Idea of justice prescribes them not to prescribe (this property being the specific property of the game of obligation in the wished dispersion), the multiplicity of justices (rules) must both depend on the regulative Idea of justice and resist it as itself totalizing. The Idea is thus always already in conflict with the generalized justice which it wants to articulate. In other words, as an *Idea* of plurality, justice is still being brought under a unifying movement. This prompts one to suggest – and there are many signs in the *style* of the work – that *Just Gaming*, like the article 'What is the postmodern?', is itself another *essai* or coup of reflective judgement, an experiment on the questions of justice given the predominantly theoretical circumscriptions of justice which it is working through and criticizing, and that the Idea of plurality with which it ends is another *analogical* way of presenting 'qu'il y a de l'imprésentable' (here matters of justice and the excess of the law of justice over *any* determination or articulation whether it be a concept *or* an Idea).

The last comment has several implications. One would need, first, to focus on a certain instability in Lyotard's use of the term 'unpresentable' which we did not attend to in any detail earlier on when looking at the feeling of the sublime and the negative aesthetics which Lyotard considers it to encourage. We recall from 'What is the postmodern?' that the artist is in the 'sublime' situation of trying to make visible negatively that there are unpresentable conceptions. Lyotard used Kant to open up the distinction between what is conceivable and what is cognitively verifiable (the 'real') and hence spoke in the Kantian terms of Ideas of reason, on the one hand, and imagination and sensibility, on the other. However, the last argument in the article and the above criticisms of Lyotard's reversal of the Idea of finality to attain a justice of multiplicity have suggested that the 'unpresentable' cannot necessarily be thought in terms of an Idea of reason. For an Idea, even if regulative, still provides a set of *rules* which end up totalizing (be it a totality of unity or multiplicity, consensus or dissensus) the conflict it is attempting to witness. This point would imply, second, – although I must state this briefly here – that Lyotard's work (post 'What is the postmodern?') is split between, on the one hand, *using* the Kantian distinction between Ideas of reason and concepts of the understanding to survey critically and judge the predominantly Marxist and communicational theory's attempts to overcome the 'bridge' between freedom and necessity (the politico-historical work of *The Differend* for example) and, on the other, attempting to think the 'unpresentable' beyond its rational, ethical orientation in Kant's very *use* of Ideas in and after the *Critique of Judgement*.[23] In relation to this second point, one would have to look carefully at the way in which Lyotard, since 'What is the postmodern?', has tended to see artistic practice as negatively presenting 'matter' or, in terms of *The Differend*, the 'arrive-t-il?' of 'that there is a sentence' (the unpresentable presentation of its *Fall*) before one determines what kind of case the sentence is (the 'il' of 'arrive-t-il?') (*D* §§131 and 132). This short excursion takes us back, precisely, to both the question of reflective judgement (how does one judge without a rule?) and to the analogical procedures of the Kantian Idea and our desire to see the idea of the Idea as an analogical (or 'negative') presentation of the *radically* unpresentable 'law' of justice.[24]

For if we have pointed to the static presentation of conflict that the meta-prescriptive 'Be plural!' ends up with, Lyotard's very critical procedure through *Just Gaming* in separating out ethics from knowledge à la Kant implies presuming 'from the start' ethics to be something like knowledge. Only on that condition – and the same point would apply to the first and second *Critiques* – can they then be separated out and distinguished. In other words, it is only by acting *as if* prescriptives are something like descriptives that one can then understand the ethical difference. If this sounds like Kant and Lyotard, there is a difference. The transcendental illusion committed, for example, in the search to justify ethical authority, as if it could be validated cognitively (as a Habermas or an Eagleton would wish), can only be described and redressed on the basis of an 'originary illusion' common to *Just Gaming and* to what it is criticizing. One has to proceed 'as if' one understands obligation or the moral law before one can *either* determine it *or* separate it out from the rules of truth and falsehood as 'undetermined'. This 'as if' before either the formulas of the Kantian categorical imperative or Lyotard's reversed version of them thus precedes the procedures of the transcendental illusion and is nothing but the originary illusion (or 'fiction') of experience itself. Now, this immediately implies that the so-called 'yawning abyss' between ethics and knowledge, prescriptives and cognitives, which Lyotard would wish to guard in order to safeguard the specificity of obligation has to be first 'crossed' before it can be 'instituted' and then crossed 'analogically'. In this sense (and again) the analogical terms themselves of 'abyss', 'bridge' and 'crossing' are not entirely applicable to the procedure of critical judgement, for one has *already* crossed the abyss in the first place in order to carve it out and construct the precarious bridge which passes over it. This does not mean, however, that one can logically cut through this paradoxical manoeuvre, as a Hegelian-type reading of either Kant or Lyotard would do by dialectizing the limit between what is known and what is unknown, or presentable and unpresentable. For dialectic ignores precisely the analogical value to the bridge even if the critical watchman's very procedure of setting it up necessarily *precedes* the opposition between ethics and knowledge.[25] (One can nevertheless sense that it is here, in this strange logic of temporality, that further 'bridges' between Kant, Hegel and Lyotard might be built beyond what Lyotard might have to say about them in, particularly, *The Differend*.)

My argument does, however, mean (since it applies to the borders between all language games) that what is at issue is the exact nature of the procedure of reflective judgement itself. Here the surveillance 'posts' of critique, which will have moved back and forward across the bridges between language games, need to be related to the 'post' of the future anterior at the end of 'What is the postmodern?' and to the argument in *The Differend* that philosophy's stakes are 'in discovering its rules rather than in supposing their knowledge as a principle'. For what else is 'philosophy', in Lyotard's determination of it earlier, than the questioning (but certainly not the dismissal) of even the principle of an *Idea* of plurality? All this demands further investigation of Lyotard's use of Kantian 'reflective judgement' and the manner in which judgement determines the 'rules' of each 'language game'. We will now try and do this by following Lyotard's complication of the 'game' of language games in an article entitled 'Introduction à une étude du politique selon Kant' which is partly reproduced as 'Kant Notice 3' in *The Differend* (pp. 130–5) and in *L'Enthousiasme: critique kantienne de l'histoire* (pp. 31f). A small and slightly dense detour through the organization and place of reflective judgement in Kantian critique is first necessary as well as a certain repetition of ideas already discussed.

IV

In the introduction to the *Critique of Judgement* the faculty of judgement is considered to be the third faculty of a priori knowledge, lodged between those of reason (in its practical use) and understanding (reason in its theoretical use). It is seen to be situated between the realm of freedom from which the a priori rules of practical reason are negatively 'deduced' (or rather, fictionalized) and the realm of nature upon which the laws of the understanding legislate. Now, if judgement, for Kant, is to be a faculty of knowledge in its own right, it must equally have its own a priori rule. This poses the problem of how judgement is to orient itself. For judgement can only be legislated upon by itself. If this principle was to be deduced, like the principles of the understanding, it would not be judgement but a technics of reason. And indeed judgement would still be necessary even then to apply such a technics to their case, so that what could be called the 'aporia of judgement' would simply reappear further up the line.[26] The faculty of judgement is singular then in having to give to itself its own rule or principle. As Kant puts it in section 4 of the Introduction:

> a transcendental principle, the reflective judgement can only give as *a law from and to itself*. It cannot derive it from any other quarter (as it would then be a determinant judgement).
>
> (*CJ* p. 19, my emphasis)

Moreover, unlike reason or understanding which are concerned respectively with their 'objects' the will and nature, it has no particular object to determine immediately. However, with its own principle, it is seen as the faculty effecting the passages (*Ubergänge*) over the 'yawning abyss' that lies 'fixed' between the realm of nature and that of freedom (*CJ* p. 14). In the context of the Introduction to the third *Critique*, these passages are, needless to say, the 'bridges' of the aesthetic judgements of taste and of the sublime and of the teleological judgement of the finality of nature.

These bridges of aesthetic and teleological judgement are acts of analogical orientation which respond to the 'call' in Kant that

> nature must . . . be capable of being regarded in such a way that in the conformity to law of its form it at least harmonises with the possibility of the ends to be effectuated in it according to the laws of freedom (*die Natur muss auch . . . so gedacht werden, dass die Gesetzmässigkeit ihrer Form wenigstens zur Möglichkeit der in ihr zu bewirkenden Zwecke nach Freiheitsgesetzen züruckstimme*).
>
> (*CJ* p. 14)

When Kant was describing in the penultimate quotation the self-legislation of judgement, it was in the *specific context* of the procedure that was needed in order to judge 'reflectively' particular laws of nature, once the determinant judgement had done its work under the a priori categories of the understanding deduced in the *Critique of Pure Reason*. Reflective judgement's search for the universal in its encountering of singularities in nature is thus placed here as a *part* within the undetermined whole of the three *Critiques*. It is acting out the 'demand' of reason that the whole of nature should be systematized according to the law of specification discussed in the chapter 'Regulative employment of Ideas' in the *Critique of Pure Reason* (*CPR* pp. 532–48). Reading Kant reading judgement, one can only presume that reason is prior to judgement in that reason demands of judgement certain rules of procedure (as was maintained by the analogy of the *self*-instituted 'tribunal' of reason in the first preface to the first *Critique*).

The a priori principle that reflective judgement gives itself is the analogical one of judging nature 'as if' nature formed, as a whole, a unity of experience. The principle is the finality of nature in its multiplicity. This principle is the unity, analogically employed, between man and nature – a unity which, according to Kant and the tribunal of reason, 'must' be presupposed and which was referred to in the last quotation. The 'demand' of reason for the regulative employment of the principle of the finality of nature is *synonymous* with the demand of reason in its practical sense that the concept of freedom 'must' actualize the end proposed by its laws. What teleologically unifies both demands is what Kant calls in §§82–4 of the *Critique of Judgement* 'Providence'. In response to the former call of reason, Nature's products are reflected upon as if they were produced purposively. In response to the latter call Nature is reflected upon as if its ultimate end (the end of all the physical ends of nature reflected upon analogically) were man, whose end is 'culture' (the setting of ends independent of nature in its mechanical sense).

From this brief sketch of the place of judgement in the third *Critique* we can see that Kant explictly locates 'reflective judgement' between the 'demand' of reason for completion and the validation of this demand by the Idea of a providential nature pursuing its ends through this very demand. For Kant, recourse to such an Idea validating the 'demand' is nothing but the 'demand' itself and yet the demand can only be validated by the Idea. It is in the turn of this vicious circle that judgement's prior intervention can be located, a judgement which is *prior* to reflective judgement and, therefore, *prior* to the *Idea* of unitary finality which regulates it, *après coup*.

Kant remarks at the end of his previous exposition of reflective judgement that the analogical orientation to the discovery of nature's particular laws is *itself* thought according to an analogy. He writes:

> The finality of nature is . . . a particular *a priori* concept, which has its origin solely in the reflective judgement. For we cannot ascribe to the products of nature anything like a reference of nature in them to ends, but we can only make use of this concept to reflect upon them in respect of the nexus of phenomena in nature. . . . Furthermore, this concept is entirely different from practical finality (in human art or even morals), though it is doubtless thought after the analogy.
>
> (*CJ* p. 20)

Kant's somewhat throw-away final remark reveals a crucial point in the development of his argument. It is a point which suggests that the reflective judgement *does* derive 'its rule from another quarter', contrary to Kant's remarks. For the reflective judgement's analogical rule of reflection is itself rooted in an analogy established

between nature and the productive causality of man. The establishment of this analogy implies that judgement has *already* intervened
before reflective judgement, in the above Kantian sense, in order to
provide it with the 'type' of rule that will rule its principle. This
judgement before reflective judgement is itself reflective because it
has to borrow from the realm of the aesthetic the rule of its production and apply it *analogically* to the procedure by which reflective
judgement orients itself in nature. Only on the basis of this first
'borrowing' can reflective judgement give, not 'from' but 'to itself',
a law of reflection which is to be used analogically.

Judgement, thus, gives to the reflective judgement of the finality
of nature the rule for its judgements. Judgement dictates: 'When
you, reflective judgement, reflect upon nature's multiplicity proceed
as if the causes in nature were final and not efficient. To think such
causality, think of nature as if it was art or as if it was a moral act.'
The dictum of the dictation is judgement's lending to the reflective
judgement the rule of causality particular to the realms of the
aesthetic and the ethical (purposive and unconditioned causality).
The reflective judgement is reflective because it will use this analogy
analogously and not constitutively. The 'reason' for the dictation is
judgement's interest in reason's unity (the Kantian promise of a
philosophical 'system'). In other words, if judgement in Kant precedes the rule of reason, it equally allows itself to judge *only* according to a unity that is systematic and guards the nature of man and
nature itself within meaning. The dictation is a fiat; that is, judgement is *immediately* 'practical'.[27] The content of the fiat is what Kant
calls elsewhere the 'need of reason' to effect itself and affect itself
in the world.[28] Judgement is constrained to judge the faculties of
knowledge and is constrained simultaneously to give them rules by
which to judge. In Kant, the way *in which* it judges, beyond its
immediate 'practicality', is to anticipate the unity, be it reflective, of
the faculties – the very thing, as we have seen, that Lyotard considers to be Kant's humanism and to be 'unjust' to the social fabric.

This pre-judgement ('pre' in the Kantian context, at least, of
reflective judgement) is itself the judgement of how to judge. In a
sense it cannot be understood as a faculty because it is nothing but
the limitation of the other faculties to their particular domains and
the method by which passages are effected between these domains,
in order for these faculties to be in a position to orientate themselves
beyond the conditions of experience and remain nevertheless *at home*
in the world. Judgement, in this sense, is the generalization of

reflective judgement across the three *Critiques*. Judgement is thus the self-legislative principle of Critique which has no domain as Kant says, but which is the 'milieu' in which the domains and realms can be instituted. To exploit another analogy Kant uses in the first *Critique* to think this institut-ion (although he would wish the latter to be, precisely, 'natural'), judgement is the founder and governor of the 'islands' of domains and realms and the 'sea', the means, by which they can commerce with each other.

Now it is precisely in these terms and in terms of this set of analogies that Lyotard reads Kant's making and unmaking of the transcendental distinction after *Just Gaming*. In doing so, Lyotard explicitly complicates the tidiness of the rules of the language games in the latter work since the critical watchman is aware of defining the 'rules' of each language game *as* his judgement delimits it and 'institutes' it as an 'island'. He is also aware that the number of islands is indefinite.

In 'Introduction à une étude du politique selon Kant', Lyotard transcribes the Kantian terminology of 'faculties' into one of 'sentences' and 'families' of sentences. This latter distinction was not clearly made in *Just Gaming* and now explicitly places the question of rule within and between each sentence, so allowing for conflict to occur between 'families' in the way they wish to validate themselves through particular sentences (a procedure generalized in the major arguments of *The Differend*). As Lyotard began to elaborate and translate in *Just Gaming*, a faculty is a 'potential' of sentences submitted to a group of rules of formation and presentation which constitute, for example, the families of sentences of reason, understanding, imagination and sensibility. The rules of validation of each faculty/ family always involve judgement since each time 'a sentence' is declared, the question of the validation of the sentence by a 'case' is necessary. Lyotard writes:

> Judgement already and necessarily intervenes each time that
> it is a question of saying 'this is the case', in order therefore
> to establish a presentation; in cognitives this takes place under
> the regime of the schema, in dialectical arguments under that
> of the symbol, and in prescriptives when it is a matter of
> evaluating responsibility and morality under the regime of the
> type [the 'as if' of the universality of laws of nature discussed
> earlier].[29]

('IEPK' p. 103)

Lyotard's interest in Kant here stems less immediately from the different forms of presentation (schematic or symbolic to follow paragraph 59 of the *Critique of Judgement*) than from the fact that it is judgement which is ensuring the passages (*Übergänge*) from one family to another in order to determine the mode of presentation particular to each family. Analogy, as we have seen in relation to Kantian ethics, is the clearest example of such a passage. The families are not 'preconstituted', but will be formed themselves through the trial and error of the mode of presentation. Only when this has taken place can the analogical borrowing from one family to another of its mode of presentation be legitimate and circumscribed and the passages be worked as paradoxical validations and not 'unifying' bridges.

What Kant calls the 'field' in the second version of the Introduction to the third *Critique*, Lyotard calls the 'archipel' (*CJ* p. 12 and 'IEPK' p. 104). For Kant, '[c]oncepts, so far as they are referred to objects apart from the question of whether knowledge of them is possible or not, have their field, which is determined simply by the relation in which their object stands to our faculty of cognition in general' (ibid.). Within this field, there are territories in which knowledge is possible for these concepts and the respective cognitive faculty, and within these territories there are realms over which the concepts and their faculty exercise legislative authority. Lyotard turns this meta-analogy of the 'field' of the third *Critique* back into an 'archipel' of islands which is now thought according to the Idea of the 'démultiplication des facultés' ('IEPK' p. 104). This procedure is clearly similar to the reversal of the Idea of unity in *Just Gaming*, but it now theorizes the conflictual play between the faculties through their attempts to validate their 'cases' and the corrections which such validations need. This is how Lyotard describes the archipel as well as the faculty of judgement which operates from and within the sea surrounding the islands:

> All these faculties find their object in this field, some delimiting a territory there, others a realm, but the faculty of judgement finds neither one nor the other, it ensures the passages between those of the others. It is rather the faculty of the milieu, within which every circumscription of legitimacy is secured. Furthermore, this is the faculty which has enabled the territories and the realms to be delimited, which has established the authority of each family on its island. And this, it

was only able to do thanks to the commerce [and war] which
it maintains between them.

('IEPK' p. 105, cf. *D* p. 131)

It is clear from the above that Lyotard has made the reflective
judgement of the third *Critique* the faculty of the 'milieu'. In a sense
it is not a faculty because it does not constitute in Lyotard's terms
'a family of sentences'. It is rather the operation of formation and
presentation of all the other families. And yet, despite the radicalization of reflective judgement effected by Lyotard's reading of the
third *Critique* in its placing of judgement before and not between
theoretical and practical reason, there remains an ambiguity in his
redescription of it which immediately recalls the Kantian problem
of the judgement of reflective judgement. For what is necessarily
unclear in Lyotard's exposition of the archipelago at this stage of
the argument is (again) the *Idea* itself of this archipelago. Despite
the conflict which he has reintroduced into the commerce and war
between 'families' of language, the Idea, as a concept which takes
its object to its logical end, cannot *think* this conflictual commerce
indeterminately; in other words it cannot think it *tout court*. It looks,
therefore, as if Lyotard is still 'presupposing' the heterogeneity of
the faculties in order to 'systematize' the operations of judgement,
just as Kant's reflective judgement is given the rule of unity to
proceed to judge singularities or cases without a rule. Lyotard is
implicitly arguing behind his description of judgement that the law
of reflective judgement, its meta-prescription, is heterogeneity and
that heterogeneity is therefore its 'ultimate end'.

The archipelago is itself the analogical or symbolic presentation
of the 'case' of the Idea of the dispersion of the faculties. It is
accordingly a 'reversal' of the Idea of philosophy that Kantian
Critique sketches out, puts to the test and tries to conform to and
which Kant describes in most detail in the 'Architectonic of pure
reason' in the first *Critique*. He writes that 'philosophy is the science
of the relation of all knowledge to the essential ends of human
reason (*teleologia rationis humanae*), and the philosopher is not an
artificer [*Vernunftkünstler*] in the field of reason, but himself the
lawgiver [*Gesetzgeber*] of human reason' (*CPR* p. 658). This philosopher is an 'ideal' in the Kantian sense, but for Kant the ideal of
his legislation is to be found in the reason with which all finite
human beings are endowed. This ideal of lawgiving prejudges at
least that the 'field' *must* be one of conformity to the law of unity,

that the essential ends of man *must* be realized. For Lyotard the Idea has become one of an open field of faculties whose rules are incommensurable with each other. Thus Lyotard's reversal of the 'end' of the Idea prejudges by the very use of the Idea as a 'guiding thread' (in the Kantian sense) the judgement of reflective judgement (how it is to operate in its passages) in the same way as Kant's judgement of reflective judgement prejudged unity. Philosophy is continuing to orient itself reflectively according to an Idea of what philosophy might be, although this idea is now one of incommensurability. In this sense, it has already found its rule.

And yet, Lyotard has equally suggested in the above quotation that the operation of judgement is *only* possible because each 'family' attempts to make claims beyond its boundaries and only at this price are its rules of validation found and delimited. Incommensurability is always a question of translation and of the limits of translatability. To push this analysis further, one could consequently say that the 'faculty of the milieu' emerges out of the differentiating and differentiated movement of 'land' (to change the analogy yet again) from which the islands *will have been* instituted. In this perspective both the islands *and* the sea (the operation of judgement) are after-effects of a more complex and intricate 'milieu'. This would be a 'milieu' *before* Lyotard's 'faculty of the milieu' and it is a way of describing, here, the radically unpresentable law of justice with which I ended my analysis of *Just Gaming*. It would also be the 'milieu' upon which judgement *decides* how to draw the map. The Idea of the archipelago already seems threatened, then, by Lyotard's own description of what is going on 'in' and 'through' it. In 'Introduction à une étude du politique selon Kant', Lyotard goes on to give several examples of how the judgemental operation of de-limitation takes place. I will move directly to the example of the 'guiding thread' of teleological judgement as we have already seen the delimitation of ethics from knowledge and the analogy of the universality of nature which simultaneously allows for the passage between the two realms. The future anteriority of the abyss carved out between different families of sentences, the future anteriority of the rules of the families and the future anteriority of philosophy's reflective judgement upon this 'milieu of the milieu' will be brought together in the example chosen.

The 'guiding thread' of teleological judgement concerns the resolution of the antinomy of the faculty of judgement in §§69–71 of the third *Critique*. Lyotard is interested, here, in the way in which

71

the operation of judgement lays out further islands in the archipel by aligning the mechanistic and teleological interpretations of nature. Kant's alignment of the mechanistic and teleological thesis is based on our inability to have an a priori determining principle of the possibility of things on mere empirical laws of nature. A reflective principle of orientation is therefore necessary in addition to an explanation based on causal nexus, as long as 'the conception of causality which it involves is a mere idea to which we in no way undertake to concede reality'. Otherwise an antinomy would arise between the two approaches to nature. Kant goes on, 'we only make use of it to guide a reflection (*man braucht sie nur zum Leitfaden der Reflexion*) that still leaves the door open for any available mechanical explanation, and that never strays from the world of sense' (*CJ* Part II, p. 40).

The specific point which Lyotard wishes to make here is that the guiding thread determining analogical orientation serves as another means by which the field of concepts in general is split into islands which borrow from each other, through judgement, their means of direct or indirect presentation. Lyotard seems to endorse the Kantian move. And yet it is at this point of Lyotard's reading of Kant that the 'institutive' role of judgement, implied from the beginning of the article, is made explicit. The judgement at work in Critique regulating the alignment and difference between schematic and analogical approaches to nature can be neither constitutive nor regulative (in the Kantian sense of determinant or reflective judgement). Indeed, it becomes quite clear at this moment in the article, given the proximity of the analysis of reflective judgement and its relation to nature, both that the judgement circumscribing and legitimating the moves of the faculties in relation to each other is anterior to reflective judgement *and* that this 'primary' judgement is at one and the same time descriptive and prescriptive of these faculty-islands and of the rules that 'bind' and 'bound' them – the point I made concerning the Idea of justice in *Just Gaming* and which we can now see more clearly through Lyotard's foregrounding of the role of judgement each time there is a case, each time there is a sentence (which is all the time). He states at the end of his commentary on the *Leitfaden*, and without further elucidation, in both the 'Introduction...' article and in *L'Enthousiasme*:

the judge decides [*trancher*] the legitimacies of each validation claim. He thereby divides [*tranche*] the transcendental subject into insular faculties and divides [*tranche*] the field of all possible objects into an archipel. However, he also looks for 'passages' which attest the coexistence of heterogeneous families and which allow for the transactions [*transactions*] between diverse parties to their satisfaction. If he shows himself thereby to be accommodating [*transigeant*], it is because he himself is nothing but the faculty of judgement, critique, and that the latter can only decide [*trancher*] if it is in the position to intervene on all the islands of the archipel, if, at least, it 'passes' without a rule 'before' the rules, analogically or otherwise, in order to establish them [*si du moins elle 'passe' sans règle 'avant' les règles, analogiquement ou autrement, pour les établir*].

('IEPK' p. 112)

The procedure of judgement described here, 'critique' itself, suggests, precisely, an unrelievable undecidability as to the procedure of its judgements and the nature of the rules which it delivers that pulls the Lyotardian re-reading of Kant away from the Idea of the archipelago that was apparently regulating its moves. The Idea of the incommensurability of families of sentences or islands is posterior to the work of separation and decision (neatly caught by the ambivalent concept of 'trancher') that judgement enacts in order that judgement can then describe, as if it was a descriptive state of affairs, the incommensurability and analogical 'passages' between these islands. The Idea of the archipelago *then* regulates this 'as if' description of '*différends*' as '*différends*'. However, judgement, as Lyotard remarks, must have been on all the 'islands' before they are described/prescribed *as* islands by judgement. This kind of paradox, the prescription of judgement's descriptions, and this kind of alogical temporality to judgement's originary orientation, confirm the suspicion that the gulfs and the bridges and passages so carefully guarded by Kant, and deepened and qualified by Lyotard, never take place in any pure or proper sense in the first place, for judgement has passed ahead 'avant les règles' to then proscribe and prescribe certain kinds of passages, certain kinds of rules of orientation. It also suggests that the 'first' case of the 'coexistence of heterogeneous families' (commerce and war) is the very ruling by which these 'insular' families appear from the differentiated and differentiating 'land' in order then to coexist with each other. For their rules are undecidably prescriptive and descriptive. In which case the very term 'co-existence', like the term '*différend*', is (again) not quite appropriate to describe what is going on here.

It is only on the prior condition of a certain and 'necessary contamination' (to use a term from Derrida's work) between the faculties of reason, understanding, imagination and sensibility that judgement can find itself and begin to sort out what rules organize which faculties and what rules organize the faculties' relations to each other. Such a sorting out will *always* be contingent and legislative in so far as the faculties and the arrangement of faculties *are* separated out. Thus the Idea of the archipelago can only be a secondary simplification of the heterogeneity which it wishes to articulate, as was the Idea of justice in *Just Gaming* and despite the complications which the latter has undergone in being rethought as the former. What is 'organizing' the 'field' before its legislative enshrinement into an *Idea* of a field or of an archipel is a tension of unity and disunity running through the 'faculties' which will allow their heterogeneity to be *either* intensified analogically (à la Lyotard) *or* synthesized analogically (à la Kant).

This last point makes it difficult for one to agree wholeheartedly (the disagreement is small but important if one is doing, as Lyotard is, philosophy) with Lyotard's final description of the 'political' in *The Differend* as a generalized archipel of sentences and families of sentences, bridged by a series of passages which serve simultaneously to articulate the 'differends' between the sentences and between the families (§§190, 194, 202 and 229). Nor can the previous analysis of judgement allow one to condone without a certain suspicion Lyotard's final remark that one should judge 'according to the idea of "passages" between heterogeneous sentences, and in respect of their heterogeneity' in contradistinction to the Kantian idea of the unity of these sentences ('IEPK' p. 134). However far Lyotard's use of the Idea of passages takes him in his analysis of the transcendental illusions committed by post-Kantian politics in the said article and *The Differend*, the suspicion remains that his own analysis of judgement takes him beyond the opposition of analogic and schematic principles of judgement. It takes him beyond judgement – into its 'pre' or 'post'.

The suspicion is further reinforced by a passage in *The Differend* which explicitly states Lyotard's own suspicion of Kant's presupposition of the guiding thread (*Leitfaden*), for reflective judgement, of the Idea of the objective finality of nature. Let me conclude with this passage. The presupposition of the natural teleology of humanity allows Kant to align the mechanical and teleological estimates of nature. This alignment of the antinomy of teleological judgement is itself, according to the Idea of nature's finality, one of the very means by which nature, as Providence, prepares its ultimate end, man's 'culture'. Thus what justifies critical judgement for Kant is the Idea of nature. What authorizes critical philosophy to have recourse to this finality to authorize itself to judge without rules on a 'case' that cannot be presented is in turn a 'case' that cannot be presented, since the Idea of nature's finality cannot be validated cognitively. Kant calls this kind of unpresentable case in the context of his historico-political writings 'signs', a term that Lyotard, I recall, exploits at length in *The Differend* and *L'Enthousiasme*. The sign validating the Idea of nature is the feeling on the part of the one who judges that he must judge in conformity to law. This feeling is the distress caused by the chaotic formlessness of empirical history. The criticist's interpretation of the feeling as a sign can only be done if the Idea of nature is already working through the feeling to allow it to appear as a sign of this nature. And yet the sign itself of this feeling serves to validate the 'practical' postulation of this very nature. Lyotard records the circularity of the argument and applies it to his own presupposition of the Idea of incommensurability and to the validation of the analogical presentation of the case of this Idea of the archipelago:

> [I]f we grant that the value signs have for the critical watchman is what leaves the play of judgement free with regard to them (finding the case for the rule and the rule for the case), that value nonetheless presupposes a kind of intention of finality on the side of what makes the sign. By means of the feeling which the philosopher has, an as-if subject would signal to him that, under the guise of this sign, a quasi-sentence [*une quasi-phrase*] has taken place whose meaning cannot be validated by procedures applicable to cognition, but must however be taken into consideration. Can one judge upon such signs without presupposing such an intention, be it problematically? That is, without prejudging that an unknown addressor not only delivers but also addresses them to us to be decoded?/ Inversely, however, if no guiding thread leads the way for judgement's expeditions, how can judgement find its way amid the labyrinth of passages? The *analoga* would be pure fictions, but forged for what needs? This itself is

impossible: the passages are what circumscribe the realms of legitimacy, and not the latter which would pre-exist the passages and tolerate them. What are we doing here other than navigating between islands in order paradoxically to declare that their regimes or genres are incommensurable?/ Whatever acceptation is given to the idea of nature, one's right of access to it is only through signs, but the right of access of signs is given by nature. Not even a denatured nature and signs of nothing, not even a postmodern a-teleology, can escape this *circulus*.

(*D* p. 135, trans. slightly modified)

It should, I hope, be clear by now that this passage brings together the problems of an idea of multiplicity, of the orientation of reflective judgement and the very rules of passage between and within the families (or genres) of sentences which we have been pursuing. The preceding has suggested as well perhaps that a way to think this *circulus* is to take into account as far as possible the future anteriority of every 'passage' and the after-effect of the 'abysses' which they will have crossed. This would be to accept that the critical sentinels or posts marking out the passages are themselves an after-effect of the contamination alluded to above; a 'post' effect of the tensions ('sublime' or otherwise) running through the families and which precludes them from being finite and determined. To recall certain sentences from 'What is the postmodern?', these *posts*, on which the critical watchman will never quite have kept his guard, 'always come too late' or 'what amounts to the same thing . . . always begin too soon' for 'their author'. The 'post' effect, or affect, of judgement signals not an 'unpresentable sign', the quasi-sentence of some sort of as-if providential subject, but the 'pre' of the messy 'land' which gave rise to the whole problem of passages in the first place. One description of this 'land' could indeed be 'language' and 'sentences', and this act of description could indeed be 'philosophy in search of its rule'. It would have to be accepted, none the less, that there will never be any presentation of this 'land', preceding as it does all distinctions between analogical and schematic presentations. It is beyond the sublime in this sense. The 'pre', for example, certainly does not address us, being interested in neither man nor 'itself'. Lyotard's placing of postmodern Providence within a 'quasi-phrase' would seem, in fact, to confirm the frailty of a sentence analysis of the social fabric at this point. For the 'pre' is not in any 'universe'.

It will only be after the event that one can describe and fail to describe it. Without this failure there would precisely be no sentence in the world. This is why the postal tensions of Critique and Lyotard's judgements and *essais* at judgement are so agitated. And this is one way to link on, in pleasure and pain, to Lyotard's 'postmodernity'.

NOTES

1 R. Boyne and A. Rattansi (eds), *Postmodernism and Society*, London, Macmillan 1990, p. 18.

2 J.-F. Lyotard, *La Condition postmoderne*, Paris, Minuit 1979; *The Postmodern Condition*, trans. Geoffrey Bennington and Brian Massumi, Manchester, Manchester University Press (1984) 1986. All future references to this book will take the form *PMC* and will be placed in the text.

3 J.-F. Lyotard, *Au juste*, Paris, Christian Bourgois 1979; *Just Gaming*, trans. Wlad Godzich, Manchester, Manchester University Press 1985. All future references to this book will take the form *JG* and will be placed in the text.

4 T. Eagleton, *The Ideology of the Aesthetic*, Oxford, Blackwell 1990, p. 398.

5 P. Dews, *Logics of Disintegration: Post-Structuralist Thought and the Claims of Critical Theory*, London, Verso 1987.

6 Indeed, given the above framework in which Lyotard has tended to be received, it can only be hoped that the recent American translation of *Le Différend*, Paris, Minuit 1983 [*The Differend*, trans. Georges Van Den Abbeele, Minneapolis, University of Minnesota Press 1988]; D. Carroll's work on Lyotard in *Paraesthetics: Foucault, Lyotard, Derrida*, New York, Methuen 1987; G. Bennington's important book *Lyotard: Writing the Event*, Manchester, Manchester University Press 1988; and the collection of Lyotard's articles in the recent *Lyotard Reader*, ed. A. Benjamin, Oxford, Blackwell 1989, will come to complicate the generally simplistic approaches to Lyotard's work. All future references to *The Differend* will take the form *D* and will be placed in the text.

7 The translator's title in *The Postmodern Condition* is 'Answer to the question: What is postmodernism?', which is, to say the least, an unfortunate rendering of the French 'Réponse à la question: qu'est-ce que le postmoderne?' (first published in *Critique* 419, avril 1982, pp. 357–67 and to be found in *Le Postmoderne expliqué aux enfants*, Paris, Galilée 1986, pp. 11–34).

8 J.-F. Lyotard, 'Introduction à une étude du politique selon Kant' is to be found in *Rejouer le politique*, ed. P. Lacoue-Labarthe and J.-L. Nancy, Paris, Galilée 1981, pp. 91–134; *L'Enthousiasme: la critique kantienne de l'histoire*, Paris, Galilée 1986. All references to the former article will take the form 'IEPK' and will be placed in the text.

9 J. Habermas, 'Modernity – an incomplete project', trans. Seyla Ben-Habib, in *Postmodern Culture*, ed. H. Foster, London, Pluto Press 1983, pp. 3–16.

10 J. Habermas, *Theory of Communicative Action*, vol. 1, trans. Thomas McCarthy, Boston, Beacon Press 1984, pp. 285ff.

11 I. Kant, *Critique of Judgement*, trans. James Creed Meredith, Oxford, Oxford University Press (1928) 1986, p. 14. All references to the work will take the form *CJ* and will be placed in the text. Where I have also quoted the German, references are to the Felix Meiner Verlag edition of *Kritik der Urteilskraft*, ed. K. Vorländer, Hamburg (1924) 1974.

12 For Kant's definition and use of this term, see the *Critique of Pure Reason*, trans. Norman Kemp Smith, London, Macmillan (1929) 1986, pp. 298ff. Very briefly, the transcendental illusion is, for Kant, the (natural) illusion of reason which goes beyond the sensible limits of possible experience (given by the forms of time and space) and attempts to apply its concepts *as if* they could designate phenomena in the world. These concepts of pure reason, stemming from reason as the 'faculty of principles', are in a sense the 'maximization' of the categories of understanding to their logical end and beyond these categories' empirical use in time and space. Kant calls these concepts 'Ideas' of pure reason and sees them as 'the totality of the syntheses of the conditioned'. The transcendental illusion is not, therefore, a *logical* illusion for Kant. The illusion rests rather on the *application* of the principles which make up the Ideas (the world, the soul, freedom, God) to the realm of experience, as if such an application could be 'objective' rather than purely 'subjective'. This is the Kantian distinction between the 'constitutive' and 'regulative' use of rules which will be important to us later on. Lyotard is clearly interested in the illusory use of rules of validation from one sphere to another in order to question so-called post-Kantian philosophy, whether its colours be Hegelian, Marxist, neo-Kantian, analytical or Habermasian. The transcendental illusion is, therefore, a crucial tool to him. As we shall see, however, he does not trouble enough (despite reversing it) the Kantian *logic* of Ideas as such.

13 It is here that Lyotard will *also* depart from Kant, given the latter's desire to see critique as a provisional step to a philosophical system with its doctrines. We'll come back to this departure.

14 See, J.-F. Lyotard, 'Judiciousness in dispute, or Kant after Marx' in *The Lyotard Reader*, pp. 324–59, at p. 328. 'Judicieux dans le différend' was originally given as a paper at a colloquium in 1982 concerning Lyotard's work, the articles of which are to be found in Lyotard *et al.*, *La Faculté de juger*, Paris, Minuit 1985.

15 The English translation of the phrase in the afterword to *The Postmodern Condition* reads 'to present the fact that the unpresentable exists', which is a little wayward (*PMC* p. 78).

16 The terms are to be found in Heidegger's *Kant and the Problem of Metaphysics*, trans. James Churchill Bloomington, Indiana University Press 1962. Heidegger's rereading of the *Critique of Pure Reason* follows the A edition of the text which does indeed suggest that the faculty of import to the deduction of the 'categories' of understanding is the transcendental imagination. Lyotard would, however, criticize the universalization of the latter's role across the different domains which form the objects of the three *Critiques* and Kant's politico-historical writings (see, especially,

Lyotard's recent *Leçons sur l'Analytique du sublime*, Paris, Galilée 1991, a series of lectures given over the past years which merits careful reading). Heidegger's subsequent move to Nietzsche's work in the 1930s could be usefully read as well through Nancy's deconstruction of 'fictional ontologies' in *La Communauté désœuvrée*, Paris, Christian Bourgois 1986 and through P. Lacoue-Labarthe, *La Fiction du politique*, Paris, Christian Bourgois 1987. Lyotard's slight impatience with Heidegger's reading of Kant and the consequences it may have on his own reading of Kant are questions which I have dealt with in my doctoral thesis, 'Community and originary finitude: thinking the political from Derrida to Kant', University of Sussex 1990, unpublished.

17 Geoffrey Bennington's *Lyotard's Writing the Event* reads both Lyotard's work up to the late 1970s and his work with Kant and Wittgenstein since the 1970s as a series of 'analogical presentations' of the 'event'. The present article owes much to the implicit approach to Lyotard in this deceptively accessible book.

18 See E. Lévinas, *Totalité et infini. Essai sur l'extériorité*, The Hague, M. Nijhoff 1961 and *Autrement qu'être ou Au-delà de l'essence*, The Hague, M. Nijhoff 1974; I. Kant, *Critique of Practical Reason*, trans. Lewis W. Beck, London, Macmillan 1956 and *Foundation of the Metaphysics of Morals*, trans. Lewis W. Beck, New York, Library of Liberal Arts 1959. All future references to the two works will respectively take the form *CPrR* and *FMM* and will be placed in the text.

19 See *Kant's Political Writings*, ed. H. Reiss and trans. H. B. Nisbet, Cambridge, Cambridge University Press 1970.

20 J.-F. Lyotard, 'L'Intérêt du sublime' in *Du sublime*, ed. Courtine *et al.*, Editions Belin 1988, pp. 149–78.

21 Kant's 'Perpetual peace' essay is to be found in *Kant's Political Writings* (1970), op cit., pp. 93–130.

22 See S. Weber, 'Afterword – Literature, just making it', the afterword to *Just Gaming*, G. Bennington's review of *Au juste*, 'August: double justice' in *Diacritics* (Fall 1984), pp. 63–71 and my review of the English version, 'Just attempts at Justice' in *Paragraph* 10 (1987), pp. 103–10.

23 As J. Sallis has shown, albeit rather obscurely, in his *Spacings – of Reason and Imagination in texts of Kant, Fichte, Hegel*, Chicago, University of Chicago Press 1987, the 'sublime' collapse of the imagination in its attempt to present Ideas of totality, and therefore its negative presentation of them through this collapse, is determined by Kant in the *Critique of Judgement within* the practical economy of reason's unity. The collapse points to Man's ethical *Bestimmung*, the capacity to conceive Ideas of reason. This last point will be picked up later with respect to Lyotard.

24 To say this is to begin to link the implications of Derrida's profound essay 'Préjugés: devant la loi' in *La Faculté de juger* (pp. 87–140) with Lyotard's concerns.

25 On Hegel's reading of the transcendental distinction in Kant, see, especially G. W. F. Hegel, *Science of Logic*, trans. A. Miller, London, Allen & Unwin 1969, vol. 1, part 1, section 2, chapter 2, 'Determinate being', pp. 111–57, esp. pp. 127–50.

26 The term 'aporia of judgement' is used at length by H. Caygill in his excellent work on Kant in *Art of Judgement*, Oxford, Blackwell 1989.

27 On this immediate practicality of judgement, see J.-L. Nancy's excellent essay 'Dies Irae' in *La Faculté de juger*, pp. 9–54.

28 On the 'need of reason', see I. Kant, 'Was heisst: sich im Denken orientieren', *Werke* V, Wiesbaden, Suhrkamp 1958, pp. 267–83.

29 This and the following quotation are to be found in 'Notice Kant 4' in *The Differend*. I have used the American translation, modifying it where necessary or appropriate.

4

THE MODERN DEMOCRATIC REVOLUTION: REFLECTIONS ON LYOTARD'S *THE POSTMODERN CONDITION*

John Keane

No sooner do you set foot upon American soil then you are stunned by a type of tumult; a confused clamor is heard everywhere, and a thousand voices simultaneously demand the satisfaction of their social needs. Everything is in motion around you; here the people of one town district are meeting to decide upon the building of a church; there the election of a representative is taking place; a little farther on, the delegates of a district are hastening to town in order to consult about some local improvements; elsewhere, the laborers of a village quit their ploughs to deliberate upon a road or public school project. Citizens call meetings for the sole purpose of declaring their disapprobation of the conduct of government; while in other assemblies citizens salute the authorities of the day as the fathers of their country, or form societies which regard drunkenness as the principal cause of the evils of the state, and solemnly pledge themselves to the principle of temperance.

(Alexis de Tocqueville, *De la démocratie en Amérique*)

I

The observation that modern societies are uniquely restless and self-revolutionizing because they invent and universalize democratic mechanisms for the interrogation and control of power has been familiar since Tocqueville's *De la démocratie en Amérique.*[1] According to Tocqueville's highly original thesis, which remains much

81

neglected in theories of modernization, a 'great democratic revolution' (vol. 1, p. 57) has begun to sweep through all spheres of modern life. In post-aristocratic societies, daily existence becomes agitated because democratic mechanisms awaken and foster a widespread passion for the equalization of power, property and status within the spheres of state and civil society. In the political realm, Tocqueville observed, everything becomes disputed and uncertain. The convincing power of sentimental tradition, absolute morality and religious faith in other-worldly aims is shaken; in this sceptical, secular age of political democracy, the stars of mythical belief fall to earth, the light of faith grows dim, and the horizons of political action become worldly, and thus subject to argument, persuasion and practical judgement. Those who live in democratic nations consequently look upon political power with a jealous eye: they are prone to suspect or despise those who wield it, and are thereby impatient with arbitrary state regulation. The state and its laws lose their divinity, coming to be regarded as necessary and/or expedient, and as properly based on the voluntary consent of the citizens. The spell of absolute monarchic power is broken, political rights are extended gradually from the privileged political classes to the humblest citizens, and political regulations and laws are subjected constantly to redefinition and alteration.

Tocqueville emphasized that distinctions and privileges are eroded gradually not only in the field of politics, but also within the domain of civil society. Modern democracies are subject to a permanent 'social revolution' (vol. 1, p. 69). Naturalistic definitions of social life are replaced by avowed conventions (Tocqueville notes, for instance, that democracy gradually destroys or modifies 'that great inequality of man and woman, which has appeared hitherto to be rooted eternally in nature' (vol. 2, p. 263); (hereditary) property is parcelled out, social power is shared ever more widely, and the unequal capacities of classes tend to dissolve. This is not to say that democracies are without concentrations of wealth. Such concentrations of property persist, but Tocqueville saw them to be vulnerable, as subject constantly to redistribution through changes in fortune, competition, legal redefinition and social pressures from the property-less. Having subverted the systems of feudalism and absolute monarchy, the democratic revolution refuses to bow before the social power of notables, merchants and industrial capitalists. The fear of losing their privileges strikes at the heart of these social groups – which is also why they have a hearty dislike of democratic mechanisms. Tocqueville evidently exaggerated the momentum and extent of this levelling process, and yet the logic of his explanation remains compelling: once certain social claims (e.g. rights to property) are defended by one group, the pressure is greater for extending them to other social groups; and after each such concession, new demands from the socially less powerful force new concessions from the privileged, until the once restricted social claims become *universal* in scope. The dilemma of modern civil societies is that they must extend social rights to everyone or to nobody. Since the latter option is an open embarrassment to democracy, the process of social levelling tends to develop an irreversible momentum of its own. Democratic mechanisms, or so Tocqueville argued, stimulate a passion for social equality which they can never quite satisfy: 'This complete equality slips from the hands of the people at the very moment when they think they have grasped it and flies, as Pascal says, an eternal flight' (vol. 1, p. 285). The less powerful ranks of civil society are caught especially in the grip of this dynamic. Agitated by the fact of their subordination and by the possibility of overcoming it, they are also irritated by the uncertainty of achieving equality; their initial enthusiasm and hope give way to disappointment and frustration, and to renewed commitment to the struggle for equality. This 'perpetual movement of society' (vol. 1, p. 261) fills the new world of modern democracy with radical scepticism and an impatient love of novelty. In this democratic maelstrom, nothing seems any more to be fixed or inviolable, except the passionate, dizzying struggle for social equality and political freedom.

II

At first sight, Tocqueville's expectation that democracy would become a universal and irresistible principle of modern life seems completely unrelated to the subject of postmodernism. Two explanations might be offered for this doubt. First, most of the recent controversies about postmodernism have severed themselves from theories of the modernization process – a symptom of which is postmodernism's relative unattractiveness in the disciplines of sociology, politics and economics. The objection to my interest in Tocqueville would be that the postmodernism discussion is concerned only with 'cultural' phenomena and not with social and political life. I am not convinced by this objection, for what is most often presented as an 'aesthetic' or 'scientific' contribution to the modernism/postmodernism debate is saturated deeply with (often implicit) political judgements about the modernization process, which is either stigmatized as corrupt (Tafuri; Jameson) or saluted as culturally, economically or politically advanced (post-war social democracy; neo-conservatism). The centrality of the prefix *post*-modernism provides a second explanatory clue as to why it might be argued that Tocqueville's theory of the modern democratic revolution is irrelevant to the subject of postmodernism: among many advocates of postmodernism *sensu stricto*, all things modern, not only modern art and scientific enquiry, but modern socio-political structures as well, are seen to be deeply problematic. From this standpoint, the modern project as a whole is a lost cause and cannot be rescued or revived; it has become (or for a long time has been) canonical, deadly and stultifying and (it is argued) it must therefore be broken, repudiated and exceeded. The original objection would therefore remain: is not Tocqueville's theory of the modern democratic revolution merely of interest, say, to antiquarians who inhabit the dark corners of museums and archives, or to traditional political philosophers searching for certitudes under fluorescent lights, but quite irrelevant to the contemporary discussion of postmodernism?

The answer I wish to defend is emphatically negative: the fundamental importance of Tocqueville's thesis is that it furnishes the (admittedly incomplete and, in places, unsatisfactory) outlines of a socio-political understanding which is both implied and (for reasons of self-consistency) required by the most advanced philosophical defences of postmodernism, among which I include Jean-François Lyotard's *The Postmodern Condition*.[2] Expressed conversely, and more paradoxically, the fundamental socio-political importance of philosophical essays such as Lyotard's lies in their *potential* call for the deepening of the democratic revolution first analysed and defended by Tocqueville. Viewed from this paradoxical angle, philosophical postmodernism of the type defended by Lyotard is not a break with the modernization project but, potentially at least, its socio-political ally, a vigorous agent of the renewal and deepening of modernity's democratic potential.

In attempting to unravel and defend this potentially intimate, if paradoxical, relationship between philosophical postmodernism and modern democracy, I shall concentrate exclusively on Lyotard's *The Postmodern Condition*. In so doing, I do not wish to make claims about its 'representativeness' of the postmodern movement as a whole. This movement is marked by a deeply protean quality; its breathtaking heterogeneity of questions and pursuits is to be expected and encouraged, not only because 'modernism', its object of criticism, is itself highly differentiated (the architecture of Le Corbusier, Abstract Expressionist painting, and the neo-positivist science of Popper are evidently not isomorphic phenomena), but also and more specifically because philosophical postmodernism, to which I am in several ways deeply sympathetic, has a justified aversion to attempted totalizations of the world, a world which is seen in fact as an infinitely complex, dynamic and linguistically charged reality that can therefore only ever be interpreted from a multiplicity of perspectives.[3] This latter point explains not only why I am not concerned to point to the 'representativeness' of *The Postmodern Condition*; it also suggests why I am concerned neither to summarize it in its own terms nor to extract from it systematic generalizations and hard-and-fast conclusions. I should like to avoid these options, preferring instead to pursue a type of hermeneutic approach which attempts to reconstruct the deliberately organized arguments of *The Postmodern Condition* in defence of postmodernism, in order to indicate the ways in which they carry the text away from the 'positions' advocated by its author – more precisely, my aim is to foreground the adventures of argumentation which lead the text to both deny (in the name of *post*-modernism) *and* sanction socio-political claims compatible with the modern democratic project outlined and defended by Tocqueville.

III

The stated concern of *The Postmodern Condition* is the altering status of science and technology within late twentieth-century – or, as Lyotard prefers, postmodern – societies. This concern functions, however, as a means of exploring a much broader repertoire of questions, such as the future of the university, social justice, the contemporary fetishism of efficiency and effectiveness, the crisis of metaphysics, systems theory, the structure and functions of narrative, the dangers of a fully computerized society, and the possibility of a postmodern science which places emphasis on discontinuity, catastrophe, non-rectifiability and paradox.

Of special interest to Lyotard is the problem of legitimacy, that is, the processes by which every particular language game seeks to authorize its 'truth', 'rightness' and (potential) efficacy – and therewith its superiority over other, rival language games – through utterances which specify, more or less explicitly to the 'bearers' of a particular language game, rules concerning such matters as the need for narration, internal consistency, experimental verification, consensus obtained through discussion, and so on. These rules consist not only of guidelines concerning how to form denotative utterances (in which the true/false distinction is central); they pertain to notions of *savoir-entendre, savoir-dire, savoir-vivre*, that is, to the ability to form and understand 'good' evaluative and prescriptive statements and, thereby, to speak and interact with others in a normative way. It is precisely consensus about these pragmatic rules, or so Lyotard argues, that permits the participants within a language game to identify each other as interlocutors, as well as to circumscribe their language game, distinguishing it from other, possibly incommensurate language games.

From this (neo-Wittgensteinian) perspective, Lyotard emphasizes that every utterance within a particular language game should be understood as an activity, as a 'move' with or against players of one's own or another language game. Utterances may in addition be understood as moves in opposition to the most formidable adversary of all: the prevailing language itself. This is Lyotard's 'first principle': to perform speech acts involves jousting, adopting agonistic or solidaristic postures towards other players or towards language itself. In this respect, players within language games are always embedded in relations of power – power here understood as the capacity of actors wilfully to block or to effect changes in speech activities of others within the already existing framework of a language game which itself always prestructures the speech activities of individuals and groups.

This point about power and language games also implies – this is Lyotard's 'second principle' – that language games must be considered as definite social practices: to perform rule-bound or rule-breaking utterances is at the same time to participate in the production, reproduction or transformation of forms of social life. Society can be understood neither as an organically arranged functional whole (Parsons) nor as a totality subject to dualistic fragmentation (Marx). Rather, the social bond resembles a complex labyrinth of different, sometimes hostile, slipping and sliding language games, which obey rules of an indeterminate variety and therefore cannot be apprehended or synthesized under the authority of any single meta-discourse. Lyotard quotes Wittgenstein (*Philosophical Investigations*, section 18) to drive home this point concerning the thousands of language games, trivial or not so trivial, that weave the fabric of our societies: 'Our language can be seen as an ancient city: a maze of little streets and squares, of old and new houses, and of houses with additions from various periods; and this surrounded by a multitude of new boroughs with straight regular streets and uniform houses.'

The aim of postmodernism, in Lyotard's view, is to accentuate this insight about the infinite and splintered character of the social. Practically speaking, this means that postmodernism is committed to the task of dissolving the dominant language games which have hitherto cemented together and 'naturalized' a particular – modern – form of social bonding. The multiplicity of language games circulating in any society cannot be transcribed and evaluated in any totalizing meta-discourse; attempts to do precisely that must therefore be countered by the practice of paralogism (*la paralogie*), that is, by attempts to defer consensus, to produce dissension and permanently to undermine the search for commensurability among nonidentical language games. In my view, Lyotard's text is at its finest and most insightful when interrogating and doubting various types of language games: the Platonic dialogue, with its patterns of argumentation oriented to reaching a consensus (*homologia*) between communicating partners; the popular narratives which define what may or may not be said and done in traditional societies; the crucial dependence of modern scientific discourse upon mainly postnarrative techniques, such as didacticism, denotation, argument- and proof-based methods of falsification and rules of diachronic rhythm; the concern of German Idealism to synthesize the various sub-branches of knowledge through a totalizing metanarrative that understood both this knowledge and itself as moments in the becoming of Spirit; the early modern theory of socio-political legitimacy, according to which the consensus of a deliberating people is a necessary condition of political liberty and justice; and recent technocratic proposals for abandoning the old ideals of liberal democratic humanism in favour of effectiveness and efficiency – *performativité* – as the sole criteria of legitimacy. These interrogations emphasize the heteromorphous and wholly conventional nature of language games, thereby raising doubts about their 'imperialistic' claims to be absolute. Lyotard's interrogations do not necessarily lead (*pace* Seyla Benhabib[4]) to a privileging of one language game – a mathematical and natural science which emphasizes discontinuity and self-destabilization – over other possibly incommensurate language games. Lyotard is not caught in a performative contradiction. He covers himself against this outcome by rehabilitating the logic of occasion as it is found, say, within the writings of the Greek sophists. The curious feature of this logic is its claim to give the lie to the logic of the one universal truth, by signalling that the latter is only a particular case of the logic of the particular, of the special case, of the unique occasion. This procedure is not at all self-contradictory, since this logic of particularity is presented as neither a more universal logic nor a 'truer truth'. On the contrary, Lyotard's interrogations consistently depend upon the logic of particularism, and consequently they contribute decisively, or so I would argue, to a revised theory of the ideological functions of language games.[5]

Under pressure from the type of paralogism defended by Lyotard, ideology can no longer be understood, nor its riddles explained and criticized, within the classical Marxian mode. Contrary to the classical Marxian schema, Lyotard's interrogations suggest that ideology is not a form of posthumous misrepresentation of a prior ontological reality of class-divided material life processes, which function (as Marx thought) as both the pre-linguistic, Archimedean point of origin of ideological forms and as the point of truth that contradicts the 'false' dissimulations of ideology. Lyotard reminds us that there is nothing specifically social – not even the labour process itself – which is constituted from such an Archimedean point 'outside' and 'below' language games. Language games cannot be conceived as simply a 'level' or 'dimension' of any social formation: they are co-extensive with social and political life as such. Further, Lyotard's interrogations remind us not only that ideology is not simply (in the most vulgar Marxian sense) a veil-like substance draped over the surface of 'real' social relations, but also that there can be no 'end of ideology' in the sense of a future society finely tuned to a 'reality' freed from the rules and effects of language games. His emphasis on the heteromorphous and wholly conventional character of language games implies a radically different, critical conception of ideology, one that abandons the search for foundations and totalizing truth and instead embraces the logic of particularity and context-dependent polytheism. From this revised, post-Marxian standpoint, ideology would be understood as a *grand récit*, as a particular type of (potentially) hegemonic language game which functions, not always successfully, to mask both the conditions of its own engendering as well as the pluralism of language games within the established socio-political order of which it is a vital aspect. In other words, the concept of ideology would be applicable to any and all particular language games which endeavour to represent and secure themselves as a general or universal interest, as unquestionable and therefore freed from the contingency of the present; ideological language games are those which demand their *general* adoption and, therefore, the exclusion and/or repression (the 'terrorizing', as Lyotard would say) of every other *particular* language game. So understood, the *critique* of ideology would break decisively with the anti-modern political aim of the classical Marxian theory of ideology, namely, its attempt to devalue the false universality of an opponent's language game by presenting its own language game as universally true and ethically justified, hence unassailable. To criticize ideology in this revised way would be to emphasize that there is an inverse, but nevertheless intimate relationship between ideology and the modern democratic revolution: to tolerate ideology is to stifle and potentially undo the very plurality of language games which, as Tocqueville first argued, this revolution has greatly facilitated and upon which it thrives.

IV

Here I admit to extending and 'politicizing' a line of thought which is at most hinted at in *The Postmodern Condition*. In general, this essay is deeply reticent about developing further its own political connotations. Lyotard may have donned 'the mask of paganism, polytheism',[6] but social and political matters are choked off constantly in this essay by the resort to obscure formulas and shapeless suggestions. In this respect, *The Postmodern Condition* resembles the bulk of postmodernist writing. One could say that, often in spite of itself, much postmodernism remains pre-political. Its political credentials – its implications for the existing distribution and legitimacy of power crystallized in state and non-state institutions – remain wholly ambiguous. Postmodernism is said to involve the practice of resistance; challenging master narratives with the discourse of others; questioning rather than exploiting cultural codes; opening closed systems to the heterogeneity of texts; becoming more sensitive to difference; emphasizing discontinuity, incompleteness and paradoxes – and yet phrases such as these remain highly amorphous, thereby marginalizing or repressing outright further consideration of socio-political questions.

JOHN KEANE

The Postmodern Condition is similarly marked by a profound uncertainty and lack of clarity about its socio-political affiliations. Symptomatic of this is Lyotard's tantalizing summary description of his essay as an outline of 'a politics that would equally respect the desire for justice and the desire for the unknown' (p. 108). Equally tantalizing is his insistence (pp. 88–97) that postmodern knowledge aims to refine our sensitivity to the heterogeneity of the rules of language games, and to reinforce our ability to tolerate their incommensurability. More troubling still are those solipsistic, deeply apolitical moments in *The Postmodern Condition* (e.g. pp. 8, 63–8) in which Lyotard proposes that we are at last entering an age devoid of grand narratives, a period of postmodern austerity, it seems, in which individuals can only laugh cynically down their noses or smile happily into their own beards at every belief taught them. This is a preposterous suggestion, for it supposes, falsely, that grand (or ideological) language games are everywhere dead, and, again falsely, that all individuals and groups presently living, say, in western and eastern European and North American systems already enjoy the full civil and political liberties necessary for defending themselves against the rise of future ideologies. Lyotard's suggestion also misleadingly supposes, by means of a lapse into a curious form of neo-romantic expressivism, that an age devoid of grand language games would lead to the withering away of power and conflict, as if the array of specifically modern democratic mechanisms for limiting serious conflicts as well as concentrations of power could be superseded, like water wheels, handicrafts and other historical curiosities, by a fully transparent and harmonious whole.

Lyotard argues persuasively that language games are intelligible and interpretable only in terms of their own or other language games' rules and that, lacking a privileged language game, there is no alternative but to recognize the *difference* among language games, the potential infinity of rules defining them. This is well and good, but if this postmodernist conclusion that language games may be non-identical is to have any political credibility; if it is to avoid sliding into an uncritical deference to the existing patterns of unfreedom and inequality of late twentieth-century societies (succumbing, that is, to the dangerous charms of Wittgenstein's maxim that philosophy must leave everything as it is); and if it is not to adopt a blasé, carefree attitude towards the achievements of modernization (evidenced in a recent essay by Lyotard, where he says, against Habermas, that 'Auschwitz may be taken as a paradigm, as a name

90

for the tragic unfinished of modernity'), then it must engage, or so I would argue, in a further questioning of its own tacitly presupposed conditions of possibility. In my view, there is potentially an intimate connection – and not a simple hiatus – between Lyotard's examination of the postmodern condition and the line of political argument defended in Tocqueville's examination of the modern condition. I am basing this claim not only on Lyotard's paradoxical (but self-consistent and highly plausible) defence of the dynamic, antirepresentational thrust of modernist aesthetics, which, as Lyotard says, is pregnant with the will to question reality as 'unreal' and to invent new and different realities.[7] My thesis is broader: postmodernism of the type defended by Lyotard does not constitute a radical (or even mediated) break with the modernization process, but instead a dialectical intensification of its democratic impulses. Expressed paradoxically, Lyotard's postmodernism implies the need for a renewal and further development of the modern democratic tradition; that is, postmodernism is a call for ultra-modernism, a defence of the dynamic and future-oriented democratic revolution identified by Tocqueville. This paradoxical equation can be established and clarified, I believe, by asking after the socio-political presuppositions of Lyotard's postmodernism, that is, by reflecting counterfactually upon the socio-political conditions necessary for its institutionalization and preservation as such.

Consider the following line of argument, which can be thought of as one possible response to Lyotard's unanswered question: 'Where can legitimacy reside after the metanarratives?' (p. 8). This question, concerning which of those gods who strive to gain power over our lives we can or should serve in an age of nihilism, is also raised (but again left unanswered) in Lyotard's earlier work, *L'Economie libidinale*. It prompts the following response. To begin with, the postmodernist thesis that language games may be incommensurable, and that they are intelligible and interpretable only in terms of their difference from, or similarity with, other language games, *implies* an opposition to all claims and contexts which thwart or deny this thesis. A self-consistent postmodernism, that is to say, is compelled to devote itself to the philosophico-political project of questioning and disarticulating all essentialist or absolutist Truth claims or what I have called ideologies. Postmodernism therefore cannot rest content with pre-political assertions about the need for tolerating the incommensurable, supporting our culture 'conversationally' through the telling of stories[8] or, in Lyotard's version, 'marvelling at the diversity of discursive species, just as we do at the diversity of plant and animal species' (p. 47). And postmodernism certainly cannot cling naïvely to the complacent view – associated frequently with various forms of ethical and cognitive relativism – that 'every belief about every matter is as good as every other'. Postmodernism rather *implies* the need for democracy, for institutional arrangements which guarantee that protagonists of similar or different forms of language games can openly and continuously articulate their respective forms of life.

Postmodernism further *implies*, no doubt, the need for *political* mechanisms (of conflict resolution and compromise) which limit and reduce the serious antagonisms that frequently issue from struggles among incompatible forms of life. Postmodernism does not imply anarchism, for active and strong political institutions, as Tocqueville pointed out against his contemporaries who dreamt of the withering away of the state, are a necessary condition of preserving the democratic revolution. Just as all speakers of a language (to appropriate Tocqueville's simile) must have recourse to definite grammatical rules in order to express themselves, so citizens living together under modern democratic conditions are obliged to submit themselves to a political authority, without which they would fall into confusion and disorder (and, it might be added with hindsight, into the peculiarly modern type of yearning for existential security and grand ideologies that is produced by the experience of temporal and institutional discontinuity unleashed by modern societies). According to Tocqueville, the need for political mechanisms is especially pressing within large and complex societies, whose common interest, such as the formulation and administration of positive law, and the conduct of foreign policy, cannot be taken care of effectively without a powerful and centralized administration.

If Lyotard's philosophical postmodernism implies the need for state mechanisms of conflict mediation, it also suggests the need for mechanisms capable of preventing absolute state power. Tocqueville's political theory, concerned as it is with simultaneously defending modern democracy and pointing to its dangerous consequences, again provides some useful hints in this respect. Tocqueville argued that, in order to prevent the yoke of administrative despotism (a popularly elected state despotism that institutes a 'well-regulated, gentle and peaceful servitude') from descending upon the modern world and paralysing its revolutionary momentum, mechanisms of several kinds are required for preventing the buildup of dangerous monopolies of power. Within the realm of *state* institutions, Tocqueville argued, the paralysis of the democratic revolution can be minimized by ensuring that political power is distributed into many and various hands. A legislative power subject to periodic elections, combined with a separate executive authority and an independent judiciary, for instance, minimize the risk of despotism by ensuring that political power frequently changes hands and adopts different courses of action, being therefore prevented from becoming excessively centralized and all-embracing. Tocqueville also stressed the very rich democratic consequences of citizens' action within state institutions, and saw the American jury system as exemplary of this principle of supplementing representative democratic mechanisms (e.g. citizens' election of representatives to the legislature) with *direct* citizen participation. The jury system, in his view, facilitates citizens' self-government as well as teaching them how to govern others prudently and fairly; they learn to be sensitive and respectful of otherness, better capable of judging their fellow citizens as they would wish to be judged themselves.

Tocqueville was certain that these kinds of *political* checks upon despotism must be reinforced by the growth and development of *civil* associations which lie beyond the control of state institutions. Tocqueville no doubt underestimated the scope and anti-democratic implications of the rise of capitalist manufacturing industry, as well as the democratic potential of workers' resistance to its grip on civil society. (In *De la démocratie en Amérique* Tocqueville does not consider workers as a separate social class but, rather, as a menial fragment of *la classe industrielle*. This point of view, defended by Hegel and criticized bitterly by Marx, was also evident among other French writers such as Saint-Simon, for whom workers and entrepreneurs comprised a single social class, *les industriels*. This partly explains why Tocqueville reacted in contradictory ways to the events of 1848; as François Furet and others have pointed out, Tocqueville both interpreted these events as a continuation of the democratic revolution and, spitefully, as a 'most terrible civil war' threatening the very basis of 'property, family and civilization'.) Tocqueville failed to consider the possibility of a *post-capitalist* civil society – a type of ultra-modern civil society no longer dominated by capitalist enterprises and patriarchal families.[9] He none the less saw correctly that forms of civil association such as scientific and literary circles, schools, publishers, inns, manufacturing enterprises, religious organizations, municipal associations and independent households – to which we could add self-managed enterprises, refuges for battered women, lesbian and gay collectives, housing co-operatives, independent recording studios, and neighbourhood police monitoring associations – are crucial barriers against both social and political despotism. Tocqueville never tired of repeating the point that the 'independent eye of society' – an eye comprising a plurality of interacting, self-organized and constantly vigilant civil associations – is necessary for consolidating the democratic revolution. In contrast to political forms of involvement (such as participation in elections or jury service) which are concerned with the wider, more general interests of the community, civil associations consist of combinations of citizens preoccupied with 'small affairs'. Civil associations no doubt enable citizens to negotiate wider undertakings of concern to the whole polity. But they do more than this: they also nurture and powerfully deepen the local and particular freedoms so necessary for maintaining democratic equality. Tocqueville acknowledged that civil associations in this sense always depend for their survival and co-ordination upon centralized state institutions. Yet freedom and equality among individuals and groups *also* depend upon preserving types of organizations which nurture local freedoms and provide for the active expression of particular interests. A pluralistic and self-organizing civil society independent of the state – a type of anti-politics – is an indispensable condition of democracy. Tocqueville anticipated, correctly in my view, that whoever promoted the unification of state and civil society would endanger the democratic revolution. State power without social obstacles, he concluded, is always hazardous and undesirable, a licence for despotism.

V

This line of argument, which is so near and yet so far from Lyotard's, suggests that philosophical postmodernism is potentially a protagonist and potential political ally of the modern democratic project. The separation of civil society and the state, as well as the democratization of each – a democratic civil society and a democratic state – are implied or counterfactual conditions of postmodern endeavours. To defend philosophical postmodernism of Lyotard's type requires a political stance which is thoroughly modern; it implies the need for establishing or strengthening a democratic state and a civil society consisting of a plurality of public spheres, within which individuals and groups can openly express their solidarity with (or opposition to) others' ideals. Understood in this way, democracy could no longer stand accused of being a substantive ideological 'ought', an Eleventh Commandment, a type of heteronomous principle or grand narrative that seeks to foist itself upon other social and political actors in the name of some universal interest. As Hans Kelsen first hinted,[10] and as my interrogation of Lyotard's text suggests, socio-political democracy is an implied, counterfactual condition of the practice of paralogism, and not a type of normative (or, as Kant would have said, imperative) language game. The type of thinking with and against postmodernism employed here suggests, however, that democracy cannot be interpreted as merely one language game among others, as if particular groups struggling to defend or institutionalize their particular language games could decide self-consistently to conform to democratic arrangements for a time, only later to abandon them. On the contrary, their rejection of democracy would constitute a lapse into ideology – it would evidently contradict the particularity of their language games. They would be forced to represent themselves to themselves and to others as bearers of a universal language game, and they would thereby cover up the wholly conventional social and political processes of conflict and solidarity through which all particular language games are practically established, maintained and altered.

From this perspective, finally, democracy could no longer be seen as synonymous with the withering away of social division and political conflict. In democratic societies, as Tocqueville recognized, the foundations of social and political order are permanently unstable. Having severely weakened the power of norms whose legitimacy depends upon either transcendental standards (such as God) or a naturally given order of things (such as cultural tradition), modern societies begin to sense the need to summon up their socio-political identity from within themselves. The processes of modernization bring about an end to the naturalistic determination of the means and ends of life; destroying the old reference points of ultimate certainty, modern social actors begin to sense that they are not in possession of any ultimates (based on knowledge, conviction or faith), and that they are continually, and forever, forced to define for themselves the ways in which they wish to live. Trotsky's remark that those persons desiring a quiet life had done badly to be born into the twentieth century in fact applies to the *whole* of the modern epoch. Modern democratic societies are historical societies *par excellence*. It becomes evident to modern social actors that theirs is a society marked by socio-political indeterminacy; they sense that so-called ultimate social and political means and ends do not correspond to an immutable and 'real' origin or essence, and that their techniques and goals are therefore always subject to debate, conflict and resistance and, hence, to temporal and spatial variation.

This is why in modern societies institutions and decisions are never accepted fully – as if controversies concerning power, justice or law could somehow be resolved once and for all through the adoption of a universal metalanguage. Democratic societies recognize the necessity of relying always on judgement, for they know of their ignorance, which is to say (cf. the Socratic attitude) that they know that they do not know or control everything. Democratic societies cannot flatter themselves on assumptions about their capacity to grasp the whole directly, for they always consist of risky and often ambiguous action in the process of self-invention in all quarters of life. To defend democracy in this sense is to reject every ideology which seeks to stifle this indeterminacy by demanding the general adoption of particular forms of life that are clothed in the familiar repertoire of old and new metaphors: every woman needs a man, as the herd needs the shepherd, the ship's crew a captain, the proletariat the Party, and the nation a Moral Majority; the end justifies the means; doctors know best; mankind is the master and possessor of nature; scientific evidence is the most rational criterion of knowledge; capitalism is the most effective and efficient (and therefore best) form of property system; and so on. To defend democracy against these and other ideologies is to welcome indeterminacy, controversy and uncertainty. It is to be prepared for the emergence of the unexpected, and for the possibility of creating the new. It is, contrary to the self-understanding of philosophical *post*modernism, to recognize the need for *continuing* the modern democratic revolution, which is incomplete, highly vulnerable, and today threatened by a world heaving with an assortment of old and new antimodern trends.

NOTES

1 *De la démocratie en Amérique*, preface by François Furet, 2 vols, Paris 1981 [1835–40]. All translations from this edition are my own.

2 Jean-François Lyotard, *La Condition postmoderne: rapport sur le savoir*, Paris 1979. All translations from this edition are my own.

3 This point remains curiously unaddressed in Fredric Jameson's writings on postmodernism. Driven by a desire for a unitary, totalizing standpoint constructed of monistic assumptions, Jameson acknowledges the protean quality of cultural postmodernism, but only in order better to criticize it as an expression of the logic of universal commodification of contemporary consumer capitalist societies. Cultural postmodernism is rejected as a blind accomplice of the (temporary) disappearance of a collectively shared sense of class-based History, as an agent of late capitalist societies' fetishism of symbolic representation and celebration of the fragmentation of the experience of time into a series of perpetual presents. See, for example, 'Post modernism and consumer society', in Hal Foster (ed.), *Postmodern Culture*, London and Sydney 1985, pp. 111–25, 'Postmodernism, or, the cultural logic of late capitalism', *New Left Review* 146 (July–August 1984), pp. 53–92 and 'The politics of theory: ideological positions in the postmodernism debate', *New German Critique* 33 (1984), pp. 53–65.

4 Seyla Benhabib, 'Epistemologies of postmodernism: a rejoinder to Jean-François Lyotard', *New German Critique* 33 (1984), p. 120.

5 Cf. my 'Democracy and the theory of ideology', *Canadian Journal of Political and Social Theory/Revue canadienne de théorie politique et sociale* 7 (1983), pp. 5–17.

6 Vincent Descombes, *Modern French Philosophy*, New York 1980, p. 184.

7 See his 'Réponse à la question: qu'est-ce que le postmoderne?', in *Critique* (April 1982), pp. 357–67, which is translated and included as an appendix to Jean-François Lyotard, *The Postmodern Condition: A Report on Knowledge*, Minneapolis 1984. Lyotard here defends postmodern aesthetics not as that which lies beyond modernism, but as an immanent dynamic within modernism: 'Modernity, in whatever age it appears, cannot exist without a shattering of belief and without discovery of the "lack of reality" of reality, together with the invention of other realities' (p. 77).

8 This view is associated with Richard Rorty's *Philosophy and the Mirror of Nature*, Oxford 1980. Aside from its failure to deal with the type of non-foundational, counterfactual reasoning sketched in this chapter, the conversational model fails to acknowledge the dangers of totalitarian language games, to which (as Claude Lefort has pointed out in his *L'Invention démocratique*, Paris 1982) modern societies are prone constantly because of their self-revolutionizing, self-questioning character. More recently ('Habermas and Lyotard on postmodernity', *Praxis International* 4 (1984), p. 34), Rorty has argued for the reliance upon a potentially anti-democratic instruction ('let the narratives which hold our culture together do their stuff'), as if the fact of existence of certain

narratives automatically implied their sacred right to an undisturbed future existence.

9 This argument is developed in *Democracy and Civil Society*, London and New York 1988, *Civil Society and the State: New European Perspectives*, London and New York 1988 and *The Media and Democracy*, Oxford and Cambridge, Mass. 1991.

10 Hans Kelsen, *Vom Wesen und Wert der Demokratie*, Tübingen 1981 [1929], pp. 98–104.

5

HABERMAS vs LYOTARD
Modernity vs Postmodernity?

Emilia Steuerman

I

Although today we are surrounded by discussions of a postmodern sensitivity or style, of postmodern social movements, and of a postmodern science, the term 'postmodernity' has been used in so many different ways that one can no longer be sure exactly what it means. It can be used to indicate non-conformative aesthetic attitudes (avant-garde movements), a refusal of grand political theories (the critique of totalitarianism), a critique of rationality and representation (Foucault, Derrida and Rorty), or a radical critique of empiricist scientific method (Feyerabend). But it has also been invoked in a more conservative defence of post-industrial societies (Daniel Bell), in defence of a new figuratism in art, or to eulogize the artificial intelligence model for a representation of knowledge. In a way, one longs for a clear-cut (re)definition both of 'postmodernity' and also, necessarily, of that 'modernity' which it is supposed to have followed or transcended. The problem, of course, is that the idea of the postmodern is itself sometimes used to challenge the possibility of a stable theory of meaning as reference or representation. Nevertheless, a review of the philosophical themes encompassed by these terms is more than ever urgent.

In such a review, the philosophical landscape is dominated by two figures: Jürgen Habermas and Jean-François Lyotard. The confrontation between these two authors is, in my view, extremely rewarding: at issue between them is the nature or definition of the modernity project, with all its philosophical, political and aesthetic implications. My own approach has been strongly influenced by Habermas. From this perspective, I find Lyotard's work the most challenging alternative, because it avoids the conservative

99

implications of premodern and counter-Enlightenment views. Habermas – and this is part of his appeal – speaks in the name of emancipation. He wants to develop the modernity project as the rational discussion and redemption of the notions of truth, justice and freedom. Habermas calls for more philosophy, for a rational discussion of values and norms. But Lyotard also asks what is the meaning of truth and justice in contemporary societies and has clearly stated the purported political dimension of his writings.[1] But whereas Habermas speaks in the name of emancipation, Lyotard warns us of the dangers of speaking 'in the name of'. He shows how one can, in defending the idea of emancipation, deny this very notion of freedom.

On the other hand, re-reading Lyotard one is surprised to see how close his analysis of the status of knowledge in contemporary societies is to that of Habermas. The conclusion I would draw from this closeness is that the postmodern condition, as characterized by Lyotard, is indeed a *radicalization* that in no way challenges the modernity project as such. Rather, it takes it further in a way that, for me, answers Habermas's plea for the development of modernity as a yet unfinished (*unvollendetes*) project. For all those familiar with Lyotard's refusal of the modernity project – for him it has been liquidated in Auschwitz – this should sound provocative and controversial enough.

I shall start with an overview of Habermas's presentation of the central themes of modernity and the problems with his attempt to ground norms on communication. I shall then discuss Lyotard's postmodern critique of modernity as the Enlightenment project and show how indebted to the Enlightenment his critique is. And, as Lyotard's critique is based on language, I shall attempt a small discussion of modernity and postmodernity from the point of view of norms and language. This discussion should further our understanding of modernity as a project and highlight the main issues at stake in the modernity-postmodernity controversy.

II

Habermas has always situated himself within the Enlightenment tradition, from Kant to Hegel to Marx, in his pursuit of a rational critique as emancipation from dogma and domination. In the famous Kantian text 'What is Enlightenment?'[2] reason is opposed to ignorance, religious or metaphysical dogma, and political domination. '*Mündigkeit*' is the task of the modern age, and *Mündigkeit*, reason's 'coming of age', is a critical rationality that no longer relies on revealed religion, past models or metaphysics for its emancipation from dogma and political domination.

This project need not be identified with a narrow definition of reason as scientific rationality. Indeed Kant's argument is that reason is theoretical (scientific) rationality but also that reason is moral-political and aesthetic. Habermas uses Kant's differentiated approach to reason and Weber's critique of means-end rationality for his famous critique of the role played by science and technology in modern contemporary societies.[3] Habermas's point is that in advanced capitalist societies reason has become reduced to instrumental reason, to means-end rationality. When this happens, the moral and the political realms are approached from the point of view of technical management and control, and the question of the good and just life disappears. Reason then becomes a legitimating principle for political domination. It is only in so far as one recaptures the differentiated realms of rationality that the possibility of critique and of emancipation can be pursued.

The Kantian critique of reason is a reflection on the conditions of possibility of these differentiated domains of rationality. These domains have now to be grounded on rational principles and can no longer rely on religious authority or political dogma. Modernity is the project of a *rational* grounding of norms for autonomous domains of rationality. The normativity problem is the problem of modernity.

Moreover, modernity is the awareness of a 'new age' that no longer relies on criteria from the past. As Hegel put it,[4] modernity is the awareness of a 'new world' that breaks with the past, a 'birth-time, and a period of transition'. Habermas likes to recall the late seventeenth-century 'querelle des anciens et des modernes'[5] as the epitome of the modernity consciousness as a consciousness of a *new, historical* age that can no longer rely on classical criteria of timeless and absolute beauty, but which has got to work out its 'new' criteria and models in a break with the past. As Habermas argues in *The Philosophical Discourse of Modernity*, 'modernity has got to create its normativity out of itself',[6] following criteria which are no longer external but historical and immanent. Indeed, in so far as modernity is the 'new' as opposed to the 'old', it has to recapitulate the break with the past in a continuous renewal. The problem of universal norms which would ground the differentiated domains of rationality

101

becomes, with modernity's awareness of time, a historical endeavour.

And finally, the last great problem I want to mention concerning modernity and normativity is that modernity's awareness of time is also modernity's *self*-awareness. The activity of critique, or the reconstruction of the conditions of possibility of the differentiated domains of rationality, is not in itself a problem for Kant. But, as Hegel has argued, the activity of critique has got to be itself accounted for and has got to be submitted to the critical gaze. The synthetic unit of heterogeneous domains of reason proposed by Kant can no longer be accepted uncritically. With Hegel, critique becomes self-conscious and the problem of rational norms is now not only a problem in time but a problem that is itself problematic.

I want to stress here that modernity's awareness of time introduces the question of historicity and relativism and that modernity's self-awareness brings to the fore the problem of reflexivity. I think it is worth stressing this because reflexivity and relativism are some of the arguments used *against* the project of modernity as the project of a rational grounding of norms.[7] More often than not we seem to forget that these are themes of modernity. And I think we forget this because it is Hegel's and Marx's solutions to the normativity problem which have become, in our memories, the theme of modernity.

Hegel's solution to the normativity problem is carried out in terms of a philosophy of the subject, that is, it takes as its starting-point a reflection on the conditions of possibility of reason in terms of a *subject* of experience. Since Kant, this subject has been double: empirical and transcendental. But in pointing out that the transcendental dimension of reason has got to be itself accounted for in terms of its empiricity, of its historicity, Hegel moved on to an idea of a universal subject in history – Absolute Reason – that would provide a totalizing unity for the diversity and empiricity of domains of rationality. However, this unity, Absolute Reason, assumed a form which was so overwhelming that in the end it denied the very problem it attempted to solve: the subject as universal denied the subject as individual and the problem of critique and normativity disappeared. As Habermas puts it, with Hegel 'the question about the genuine self-understanding of modernity gets lost in reason's ironic laughter. For reason has now taken over the place of fate and knows that every event of essential significance has *already* been decided.'[8]

If one follows this path – and Marx in his materialistic re-reading of Hegel faces the same problem – modernity becomes the symbol of totalitarianism. One should indeed beware of the political consequences of a totalizing absolute reason embodied in a universal subject, be it the state or the proletariat.[9]

However, it is important to stress that, although Habermas approached Hegel as the philosopher of modernity, he is extremely critical of Hegel's solution to the normativity problem. Indeed, Habermas distances himself from Hegel and – to a certain extent – from Marx. In order to recover the emancipatory dimension of reason, Habermas proposes to restore the differentiated realms of reason which had been dissolved in Hegel's idealist solution (Absolute Reason) and in Marx's materialist solution, which also reduced reason to one dimension of human action – labour. This was Habermas's initial project in *Knowledge and Human Interests*. But given the problems he encountered,[10] Habermas has been trying to rework this project in terms of an analysis of the necessary conditions of possibility of communication. Implied in this move is a recognition that the problems encountered in his initial project were due to a framework still too indebted to a philosophy of the subject, that is, to a reflection on the conditions of possibility of reason and action which did not acknowledge that the very possibility of reflection is not a subjectivity turned onto itself but an intersubjectivity of discourse, of language, of communication. Habermas therefore now stresses the necessity of overcoming the framework of a philosophy of the subject in terms of a philosophy of *intersubjectivity*, of language. To this end, he proposes an analysis of the conditions of possibility of communication as the starting-point for a critical theory.[11]

This analysis reconstructs the three domains of rationality (theoretical, practical, aesthetic) in terms of three modes of communication (cognitive, interactive, expressive). In so far as one speaks, one always necessarily raises three validity claims: truth, rightness and truthfulness, as well as an intelligibility claim which can be left aside in this chapter. These claims are presupposed by every act of communication. They can be rationally redeemed in a situation of discourse, where only reason prevails. These validity claims form a structure of linguistic rationality which is necessarily and universally presupposed and anticipated by every act of communication. For Habermas, in communication the speaker raises validity claims that are accepted or rejected by the hearer(s). The framework of the three validity claims and the ideal speech situation as the situation of pure discourse where these claims would be met without internal or external constraints form not only a structure of rationality which is presupposed by communication: for Habermas they are the *very* possibility of communication.

Now, Habermas is clever enough to point out that this presupposition (*Unterstellung*) – the ideal speech situation – is not an empirical reality or an ideal construct. His point is more subtle: what he is saying is that every time we engage in communication we must inevitably assume, *even as an illusion*, a 'transcendental illusion', that we are speaking the truth, being truthful and following legitimate social rules. The possibility itself of telling a lie, deceiving or evading a norm rests on the supposition that these claims form a necessary background for communication. And, because there is such a background, we can ultimately question our interlocutors about the truth, truthfulness and rightness of their acts (and ours). In order to communicate at all, we have to presuppose that we are able to distinguish between truth and falseness, truthfulness and deceit, rightness and distortion, rational and illusory consensus, even if, in order to do so, we have to resort to a promise not yet fulfilled, to argumentation, to discourse as the rational validation of the three validity claims. The possibility of communication is based on this presupposition, which also works as a 'critical standard with which every factually reached consensus can be questioned and examined'.[12]

Habermas's solution of grounding critique on language is an attempt to maintain the differentiated domains of rationality in a framework of intersubjectivity. Habermas therefore assumes that there is a universal and necessary consensus in language, even if this consensus is a counterfactual one. The ideal speech situation is the 'effective anticipation' of a pure structure of rationality, with no internal, external or social constraints, where we could therefore agree on truth, norms and authenticity.

Habermas has been criticized for this idea of consensus.[13] However, it is important to stress that this consensus is a counterfactual one, a promise not yet fulfilled. What Habermas is saying is that language, as a structure or intersubjectivity, implies that we share a form of life, is indeed itself a form of life, to use Wittgenstein's words.[14] In order to disagree, we are still within language, language here being more than a collection of words: language here should be understood as an intricate network of words and practices. For Habermas, this agreement is continually open to disagreement.

Still, language itself is the promise and the possibility of realizing this agreement.

But Habermas takes one step further. He wants to show that every speech act in actual language demonstrates the possibility of reaching a rational consensus. In order to do so, he has to show that every speech act actually raises the above-mentioned validity claims. But, in doing so, Habermas has to reduce his analysis of communication to communicative action, thus excluding from his analysis *strategic action*.[15] But this is, to say the least, a very problematic move because in so doing he is excluding from his analysis those instances of communication where the use of power leads to a distortion in communication. His argument is that strategic action is *derivative* from communicative action. But strategic actions are precisely those instances where the use of power *excludes* the possibility of a rational discourse.

Moreover Habermas further reduces his analysis to explicit speech acts of the standard form F(p), where F is the illocutionary act (the act of promising, announcing, inviting, etc.) and p the propositional content ('He promises *that he will come*').[16] He does this in order to show that every speech act always introduces a cognitive dimension through the objectivating attitude of the propositional content (validity claim of truth), an interactive dimension through the performative attitude of the illocutionary act (validity claim of rightness) and an expressive dimension in the authenticity of the speaker's intention (validity claim of truthfulness). This is a very important point if Habermas wants to maintain that the dimensions of truth, rightness and truthfulness are universal and necessary conditions of *every* speech act and therefore that discourse is the rational validation of these claims raised in speech. But not every speech act is of the form F(p).[17] Habermas's attempt to justify this type of analysis rests on the problematic principle of expressibility of Searle. I shall not go here into the criticisms in the linguistic literature of this principle.[18] Suffice it to say that this reduction of analysis to explicit speech acts of the form F(p) excludes from the analysis most of the cases of day-to-day communication, where communication is not synchronic, not transparent and not explicit. And finally, although Habermas recognizes the background context implicit in every act of communication, his analysis does not take this context into account as, for him, it can always be made explicit in terms of the linguistic structure of human rationality. But again this is a way of approaching the background context – the form of life in Wittgenstein's words – as reasons in discourse. The Wittgensteinian agreement on the form of life which is necessary for communication becomes, in Habermas's terms, an agreement on the consensus theory of discourse. In other words, Habermas's idea of an agreement in language is an agreement about the commitment to provide reasons for the claims raised in communication. Wittgenstein's point about the agreement on a form of life is rather different. He in fact stresses that giving reasons is one possible language game and not the foundation of all possible games. In *On Certainty*, Wittgenstein says:

> I am told, for example, that someone climbed a mountain many years ago. Do I always enquire into the reliability of the teller of this story, and whether the mountain did exist years ago? . . . What stands fast does so, not because it is intrinsically obvious or convincing; it is rather held fast by what lies around it.[19]

I shall come back to these points in my discussion of Lyotard. For the moment it is sufficient to stress that Habermas's analysis implies an approach to language which reduces communication to communicative action, speech acts to explicit acts of the standard form $F(p)$, and the background context of human practices (forms of life) to giving reasons in language. These reductions question the universality and necessity of Habermas's analysis.

But if one takes seriously Habermas's idea that the ideal speech situation is a 'transcendental illusion',[20] and 'unavoidable fiction',[21] one need not show that this fiction is a universal and necessary condition of every speech act in its empiricity. What one needs to show is that this illusion is what enables us to pursue a rational discussion on values and truth, even though the idea of a situation of pure discourse, where truth, justice and freedom would be rationally met without any internal or external constraints, must remain an illusion. Indeed, the anticipation of this ideal constitutes a form of life, it enables us to pursue a discourse on truth and justice, and it provides the criteria for a rational discussion. Of course, this ideal remains an illusion, a fiction, albeit a transcendental and unavoidable one in so far as we share language as a structure of intersubjectivity. The ideal speech situation is a transcendental illusion in the sense that this illusion constitutes the 'appearance of a form of life'. Needless to say, this appearance is not an empirical reality. However, the idea itself of such a form of life, implicit in language, constitutes the possibility of a rational discussion of the values anticipated. It does not matter here if this illusion is a delusion. What is important is the recognition that in language we are given this idea. And if one wants to pursue a discourse on truth and values, one has to assume, even as an illusion, an idea of truth, justice and freedom, *given by language and in language*, which can be rationally pursued. The problem is when we move from this 'unavoidable fiction', from this 'transcendental illusion', to an analysis that wants to show how we indeed anticipate an idea of truth, justice and freedom in *every* speech act.

The great asset of Habermas, in my view, is how he puts back into the agenda the problem of normativity. For Habermas, a reflection on the meaning of rational validation of truth, justice and freedom is more than ever urgent. This reflection entails a discussion of what sort of grounding and criteria one needs to pursue such validation. Habermas's concern with these themes makes him dismissive of what he calls the premodern and the counter-Enlightenment positions. The 'premodern' chooses to regress to religious or fundamentalistic approaches to values (neo-conservatism). The 'counter-Enlightenment' cannot avoid surrendering altogether the values of modernity (truth, justice and freedom) in its critique of rationality. And then, asks Habermas, how is critique (of modernity and rationality) itself possible? And how is political critique possible if we abandon altogether a notion of truth and justice?[22]

This is precisely why I think Lyotard is the most interesting challenge to Habermas's project. Indeed, Lyotard's question is the question of the meaning of justice and knowledge in contemporary societies. And I want to show now how close Lyotard is to Habermas, the modernity philosopher. But I also want to show where their views part, and it will be on their analysis of language. I shall then draw some conclusions about the meaning of a modernity–postmodernity controversy.

III

Like Habermas, Lyotard also starts his analysis from the recognition of a change in the status of knowledge in advanced industrial societies. (I am here quite deliberately avoiding the terms postmodern age, postmodern societies.) This change has been brought about mainly by the impact of technology and information technology in knowledge research and knowledge transmission. Knowledge is no longer associated with *Bildung*, with the 'formation of spirits'. Rather, knowledge has become technically useful knowledge. The criterion of technically useful knowledge is its efficiency and its translatability into information (computer) knowledge. Therefore the questions 'Is it true?', 'Is is just?', 'Is it morally important?' become reduced to 'Is it efficient?', 'Is it marketable?', 'Is it sellable?', 'Is it translatable into information quantities?'. Through this reduction, a dimension of knowledge as a '*savoir-faire*', '*savoir-vivre*', tends to disappear or to be translated in terms of efficiency. Moreover, as knowledge becomes a commodity and produces commodities, it also changes its relation to nation-states. Knowledge as a force of production becomes one of the central tenets of power and what is at stake ('*l'enjeu*') for political domination.

The understanding of society, given this approach to knowledge, follows the paradigm of an efficient machine. Society becomes a system regulated by inputs and outputs, and its criteria only efficiency. Society – and we are familiar with this functionalist approach – is a technocratic system where the hopes and needs of groups and individuals, the ethical and political life, tend to disappear inside the optimization of the system's performativity. Crises are merely rearrangements of the system's optimization of the general relation between inputs and outputs.

This thesis, as Lyotard himself recognizes, is not new and indeed is a central theme in the work of the Frankfurt school and of Habermas. The problem is how to produce a critique of this functionalist approach, given the role played by science and technology in contemporary developed societies. And although Lyotard disagrees with Habermas's recourse to a consensus theory, there is no doubt that he is on Habermas's side. In discussing Habermas's arguments against Luhmann's *Systemtheorie*, Lyotard says that 'Habermas's cause is good'. And although consensus is, for Lyotard, an 'outmoded and suspect value', the question remains of producing an 'idea and a practice of justice that is not linked to that on consensus'.[23]

However, the parallel does not stop here. Indeed, both Lyotard and Habermas recognize that the central problem is the problem of norms, of criteria, what Habermas calls the *normativity* problem and Lyotard the *legitimation* problem.

Both claim that, in order to criticize technical rationality and its criterion of efficiency, one has to have a broader approach to knowledge. In Habermas's terms, rationality is not reducible to instrumental rationality. In Lyotard's terms, knowledge (*savoir*) is not reducible to science (*connaissance*). Both stress the diversity of human linguistic competences already implied by the language game of science. Science restricts its linguistic scope to denotation (or mainly to denotation), but this game is only possible in language and it presupposes a wider range of competences, as for instance a '*savoir-faire*', a '*savoir-dire*' and a '*savoir-écouter*'. It is the stress on the different competences that gives them both an edge for their critique of instrumental rationality. But, in so far as one recognizes the diversity of language games, one also recognizes the rule-governed character of those localized practices. And the problem of modernity is precisely the problem of normativity, the problem of criteria, of what rules govern our practices.

As I mentioned before, Habermas uses the 'querelle des anciens et des modernes' as the paradigm of modernity's consciousness. Once the differentiation of domains of rationality has been accomplished and art stands as an autonomous domain, what are its criteria of beauty if one can no longer rely on the models of the past? How is critique possible if one no longer relies on a trans-cendental ahistorical subject? What are the norms for a critical activity once one recognizes the immanence of norms for critique itself?

Lyotard has a story that captures in an exemplary way the problem of legitimation or, in Habermas's terms, the normativity problem. But instead of being a paradigm of modernity, the Cashinahua narrative stresses a different set of pragmatic rules.

A Cashinahua tells a story. He starts it with the fixed formula: 'Here is the story of Z, as I've always heard it told. I will tell it to you in my turn. Listen!' And he ends it by saying: 'Here ends the story of Z. The man who has told it to you is X [Cashinahua name], or Y to the Whites [Portuguese or Spanish name].'[24] Here there are pragmatic rules which decide who can tell the story (a male Cashinahua), who can hear the story (a bearer of a Cashinahua name, a male Cashinahua or a pre-puberty Cashinahua girl) and who can be the theme of the story (all Cashinahuas). But in this form of narrative, the truth, the truthfulness and the rightness (in Habermas's terms) of the story are not a problem. It is the repetition of the story, the endless and timeless repetition which gives it its legitimacy. The questions about the reliability of the speaker and the truth of the story are absent. Although the story might change in its continuous retelling, the telling itself has a timeless quality that forbids the problem of the author and his legitimacy. In Lyotard's terms, there is an 'immemorial beating'[25] that prevents a differentiation between diverse historical times. But in the narrative of modernity, modernity's self-consciousness in time opens up the dimension of norms in history. Therefore the legitimacy of the pragmatic rules *themselves* becomes a problem. The question of modernity is the question about the conditions of possibility of a discourse historically and contextually situated once the norms for deciding the norms become themselves a problem. In other words, who (but this might be misleading for it is not a 'who') decides what counts as knowledge but also who decides who is going to decide?

I think the Cashinahua story and, for that matter, the Jewish narrative discussed in *Just Gaming*[26] should be approached carefully. Rather than a theory about 'other (better) cultures' (Jewish or primitive) I think they should be used, in a Wittgensteinian way, to 'show' something. They are a way of talking about the legitimation and double-legitimation problem of modernity. Any reading of these other types of narrative as a theory about other ('better') societies will assume that Lyotard is nostalgic or romantic. In this type of reading, modernity is reduced to the grand narrative, to the narrative of an author or a hero, spirit or proletariat. Then modernity's mistake is the search for a grand narrative that would ground all other narratives. This search for a totalizing unity stems from the idea of a subject as author or hero of the narrative. However, this unity is no longer possible in postmodernity, given the fragmentation of our localized practices and the suspicion about a unitary subject or author. Although in many ways *The Postmodern Condition* lends itself to this type of reading, Lyotard's critique of modernity becomes much more interesting and complex once we abandon the facile idea that modernity is the legitimation through a grand narrative and postmodernity the suspicion of the great narrative.[27] In order to understand this point, it is useful briefly to recall Habermas's remarks on modernity.

Habermas stresses that the problem of modernity is the problem of norms and criteria in an age that sees itself as continuously breaking with the past. Modernity can no longer rely on any 'given' criteria. Reason's coming of age is precisely the suspicion of narratives through the awareness of the immanence of norms. In *The Postmodern Condition*, Lyotard sometimes does speak of modernity as the resort to a great narrative, a narrative of a hero, spirit of praxis. Habermas's remarks on modernity help us to differentiate between the normativity problem of modernity and the Hegelian or Marxist solutions in terms of a totalizing unity of a subject. Thus one could say that the postmodern suspicion of the great narrative is *modernity's challenge* rather than a challenge to modernity.

In the paper 'What is postmodernism?', ingeniously included in the English translation of *La Condition postmoderne*, Lyotard takes up this point. Indeed, in this paper he no longer concentrates on 'the great narrative' and 'small narratives' as characteristics of the modern and postmodern conditions. Rather, he now develops the strategy of language games as a non-reconciliatory strategy, as a way of answering the modernity challenge without resorting to a philosophy of the subject, to a hero, or to the totalizing unity of heterogeneous domains of rationality.

As I mentioned before, Habermas also moves to language as a way of avoiding a dissolution of differentiated domains of rationality in a totalizing unity. But in his attempt to show that every speech act always raises the validity claims of truth, truthfulness and rightness, Habermas has to restrict his analysis of communication to a certain type of speech act. In the end, Habermas reduces language to giving reasons in discourse, thus overemphasizing the cognitive dimension of language to the exclusion of other language games. Lyotard's strategy is different. Rather than taking language games to mean that one always already anticipates the possibility of a rational discourse, Lyotard stresses the *agonistic* aspect of games. The agonistic aspect stresses the strategic dimension of speech acts where '*l'enjeu*', what is at stake, is never decided in advance, but is always being fought over. The moves in language are therefore never predetermined but are continuously being made. The problem for Lyotard is the problem of moves, of definition of rules and criteria through moves. The problem is the problem of invention, of imagination, of judgement, of new moves (rather than the grounding or foundation of rules) in a game which, although rule-governed, does not have a fixed or transcendental set of rules. In *Just Gaming*, Lyotard mentions Aristotle's judge who has no true model or criteria to guide his judgements.[28] The problem of judgement is precisely the problem of having to make a good judgement *without* resorting to epistemology or ontology. The approach to language games as agonistic stresses that the rule-governed character of language is constituted in the practice itself of language through moves rather than grounded on a transcendent set of rules as its criteria.

Now, this approach to language stresses the invention of rules rather than the *absence* of rules. Postmodernity in this view is not an overcoming of rules but the recognition of the problem of normativity once one no longer relies on a fixed set of rules. Aristotle's judge is the best example here. As I said before, this is modernity's challenge, and Lyotard seems to accept this point. He says that modernity rather than postmodernity is the recognition of how little reality there is in reality (the *'peu de realité'*). What is to count as reality in a certain language game is fought over in language. Reality is constantly being invented and fought over in localized games. The challenge of modernity is the invention of rules. Postmodernity is the taking up of this challenge.

I think at this point one could ask whether it really matters if one approaches postmodernity as the overcoming of modernity or as the radicalization of modernity. And I think this is very important for what is at stake here is how one approaches the modernity–postmodernity controversy. Indeed, what is at stake here is the meaning of doing philosophy, of political views, of moral values. If one approaches postmodernity as an overcoming of modernity, the danger is to give up the problem of normativity altogether and in so doing to play into the hands of a technological society where the ethical, the political and the philosophical become the efficient technology. Moreover, this approach to postmodernity as an overcoming of modernity also relies on a superficial critique of representation and rationality that in discovering – two centuries later – the historicity and contextuality of a discussion of values and norms says that every story is nothing but a story amongst other possible stories. I think Habermas is right in calling this position premodern and conservative. Indeed, nothing is more nostalgic than the disappointment of a pseudo-postmodern position which, when recognizing the impossibility of an absolute grounding of norms, dismisses the problem of normativity and therefore the problem of critique in an 'anything goes'. I believe that, as one adopts this position, one is indeed saying that there is no difference between a true and an illusory consensus, a just and an unjust society, a good and a bad action. Again, I believe that if one adopts this position, one is playing into the hands of the efficiency criterion of a technological society that says anything goes – as long as it is efficient. Here the work of Habermas is extremely important for it stresses the need for *more* rather than less philosophy, the need for working out what a moral, an aesthetic and a cognitive rationality could be, rather than dissolving them into a meaningless relativism or into a discourse of technical efficiency.

On the other hand, if one does not take modernity and post-modernity as norms versus absence of norms, in other words if one takes modernity as the normativity challenge and postmodernity as the taking up of this challenge, postmodernity is the continuous critique demanded by modernity. And here the problem becomes how to produce a discourse on justice, on truth and on art when one no longer relies on ontology or epistemology. The move to language for both Habermas and Lyotard is a way of answering modernity's challenge. But whereas Habermas has to reduce the scope of his analysis in order to argue that communication is grounded on the possibility of giving reasons in language for the claims we raise in speech, Lyotard's approach to language as strategic games stresses the dimension of language which, although rule-governed, is not reducible to rational validation. Going back to the quotation of Wittgenstein given above, giving reasons in language is a possible language game and not the foundation (even as an 'anticipation') of all language games. In other words, where Habermas still relies on a theory of knowledge – now disguised in terms of a linguistic rationality – in order to ground an ethical and a philosophical discourse, Lyotard stresses the need for the invention and creation of new rules – how, for instance, Aristotle's judge is a good judge precisely because he does not rely on a theory or models. This is, however, not episteme: it is techne, it is art.

IV

I would like to make a few comments on Lyotard's strategy of moves and invention of rules. I think that while this point has been generally overlooked, it is here that the possibility of a critical discourse on modernity lies. For this is the attempt at producing a discourse on norms which, although critical, would no longer rely on a theory or an ontology. And it is Kant rather than Nietzsche who inspires Lyotard's remarks. He uses Kant's idea of the sublime as a way of approaching rules, modernity and postmodernity.

The sublime for Kant[29] is the distance between the faculty of conceiving and the faculty of presenting an object in accordance with the concept. We have the Idea of a world, of the simple, of the absolutely big or the absolutely powerful, but we do not have the capacity to show an example of these ideas. Indeed, these ideas have no possible presentation, they are unpresentable and therefore not related to our faculty of understanding (cognitive). The idea of presenting what is unpresentable, Kant's idea of the sublime, is Lyotard's idea of what is at stake in modern art. But how is one to show what can be conceived but cannot be seen? Kant himself shows the way when he quotes Exodus 20:4, 'Thou shalt not make unto thee any graven image' as the 'most sublime' passage in the Bible, for it forbids all presentation of the absolute. It is only through the absence of form, the empty abstraction, the negative presentation, that one can present the impossibility of presenting an idea which is still conceivable.[30]

But this impossibility of presentation of the unpresentable but yet conceivable can take two modes. One, which Lyotard calls 'melancholic', stresses the *impotency* of our faculty of presentation and dwells in the nostalgia of the presence. The other mode, which Lyotard calls 'novatio', stresses the *potency* of the faculty of conceiving which is not the faculty of understanding. This mode stresses the invention of new rules, of new forms in a pictorial, artistic or philosophical game. The invention of new forms is not a matter of pleasure or a nostalgia of the presence. It is a matter of mixed pleasure and pain for it is the extension of our capacity of conceiving and, if anything, it *widens* the gap between what is presentable and what is conceivable. It is not a matter of providing an unpresentable reality but of inventing allusions not to the unpresentable but to the unpresentability of the unpresentable. And these two modes of the modernity theme, the nostalgic and the innovative, are for Lyotard the modern and the postmodern modes. Postmodernity is therefore a radicalization of the modernity theme, the refusal of a nostalgic reconciliation of conceiving and presenting in the illusion of a totality. In this sense postmodernity is not the other or the overcoming of modernity, but its radicalization: postmodernity is the 'futur antérieur' of modernity.[31]

I think this approach to postmodernity stresses the need for a discourse on rules which does not rely on the faculty of understanding. Here language would have to be approached as a language game, to use Wittgenstein's terminology; that is, language as a practice which involves various skills and forms of knowledge, rather than language as a deep structure of rules which could be reduced to theoretical knowledge (episteme). Wittgenstein's own remarks on rules and rule-following are extremely rewarding for such discussions.[32] I do not have enough time to develop these ideas here but I would like to mention briefly a few points.

Wittgenstein's approach to language has to be read in the overall context of his critique of a general theory of language in the lines of the *Tractatus* (language is not just cognition). 'A picture held us captive',[33] he says, and this picture, this bewitchment of theory, is the idea that language is grounded on a deeper structure of norms and on rules. Thus the search for the theoretical foundation of language. In *On Certainty* he argues that it is the epistemological approach to language as cognition, as propositional knowledge, that leads to philosophical paradoxes. The problem therefore is how to avoid offering a 'better' (because more accurately depicting this deeper structure) theory of language without being reduced to silence. The way out of this dead end is recognizing that language is not just theory, not just theoretical knowledge, cognition, rational justification. Indeed the idea of language as a form of life is the refusal to reduce language to rational justification, to cognition, to knowledge.

But the recognition that language is not everywhere bound by theoretical definitions does not mean that language is vague or meaningless. Wittgenstein's remarks on rules and rule-following are meant to show (rather than theoretically argue) the rule-governed character of language which, although making language possible, does not predetermine the game. Rule-following is not the application of a deeper set of rules. Rule-following is itself a practice and it is the practice of the game that defines the interpretation of the rule and what counts as a rule in a certain game.

One of the most rewarding points of Wittgenstein's remarks on rule-following is how it warns us against an approach to language games as *competences*, even as localized, fragmented competences. The idea itself of 'competence' implies a deeper set of rules that grounds the application, the performance of a game. And although Lyotard seems to point to a fruitful way of discussing norms, he still approaches games as localized competences. This is not enough, for it still holds on to an idea of a deeper set of rules, although now these rules govern localized, fragmented practices. It is in so far as one moves away from the idea of a theoretical foundation of games that one indeed moves towards a discourse on rules that stresses the innovative rather than the applicatory character of rules and language as a human practice, as a form of life. But again, it is only in so far as one recognizes that the possibility of a rational discussion on norms and rules is implicit in language, implied by the very possibility of communication, that one can take up the challenge of modernity as an unfinished project. The definition of rationality itself changes when one moves from a philosophy of subjectivity centred on a knowing subject to a philosophy of inter-subjectivity which recognizes the linguistic dimension of human rationality. Here human rationality is no longer just knowledge, theory or episteme, but also techne, art, phronesis.

NOTES

1 See, for instance, W. van Reijen and Dick Veerman, 'An interview with Jean-François Lyotard', *Theory, Culture and Society* 5 (1988), pp. 277–309.

2 H. Reiss (ed.), *Kant's Political Writings*, Cambridge, Cambridge University Press 1970.

3 J. Habermas, 'Technology and science as ideology', in *Toward a Rational Society*, London, Heinemann Educational Books 1980, pp. 81–122.

4 G. W. F. Hegel, *The Phenomenology of Mind*, London, Allen & Unwin 1966, p. 75.

5 The 'Querelle' was a dispute between two factions in the Académie française, the 'Anciens', led by Boileau (1636–1711), and the 'Modernes', led by Charles Perrault (1628–1703), concerning the aesthetic rules and criteria for a literary work. Whereas Boileau defended the classical criteria as absolute and timeless, Perrault argued that the new age required the invention of new standards.

6 J. Habermas, *The Philosophical Discourse of Modernity*, Cambridge, Polity Press 1987, p. 7.

7 See, for instance, H. Lawson, *Reflexivity – The Post-Modern Predicament*, London, Hutchinson 1985.

8 Habermas (1987), op. cit., p. 42.

9 The political consequences of privileging the subject as universal, that is, the state, over the subject as individual, as Hegel does in *Philosophy of Right*, are well known. To challenge, to question, or to work against a state which embodies the concrete universal is to move against reason itself.

10 The criticisms were various and they were acknowledged and sometimes answered by Habermas himself in his 'A postscript to *Knowledge and Human Interests*', *Philosophy of the Social Sciences* 3 (1973), pp. 157–89, as well as in the preface of *Theory and Practice*, London, Heinemann Educational Books 1977. The most relevant criticism for the present discussion is that Habermas's idea of a critical discourse, which sought to overcome Hegel's idealism and Marx's materialism, was based on the problematic notion of self-reflection. As many commentators pointed out (see for instance F. Dallmayr, 'Reason and emancipation: notes on Habermas', *Man and Society* 5 (1972)), the notion of self-reflection was

still too idealistic – and therefore did not achieve the overcoming of the dichotomy between theory and practice – and, moreover, led to authoritarian political consequences that denied its emancipatory purpose; here the critical theorist, endowed with self-reflection, becomes the avant-garde and judge of emancipatory political movements.

11 J. Habermas, *The Theory of Communicative Action*, vol. 1, Boston, Mass., Beacon Press 1984; vol. 2, Cambridge, Polity Press 1987.

12 J. Habermas, 'Wahrheitstheorien', in *Wirklichkeit und Reflexion*, ed. H. Fahrenbach, Pfullingen, Neske 1973, p. 258. See also J. Habermas, 'Vorbereitende Bemerkungen zu einer Theorie der kommunikativen Kompetenz', in J. Habermas and N. Luhman, *Theorie der Gesellschaft oder Sozialtechnologie – Was leistet die Systemforschung?*, Frankfurt, Suhrkamp 1971.

13 See for instance J.-F. Lyotard, *The Postmodern Condition*, Manchester, Manchester University Press 1986.

14 ' "So you are saying that human agreement decides what is true and what is false?" – It is what human beings say that is true or false and they agree in the language they use. That is not an agreement in opinions but in form of life.' (L. Wittgenstein, *Philosophical Investigations*, Oxford, Blackwell 1974, §241).

15 In communicative action, 'participants share a tradition and their orientations are normatively integrated to such an extent that they start from the same definition of the situation and do not disagree about the claims to validity that they reciprocally raise'. In strategic action (conflict, competition, manipulation and systematically distorted communication), it is not possible to reach a direct understanding orientated to validity claims. J. Habermas, 'What is universal pragmatics?', in *Communication and the Evolution of Society*, London, Heinemann Educational Books 1979, p. 209.

16 ibid.

17 J. B. Thompson gives a number of examples of speech acts which cannot be represented by a performative expression and a propositional content. He also argues that in cases such as reading a poem, telling a joke, greeting a friend, or even in the common case of saying 'The sky is blue this morning', we cannot show that the speaker is raising the three validity claims of Habermas's scheme (J. B. Thompson, 'Universal pragmatics', in J. B. Thompson and D. Held (eds), *Habermas – Critical Debates*, London, Macmillan 1982, p. 126.

18 Searle's principle of expressibility – J. Searle, *Speech Acts*, Cambridge, Cambridge University Press 1972 – states that every speech act can be reanalysed in the form F(p). This principle has been widely criticized in the linguistic literature. D. Stampe for instance argues that to say 'I'll come' with the force of a promise is not the same as saying 'I hereby promise that I'll come' ('Meaning and truth in the theory of speech acts', in P. Cole and J. Morgan (eds), *Syntax and Semantics*, vol. 3, *Speech Acts*, London, Academic Press 1975).

19 L. Wittgenstein, *On Certainty*, Oxford, Blackwell 1979, §§143–4.

20 Habermas (1973), op. cit., p. 259.

21 Habermas (1971), op. cit., p. 120.

22 J. Habermas, 'Modernity versus postmodernity', *New German Critique* 22 (1981). See also Habermas's critique of Derrida in *The Philosophical Discourse of Modernity*, pp. 161–84. On the need for an idea of truth for political critique, see V. Havel, 'The power of the powerless', in J. Keane (ed.), *The Power of the Powerless*, London, Hutchinson 1985.
23 Lyotard (1986), op. cit., p. 66.
24 ibid., p. 20.
25 ibid., p. 22.
26 J.-F. Lyotard and J.-L. Thébaud, *Just Gaming*, Manchester, Manchester University Press 1985.
27 This is Rorty's reading of Lyotard (R. Rorty, 'Habermas and Lyotard on postmodernity', in R. Bernstein (ed.), *Habermas and Modernity*, Cambridge, Polity Press 1985).
28 Lyotard (1985), op. cit., p. 26.
29 I. Kant, *The Critique of Judgement*, Oxford, Clarendon Press 1952.
30 Lyotard (1986), op. cit., p. 78.
31 ibid., p. 81.
32 Wittgenstein, *Philosophical Investigations* and *On Certainty*. See also G. P. Baker and P. M. S. Hacker, *Wittgenstein Meaning and Understanding*, Oxford, Blackwell 1983.
33 Wittgenstein (1974), op. cit., §115.

6

THE POSTMODERN KANTIANISM OF ARENDT AND LYOTARD

David Ingram

[O]nly a redeemed mankind receives the fullness of its past –
which is to say, only for a redeemed mankind has its past
become citable in all its moments. Each moment it has lived
becomes a *citation à l'ordre du jour* – and that day is Judgment
Day.[1]

(Walter Benjamin)

The past decade has witnessed an extraordinary resurgence of
interest in Kant's writings on aesthetics, politics and history. On
the Continent much of this interest has centred on the debate
between modernism and postmodernism. Both sides of the debate
are in agreement that Kant's differentiation of cognitive, practical
and aesthetic domains of rationality anticipated the fragmentation
of modern society into competing if not, as Weber assumed, opposed
lifestyles, activities and value spheres, and that this has generated
a crisis of *judgement*. Tradition is deprived of its authority as a
common reference point for deliberation; judgement appears to be
all but submerged in the dark void of relativism. Yet, having both
accepted Kant's differentiation of reason as emblematic of the
pluralism of modern life, modernists and postmodernists remain
divided in their response to its implications. Modernists – Habermas
and Arendt too, I believe, can be classified under this rubric –
attempt to circumvent the relativism of cultural fragmentation by
appealing to a universal ideal of community. This solution recalls
Kant's own grounding of judgements of taste in the notion of a *sensus
communis*. By contrast, postmodernists such as Lyotard embrace
relativism. Whereas the modernist emphasizes the capacity of
rational agents to rise above the parochial limits of local community
in aspiring towards an autonomous perspective, the postmodernist

denies the possibility of impartiality altogether, thus binding judgement to the traditional constraints of practice.

This way of viewing the debate, I shall argue, neglects the fact that the postmodernist, no less than the modernist, must acknowledge a higher community of discourse, and for two reasons: first, because the constant state of revolution endemic to the postmodern condition fosters an autonomous perspective oriented towards the idea of indeterminacy and conflict, in short, towards plurality for its own sake; second, because the affirmation of pluralism implies the idea of a community wherein everyone agrees to disagree. If this analysis is correct, the distinct advantage of the postmodernist position would reside in its capacity to combine – in however paradoxical a manner – both practical and aesthetic moments of judgement: both the Aristotelian notion of phronesis, or the application of general rules heteronomously determined by local habits of thought, and the Kantian notion of taste, or the free, reflexive discovery of rules in the light of indeterminate, transcendent ideas of community.

Taking the philosophies of Hannah Arendt and Jean-François Lyotard as representative of modernist and postmodernist responses to the crisis of judgement respectively, I intend to show that neither adequately explains the possibility of truthful evaluation. Whereas the modernist approach escapes the dilemma of relativism only at the cost of aestheticizing or depoliticizing judgement, the postmodernist alternative affirms the political reality of judgement by delivering it to the vicissitudes of changing circumstance. I therefore concur with Jean-Luc Nancy that judgement must ultimately be located in the prediscursive nexus of habits and meanings that precedes propositionally differentiated language.

The first section reviews Kant's contribution to the debate, especially his resolution of the conflict between theoretical and practical reason in the third *Critique*. The mediation of nature and freedom in aesthetic judgement is of cardinal importance for Arendt and Lyotard since it provides them with a non-teleological model for reconciling the standpoints of actor and philosopher-spectator. In addition, the judgemental disclosure of analogical relationships between distinct fields of rationality suggests a possible grounding for philosophical rationality which, as we shall later see, is exploited to good advantage by Lyotard. Clearly, the delimitation of fields of rationality undertaken by the critical philosopher cannot be grounded exclusively in any particular field. Philosophical no less than aesthetic judgement must remain autonomous, or detached from particular theoretical and practical interests, since its aim is to regulate in as impartial a manner as possible the conflict arising from them. Such impartiality, however, can only be secured by invoking a universal community of discourse. The second section discusses Arendt's use of this principle in addressing the crisis of judgement besetting the modern age. She is less concerned with the problem of justifying global philosophical judgements about rightful boundaries and more interested in the meaning of history. In particular, she hopes to show how judgement can 'redeem the past' without resorting to teleological interpretations that deny the autonomy of actor and spectator. The problem with this solution, which involves transferring the model of aesthetic judgement developed by Kant to the political and historical sphere, is that it ends up depoliticizing judgement. The postmodern alternative of Lyotard discussed in the third section seems to circumvent this difficulty in that it reinstates the practical dimension of judgement (phronesis) alongside the aesthetic. However, the tension between these two poles is once again resolved in favour of the aesthetic. Deprived of prescriptive force and decentred (or, if one prefers, centred on a wholly indeterminate ideal of community), judgement ceases to discriminate or discriminates in a manner that constantly vacillates depending on local circumstances. I conclude that this radical relativism can be mitigated and the truthfulness of judgement accounted for only if one acknowledges the continuity of effective history as an ontological ground supporting radical heterogeneity.

I

It is vexing to expositors of Kant that he left unclarified what is arguably the most important concept in his philosophy: judgement. Doubtless he meant many things by this term: a 'faculty of thinking the particular as contained under the universal', common to cognitive, practical and aesthetic modes of experience; a capacity for finding analogical passageways linking these disparate modalities; a distinct faculty of taste.[2] It suffices to note for our purposes that, notwithstanding its designated role within Kant's system, a species of judgement was identified by him that may be described as evaluative in the broadest sense of the term and one, moreover, that he himself thought to exercise in coming to grips with the political events of his day. The most detailed discussion of judgement occurs in the *Critique of Judgement*, where it is introduced in conjunction with two problems.[3] The former concerns the need to bridge the 'immeasurable gulf' separating 'the sensible realm of nature and the supersensible realm of the concept of reason'. This 'gulf' was a by-product of Kant's famed resolution of the problem of free will and determinism in the *Critique of Pure Reason*. Since understanding (the faculty of natural concepts responsible for causality) and reason (the faculty of supersensible ideas responsible for freedom) have their source in the subject, it is entirely possible, Kant concluded, that they exercise 'two distinct legislations on one and the same territory of experience without prejudice to each other' *(CJ* p. 12). He later realized, however, that this resolution of the problem was not entirely satisfactory, for the categorical distinction between heterogeneous orders of reality, *phenomena* and *noumena*, belies the integral experience of the embodied moral agent for whom 'the concept of freedom is meant to actualize in the world of sense the purpose proposed by its laws'. Nature, Kant reasoned, 'must be so thought that the conformity to law of its (causal) form at least harmonizes with the possibility of the purposes to be effected in it according to laws of freedom *(CJ* pp. 11–12). Somehow we have to imagine the possibility of a supersensible ground of freely willed purposes producing causal effects in nature. Though such production is beyond our ken, Kant insisted that it is presupposed whenever we try to explain a complex event in terms of natural teleology or judge nature to be beautiful. As regards the latter case – of signal importance for understanding the possibility of a global judgement capable of delimiting the rightful boundaries of distinct domains of action and discourse – the underlying feeling of pleasure announces a kind of harmony between understanding and reason arising from the non-cognizable purposiveness of nature with respect to our subjectivity.

As a solution to the conflict of faculties this appeal to taste seems at first highly disingenuous since evaluative judgements are one and all subjective. The tendency to conclude that judgements of this type are merely arbitrary opinions is none the less resisted by Kant, who follows Shaftesbury and Burke in defending their presumption of intersubjective validity. It would be folly, Kant notes, to reprove another person's judgement of what is gratifying in an immediate, non-reflective way, since 'as regards the pleasant . . . the fundamental proposition is valid: everyone has his own taste (the taste of sense)'. Thus 'he is quite contented that if he says "Canary wine is pleasant", another man may correct his expression and remind him that he ought to say, "It is pleasant to me." ' It is otherwise in the case of pure aesthetic judgements:

Many things may have charm and pleasantness – no one troubles himself at that – but if he gives out anything as beautiful, he supposes in others the same satisfaction; he judges not merely for himself, but for everyone, and speaks of beauty as if it were a property of things. Hence he says, 'The thing is beautiful,' and he does not count on the agreement of others with this his judgement of satisfaction, because he has found this agreement several times before, but he *demands* it of them.

(*CJ* pp. 46–7)

Judgements of taste, then, are at once evaluative and cognitive, that is, they refer a subjective feeling to an object in a manner conducive to bringing about an expectation of universal agreement. However, unlike judgements of the good, which produce similar expectations, the ground of aesthetic judgements cannot be conceptually represented and objectively demonstrated; one cannot show that a painting is beautiful in the same way that one can show that a saw is useful, a square perfect, an action worthy or an end universalizable. For to say that something is beautiful is to say nothing at all about its possible utility, worthiness, perfection or purposiveness with respect to any conceivable end.

But how can judgement lay claim to universal validity if its source is subjective pleasure? One might suppose that an appeal to transcendental grounds would help here, for on Kant's reading of the matter, transcendental judgements attributing categorical properties to objects have their origin in the subject too. The appeal can be made but not, Kant adds, without encountering difficulties arising from the peculiar reflexivity that distinguishes aesthetic from categorical judgements. The categorical properties predicated of objects of knowledge, such as causality and substance, can be proved to be universally and necessarily valid as a priori conditions for the possibility of objectivity. Ascriptions of this sort are instances of what Kant calls *determinant* judgement, or predication which subsumes a particular under a *pre-given* universal. Judgements of taste clearly do not determine their object in this way; one does not judge this diamond to be beautiful because it has been universally established in advance that all diamonds are beautiful. Rather, one judges it so only after associating its particular formal attributes with feelings of pleasure. Stated differently, such *reflective* judgements discover the universal (or the beautiful, or the sublime) which best captures our subjective response to a given particular.

For Kant, it is the *disinterested* contemplation of an object solely in regard to its *pure form* alone independent of any purpose it might serve (be it subjective gratification of the senses or objective conformity to some concept) that suggests a way out of the grounding dilemma. Might there not be a priori formal conditions of aesthetic pleasure analogous to the formal unity of cognitive faculties underlying the possibility of objective knowledge? The deduction of such a ground cannot, of course, aspire to rigorous demonstration in accordance with concepts or other determinate criteria, since we are here talking about the *exemplary* necessity and universality of certain subjective states of pleasure – our general feeling that all persons of disinterested mind ought to agree in matters of taste – not the apodeicticity of categories of possible objective knowledge. What is at issue here is the existence of a common sense (*sensus communis*) which enables feelings to be communicated as universally as cognitions. According to Kant, there would be no agreement in people's feelings or cognitions unless they shared the same cognitive faculties and the same 'state of mind' affected by acts of judgement (*CJ* pp. 75–6). Now judgement involves the subsumption of a particular under a universal, a process bringing into play the imagination (the faculty of representing sensible intuitions) and the understanding (the faculty of concepts). As for logical judgements of cognition, or judgements which ascribe a universal property such as causality to a particular object, a sensible intuition is schematized by the faculty of imagination in prior conformity to the laws of the understanding. In the case of aesthetic judgements, however, the predicate ascribed to the object does not refer to an objective concept, but to a subjective feeling. Here the formal unity of understanding and imagination is not predetermined by understanding. Instead, the imagination, representing only the mere form of a particular intuition apart from any sensuous or conceptual content, harmonizes with the understanding spontaneously (*CJ* pp. 128–32).

The feeling of pleasure arising from the *free play* of cognitive faculties permits us to judge the subjective purposiveness, or beauty, of an object in a manner that leads Kant to formulate a new solution to the conflict of faculties. Not only is the imagination in its freedom harmonized with the understanding in its conformity to law, but as

Kant later notes, beauty – especially natural beauty – can also be said to symbolize, and thereby harmonize with, morality. For Kant, symbols function as indirect representations and, more specifically, as concrete *analogues* of rational ideas to which no direct sensible intuition corresponds. In his opinion, nature in the wild, independent of any conceptual or utilitarian associations, excites those pure aesthetic feelings whose underlying formal structure – implicating, free, immediate, universal and disinterested pleasure – is analogous to the feeling of respect accompanying our fulfilment of moral duty. Hence there is a sense in which the symbolizing of moral ideas such as freedom and the kingdom of ends by means of aesthetic 'ideas' implies a supersensible ground (sometimes referred to as *Geist*) identifiable with neither nature nor freedom taken singly (*CJ* pp. 196–9).

II

Those who have followed the discussion thus far may well wonder what Kant's aesthetics has got to do with postmodern political thought. To begin with, the conflict between theoretical and practical reason motivating much of Kant's discussion of judgement crops up again in the postmodernism debate. True, one no longer talks about reason *per se*, yet the issue of fragmentation and conflict – in this case involving domains of discourse and action – is the same. Two questions arise concerning this fragmentation: What place does philosophy occupy in this scheme? And to whom can the political actor appeal in deciding what is right? Lyotard is interested principally in the former, that is, he is concerned with the legitimacy of a discipline that aspires to the status of an impartial tribunal regulating the rightful boundaries of heterogeneous language games. In particular he wonders whether it makes sense to appeal to a transcendent (or transcendental) notion of reason, or community, in defending philosophy's right to judge in these matters. If the philosopher, like the aesthetician, must judge without claiming a privileged standpoint outside the relativity of language games and must discover at each moment the universal which best fits the particular case independent of determinate criteria, then whatever regulative idea he or she invokes must necessarily remain formal and empty. Perhaps a universal idea of community is operational here, but if so, what kind? One conforming to the harmonistic model underwriting judgements of beauty or one conforming to the transgressional aesthetics of the sublime? Lyotard, as we shall see, hopes to avoid a politics of terror (or totalitarianism) by opting for the latter. The second question is of concern to both Lyotard and Arendt, though it is Arendt who initially formulated it. Given the unreliability of conventional authority and the constraints of action in the modern age, is it not wiser (*contra* Lyotard) to reserve judgement to the spectator whose aesthetic distance on life secures a semblance of impartiality? If so, then would such a notion not imply something like an ideal community of speakers capable of agreeing with one another?

I shall begin with Arendt's diagnosis of modernity, which focuses on the devastating impact the Industrial Revolution had on traditional societies 'held together only by customs and traditions'.[4] This impact was immediately registered in the degradation of cultural goods to the status of exchange values serving the social aspirations of philistine *parvenus*. With the advent of mass society, concern with cultural fabrication (work) gave way to the functional production of entertainment and other consumer goods (labour). Absorption of culture into the life process was not without political implications since the public sphere – the stage on which the drama of political life is acted out and recorded before an audience of spectator-judges – is itself constituted by the narratives, artistic images and other cultural artefacts that lend it permanence:

> Culture indicates that art and politics, their conflicts and tensions notwithstanding, are interrelated and even mutually dependent . . . [T]he fleeting greatness of word and deed can endure in the world to the extent that beauty is bestowed upon it. Without the beauty, that is, the radiant glory in which potential immortality is made manifest in the human world, all human life would be futile and no greatness could endure.[5]

Inasmuch as political action depends for its enduring appearance, its meaning and purpose, on the sound judgement and judicious understanding of a public, the 'crisis in culture' is a political crisis as well. Gone is the man of action, replaced by a mass man whose 'capacity for consumption [is] accompanied by inability to judge, or even to distinguish'.[6]

Symptomatic, too, of the crisis in culture is the widespread dissemination of scientific and technological modes of thought. The rational questioning of cultural tradition and authority and the concomitant spread of what, since Nietzsche, has come to be known as nihilism – scepticism regarding the existence of absolutes, devaluation of values claiming universal assent, and resignation to a life devoid of meaning and purpose – has had the further consequence of depriving judgement of any reliable standards. In conjunction with the rise of state bureaucracy devoted to global economic management, the demise of community based on shared values and the attendant withering away of common sense also play important roles in Arendt's account of the emergence of totalitarianism. Having 'clearly exploded our categories of political thought and our standards of moral judgement', totalitarianism challenges not only the capacity of the actor to discern right from wrong, but also the capacity of the historian to understand.[7]

The Eichmann trial in the 1960s seemed to confirm her thesis. Not Eichmann's diabolical nature (if he possessed one) but his banal thoughtlessness, his failure to engage in responsible judgement by blindly obeying the orders of others, was the root cause of his evil. Consequently, Arendt felt that it was all the more imperative that we ascribe to each and everyone 'an independent human faculty, unsupported by law and public opinion, that judges anew in full spontaneity every deed and interest whenever the occasion arises'.[8] But how can one judge or understand the unprecedented inhumanity of totalitarianism? What gives the historian the right to judge actions whose circumstances are so novel as to defy comprehension? Is not the actor better qualified to judge than the historian? This question was raised by Gershom Scholem with regard to Arendt's harsh judgement of those Jewish Elders who had urged compliance with Nazi authorities. Had she not presumed first-hand knowledge of their plight? While conceding that it might be too early for a 'balanced judgement', Arendt replied that 'the argument that we cannot judge if we were not present and involved ourselves seems to convince everyone, although it seems obvious that if it were true, neither the administration of justice nor the writing of history would be possible'.[9] The moral of this story is that if the historian must judge, the actor must understand, or insert his or her own judgements into the broader framework of a community of persons united by common narratives, meanings and goals. Eichmann was evil because he lacked the imagination to take into account other persons' interests save those of his own chosen company.[10] In the words of Arendt, 'understanding becomes the other side of [political] action' engaged in making a new beginning, for one must 'eventually come to terms with what irrevocably happened and to what unavoidably exists', including, one would think, the provenance of one's own identity and that of the community to which one belongs.[11]

A crisis of meaning and judgement likewise clouds political action aimed at initiating fundamental change. To appreciate the role of understanding in coming to terms with action of this sort one must turn to Arendt's transcription of Kant's system in *The Life of the Mind*. After treating the *vita activa* – the life of labour, work and political action – in *The Human Condition*, Arendt returned to some of her earlier concerns pertaining to thinking, willing and judgement – the triad comprising the *vita contemplativa*, or 'life of mind', modelled on Kant's three *Critiques*. Kant's distinction between *Vernunft* and *Verstand* is preserved in her distinction between *thought*, which 'deals with invisibles, with representations of things that are absent' (the combined capacities of abstraction, critical reflection and imaginative reproduction and synthesis), and *intellect* which involves the necessary conditions for cognition.[12] Thinking endows life with meaning by weaving experience into a coherent narrative; cognition, which depends on thinking, aims at demonstrable truth. The other, non-cognitive faculties of mental life – willing and judging – are also dependent on (but irreducible to) thinking.

Now Arendt no less than Kant must contend with the conflict of faculties. The freedom to initiate fundamental political change imposes a responsibility – the need to legitimate the new order – that can only be accomplished by situating the founding act within a historical narrative connecting it to a prior foundation in the past.[13] One is tempted to recount a story of progress in which the revolutionary event is justified as inevitable or necessary, but this cannot be done without denying freedom of the will. Two alternatives remain: one resigns oneself to nihilism or redeems the meaningfulness of the past (along with hope in the future) without any appeal to ultimate ends. Nietzsche, in Arendt's opinion, tried to do both and failed. According to Nietzsche, in order for the will to affirm nihilism as a positive expression of its freedom and power it would (so it seems) have to deny the past – that residue of congealed meaning weighing upon the present and future like a 'stone'. 'Powerless against what has been done', the will, Nietzsche tells us, 'is an angry spectator of all that is past'.[14] Short of denying time itself (which would usher in the extinction of the will), Nietzsche can only affirm its inherent purposelessness – the 'innocence of all

Becoming' – in the doctrine of Eternal Recurrence.[15] A better solution – one which does not end up denying the temporal openness necessary for freedom – would require redeeming each moment of the past by disinterested judgement.

At this juncture Arendt turns to Kant. She here notes two ways in which he sought to apply the concept of judgement in order to retrieve meaning out of political chaos, each demarcating distinct philosophies of history. The first departs from the central tenets of the *Critique of Practical Reason*: we are enjoined by practical reason to strive for moral perfection; such a state presupposes the realization of a universal kingdom of self-legislating agents regarded as ends in themselves – an ideal condition that cannot be attained by imperfect, mortal beings; yet 'ought' implies 'can' – we can only be obliged to strive for what we have reasonable hope of attaining; hence, we must postulate as regulative ideas the immortality of the soul and divine providence. The pursuit of moral perfection on earth is taken up further in Kant's miscellaneous writings on history, where he argues that the achievement of a cosmopolitan federation of republics in a state of 'perpetual peace' is a precondition for the free exercise of practical reason (*CJ* p. 284). The question is posed whether we have any reason to hope that such a state can be brought about by a species naturally inclined to pursue its own selfish interests. For the moral agent caught up in the vicissitudes of action, the answer would appear to be negative.[16] However, from the vantage point of the spectator-judge surveying the totality of human history, the situation is quite different. The basis for this optimism (following the strategy outlined above) resides in the Idea of nature as a supersensible realm of final ends. In response to the question raised in the second half of the third *Critique* – Why is it necessary that man should exist at all? – Kant defends the view that humanity, like any other class of living things, must ultimately be accounted for in terms of teleology, since 'absolutely no human reason . . . can hope to explain the production of even a blade of grass by mere mechanical causes' (*CJ* p. 258). On this reading, our natural self-interestedness is judged to be so providentially designed as to force us out of a state of nature (which Kant, following Hobbes, conceives as a state of war) and into a political condition compelling lawful behaviour culminating in 'a moral predisposition'. Man's natural 'unsocial sociability' is here understood as causally effecting the progressive advent of an unnatural (i.e. moral) state of peace and harmony in accordance with an Idea of reason. It is this teleologically based interpretation of natural history, then, which perhaps explains how Kant could wax enthusiastic over the sublimity of the French Revolution as a symbol of eternal moral progress while yet condemning the lawlessness of its leaders.[17]

The appeal to reason notwithstanding, Arendt finds this use of teleological judgement in resolving the dilemma of nature and freedom, and explaining the superior insight of the philosopher-historian questionable, since it relegates moral agents to the undignified status of means in attaining prior ends.[18] Elsewhere, however, the aesthetic strain prevails in Kant's conceptualization of historical judgement, and it is here, she believes, that the core of Kant's political thought resides. The 'wishful participation that borders closely on enthusiasm' which Kant detects in his positive judgement of the French Revolution is described as consisting in 'simply the mode of thinking of the spectators which reveals itself publicly in this game of great transformations, and manifests such a general yet disinterested sympathy for the players on one side against those on the other, even at the risk that this partiality could become very disadvantageous for them if discovered'.[19] Implicit in this description is an aesthetics of judgement which Arendt characterizes as essentially imaginative, dialogical and communitarian.[20] To begin with, there is the idea that the aesthetic attitude of the spectator is superior to the moral attitude of the actor. From the standpoint of the actor, revolution 'is at all times unjust' since its success would involve violating the principle of publicity. As Kant puts it, a 'maxim which I cannot divulge publicly without defeating my own purpose must be kept secret if it is to succeed; and, if I cannot publicly avow it without inevitably exciting general opposition to my project, the . . . opposition which can be foreseen a priori is due only to the injustice with which the maxim threatens everyone'.[21] This perspective seems to clash with that of the spectator-judge for whom the sublimity of the ends takes precedence over the ignominy of the means – in this regard, at least, war is by no means a handmaiden to the 'commercial spirit . . . low selfishness, cowardice, and effeminacy' wrought by a successful peace (*CJ* p. 102). Arendt goes on to say, however, that in so far as 'publicness is already the criterion of rightness in (Kant's) moral philosophy', the opposition between the practical and aesthetic standpoints and with it, 'the conflict of politics with morality', is partially resolved.[22] The 'political moralist', whom Kant sees as forging 'a morality in such a way that it conforms to the statesman's advantage', is the one who takes the narrow view of history as a 'mere mechanism of nature'. The moral politician, by contrast, is capable of viewing history, if not as a natural process progressively striving to realize a final end, then at least as a theatre of moral purposes in which his or her own freedom is tested and affirmed.[23] In this instance the possibility of taking up the moral standpoint, far from opposing the aesthetic distance of the spectator-judge, actually presupposes it. Publicity not only becomes the great regulator of moral actions; it also anticipates an ideal public of spectators who transform their solitary perspectives by communicating with one another.

Arendt proceeds to unpack the meaning of this ideal in terms of the disinterestedness of the spectator. Of the three 'maxims of common human understanding' mentioned by Kant – think for oneself; think from the standpoint of everyone else; and think consistently – it is the second, the maxim of 'enlarged thought', that specifically applies to the disinterestedness of the spectator's judgement. A person of enlarged mind 'detaches himself from subjective personal conditions of his judgment, which cramp the minds of so many others, and reflects upon his judgment from a universal standpoint (which he can only determine by shifting his ground to the standpoint of others)' (*CJ* pp. 136–7). The importance of enlarged thought for the problem of judgement hinges on the role of imagination. In her earlier essay, 'Understanding and politics' (1953), Arendt writes:

> Imagination alone enables us to see things in their proper perspective, to put that which is too close at a certain distance so that we can see and understand it without bias or prejudice, to bridge abysses of remoteness until we can see and understand everything that is too far away from us as though it were our own affair.[24]

Imagination enables one to 'represent something to oneself that is no longer present'; thinking subjects the representation to the critical dialogue of the mind. Judging, by contrast, does not deal with representations (universal or otherwise) but 'always concerns particulars and things close to hand'. None the less, it is 'the by-product of the liberating effect of thinking' and 'realizes thinking, makes it manifest in the world of appearances'.[25] The thoughtful distancing of imagination 'cannot arise unless we are in a position to forget ourselves, the cares and interests and urges of our lives, so that we will not seize what we admire but let it be as it is, in its appearance'.[26] As Ernst Vollrath and Ronald Beiner have pointed out, the kind of impartiality intended here should not be confused with scientific objectivity.[27] If anything, it is more kindred to phenomenological openness; things are to be judged afresh in all their phenomenal richness and inexhaustibile particularity without being subsumed in advance under conventional universals or habitual modes of classification. Still, without some mediation of universal and particular neither perception nor judgement would be possible. In the case of phenomenological description particular appearances are elevated to the rank of exemplary universals (essences) through a process of imaginative variation and eidetic intuition. Something similar happens to particular events when judged; brought into relief with the aid of narrative understanding and imaginatively interpreted with an ideal audience in mind, human actions come to exemplify what is best or worst in us, what should or should not be emulated. This is how 'redemptive' judgement resolves the antinomy of freedom and necessity, willing and thinking; reconciliation with the past is made possible by endowing the contingent particular with intrinsic meaning and worth.

The work of imagination is captured further by Kant in terms of an ideal community, or audience of interpreters who are thought of as striving to reach impartial agreement and mutual understanding:

> [U]nder the *sensus communis* we must include the idea of a sense common to all, i.e., of a faculty of judgment which, in its reflection, takes into account (*a priori*) the mode of representation of all other men in thought, in order, as it were, to compare its judgment with the collective reason of humanity . . . This is done by comparing our judgment with the possible rather than the actual judgments of others, and by putting ourselves in the place of any other man, by abstracting from the limitations which contingently attach to our own judgment.
>
> (*CJ* p. 136)

Implicit reference is here made to the importance of publicity. In Kant's opinion, it is not enough to possess a right to the private use of one's reason, for even the most conscientious exercise of judgement will be biased unless it is exposed to public examination. Hence, the principle of aesthetic judgement has as its corollary freedom of speech and press.[28]

III

One wonders just how successful Arendt's reconstruction of Kant's 'other' political philosophy is in dealing with the crisis of judgement symptomatic of the postmodern condition. If the postmodern condition renders reason and tradition equally suspect as authoritative reference points for judgement, then what can be the basis for saying that the standpoint of the spectator is any better than that of the actor? Can community still provide an 'impartial' touchstone for judging our fragmented, alienated and anomic condition? Before answering this question I would like to return again to Arendt's choice of Kant's aesthetics as a model of political judgement. This model, as we have seen, privileges the standpoint of the spectator over that of the actor. Although she herself would like to believe that the perspectives of actor and spectator coincide, it is clear from her own remarks that such is not really the case. Though both categorical imperative and *sensus communis* enjoin the universalizability of perspectives, the former compels the judgement of particular actions in isolation from unintended consequences, the latter does not. Interestingly, some of Arendt's earlier writings anticipate a way out of this dilemma in their fusion of Aristotelian and Kantian motifs. In 'The crisis in culture', for example, Arendt discusses the role of phronesis in judgement:

> That the capacity to judge is a specifically political ability in exactly the sense denoted by Kant, namely the ability to see things not only from one's own point of view but in the perspective of all those who happen to be present, even that judgment may be one of the fundamental abilities of man as a political being insofar as it enables him to orient himself in the public realm, in the common world. . . . The Greeks called this ability *phronēsis*, or insight, and they considered it the principal virtue or excellence of the statesman in distinction from the wisdom of the philosopher.[29]

The juxtaposition of Aristotelian and Kantian motifs is quite surprising given Kant's own conviction that prudence, or *prudentia* (following Aquinas's Latin translation of phronesis, ought to be excluded from the moral-political realm as a 'heteronomous' exercise of will. This decision rests on narrowly interpreting the prudence of the 'political moralist' as a purely theoretical (or technical-practical) skill involving the calculation of means for efficiently bringing about desired ends, such as 'exercising an influence over men and their wills' for the sake of advancing interests of state (*CJ* p. 8). Aristotle, however, was careful to distinguish phronesis from techne and episteme, and accorded it the title of practical wisdom, by which he meant deliberation over ends as well as means. This activity clearly has certain features in common with Kant's notion of reflective judgement; it is 'concerned with particulars as well as universals', not simply in order to subsume the particular under the universal (application), but to discover the universal, or rather, the proper mean, appropriate to a given situation; and its exercise involves considering the good of the community as well as one's own.[30] One reflects on the particular situation and the opinion of one's fellow citizens in qualifying the universal, and in this regard, at least, prudence is more open to the particular and less rigidly determined by the universal than Kant's 'law-testing' approach to moral judgement (as Hegel referred to it). Still, it is quite opposed to Kant's notion of reflective judgement in its focus on the substantive qualifications of statesmanship – experience, cultivation of virtuous character, formation of sound habits, and so on – which, presupposing active membership within local political communities bound by common customs, cannot fulfil ideal conditions of impartiality, universalizability and autonomy.[31]

One wonders why Arendt ever abandoned this classical conception of judgement, since it comports much better with the presumed truthfulness of political opinion – a presumption whose basis resides in the shared convictions of a community rather than in the demonstrations of moral theorists.[32] Yet for a civilization whose identity has become so abstract as to verge on total disintegration, the only community capable of serving as touchstone for judgement may well be that disinterested ideal mentioned by Kant. Despite formalistic shortcomings, the 'aestheticization' and concomitant 'depoliticization' of *sensus communis* for which Gadamer rebukes Kant is possibly a better gauge of how things really stand with us than he or any other neo-Aristotelian would care to admit.[33]

Now, no contemporary thinker of repute has capitalized on this aspect of Kant's thought to the extent that Lyotard has. The aestheticization of science and politics which his philosophy proclaims is clearly descended from that great fragmentation of value spheres animating German thought since Kant. Yet notwithstanding the somewhat cynical manner in which Lyotard embraces the debasement of value to exchange commodity, his otherwise positive, Nietz-

schean paean to iconoclasm and innovation is at least tempered by
a strong moral proclivity which owes as much, perhaps, to the
'pagan' notion of phronesis as it does to the modern deontological
ethics of Kant. This postmodern disrespect for stylistic boundaries,
whose very eclecticism mocks the rational demand for consistency,
purity and progress, would appear to put Lyotard on the side of
relativism were it not for his retrieval – highly uncharacteristic of
most poststructuralism – of universal notions of justice and judgement.

I will not bother repeating what I have said elsewhere about
Lyotard's vision of postmodern society.[34] It suffices to note that the
fragmentation of persons and institutions into so many atomic roles
and incommensurable language games bears witness to a new legitimation crisis. According to Lyotard, the local nature of radically
incommensurable language games essentially frustrates any attempt
to uncover overarching rules of communication. Indeed the rules
internally regulating any given language game are themselves continually contested; for in science, as in daily life, conflicts between
competing descriptive, prescriptive and expressive language games
go well beyond inducing the sorts of innovations generated within
the rules of normal discourse.[35] Since the postmodern condition
fosters an incessant search for the new, the unknown, the anoma-
lous, the subversive, the eclectic – in short, dissent from dominant
conventions and decentralization of subjectivity – Lyotard concludes that only a 'legitimation by paralogy' can satisfy 'both the
desire for justice and the desire for the unknown'.[36] Consequently,
the democratic demand that social practices conform to a universally binding consensus as a condition of their legitimation – the
modernist position defended by Habermas and Arendt – strikes him
as nothing less than totalitarian.

What are the implications of this analysis for a theory of judgement? Because there is no overarching community of discourse
Lyotard maintains that judgement is bound by conventional standards of taste possessing at most local validity. The accent here is
on competencies related to phronesis; since standards are general
– prescribing only the limits of possible judgement – their application in any given situation and, therewith, their specific meaning
and validity, will also be undetermined, at least with respect to
these limits. It is at this juncture, however, where practical (pagan)
competencies for judgement and action lead to a more modern, aesthet-
icized notion of the Kantian type. The heteronomy (habitualness)

and parochiality (determinateness) of conventional judgement is itself permanently relativized *vis-à-vis* the judge's freedom to re-interpret the content of standards. As Lyotard puts it, 'the veritable nature of the judge is just to pronounce judgments, *hence prescriptions*, without criteria'.[37] In other words, the limits which immediately determine judgement are violated as soon as they are imaginatively reinterpreted in the light of an indefinite horizon of possible situations. This spectatorial horizon is likened by Lyotard to a regulative idea which postulates neither the convergence of all possible judgements nor the universalizability of any standard, but only the autonomy of judgement – its capacity to 'maximize opinions', or generate new possibilities.[38] If a communitarian ideal is implicated here it is that wherein the *plurality of voices* (or language games) would be preserved without the violence of hegemony.

Lyotard first hinted at combining Aristotelian and Kantian notions of judgement in his 1979 interview with Jean-Loup Thébaud. Shortly thereafter critics such as Jean-Luc Nancy pointed out the paradox inherent in this position. Defending an Aristotelian perspective, Lyotard denied any possibility of grounding judgements claiming universal validity. Yet his self-acknowledged willingness to play 'the great prescriber' who judges the proper limits governing all language games from the detached perspective of the spectator clearly presupposed such a possibility, otherwise his own critique of scientism and discursive hegemony would have been without foundation. Moreover, by prescribing very determinate boundaries to the prescriptive and descriptive language games of morality and science respectively he may have confused (so Nancy argues) determinant and reflective judgement.[39] On this reading Lyotard overstepped the boundaries of aesthetic judgement. The latter may well be guided by an indeterminate idea of community, but this universal is not of the order of something that can be prescribed as a definite purpose to be striven for. Having thus succumbed to a kind of transcendental illusion, Lyotard became entrapped in a totalitarian logic of his own making – that of absolute pluralism.

One need not accept Nancy's contention that Lyotard confused phronesis and reflective judgement to see the problem implicit in playing the 'great prescriber'. Even if, as Gadamer and other her-meneuticists have claimed, every valid application of a general rule to a concrete situation involves reinterpreting the rule in the light of the peculiar circumstances of the situation while relativizing these same circumstances with respect to an indeterminate ideal of community, that is, even if every determinate judgement presupposes a reflective judgement and vice versa, such application does not always or necessarily entail prescription. This objection was finally acknowledged by Lyotard in *Le Différend* (1983), where he once again returned to Kant in order to clarify the notion of a community of heterogeneous faculties 'without which (the partisans of consensus, or beautiful harmony, or the partisans of conflict, or sublime incommensurability) would not even be able to *agree* that they are in *disagreement*'.[40] Lyotard's preferred symbol for this new conception of community is an archipelago:

> The faculty of judging would be at least in part like a ship owner or an admiral who would launch from one island to another expeditions destined to present to the one what they have found (discovered in the old meaning of the term) in the other, and who could serve up to the first some 'as-if' intuition in order to validate it. This force of intervention, war or commerce, hasn't any object, it has no island of its own, but it requires a milieu, the sea, the archipelago, the principal sea as the Aegean Sea was formerly named.[41]

The third *Critique* takes note of symbolic or analogical passages (*Übergänge*) linking what are otherwise heterogeneous moral, aesthetic and cognitive faculties. Lyotard curiously finds in this 'oceanic' simile something like a higher ground on which to base the critical judgement of the philosopher – a common place (the sea) in terms of which competing islands of discourse can be relativized (located) with respect to their particular domains of validity – though he characteristically interprets it in a manner that brings into relief an underlying tension. In *The Strife of the Faculties* (1798), Kant no longer conceived critical philosophy as a neutral tribunal that delivers final verdicts (prescriptions) without incurring new wrongs. We find instead the notion of a guardian who, while not a litigant in the dispute, intervenes indirectly on behalf of the weaker party by judging what is 'just', or conducive to an agreement to disagree. The dispute in question is the conflict of faculties – in the first instance, between the 'higher' university faculties of theology, law and medicine and the 'lower' faculty of philosophy; and in the second, between opposed cognitive and practical mental faculties laying claim to the same territory, human nature. One cannot regulate the various injustices (or *différends*, as Lyotard prefers to call them) which arise when conflicting 'discourses' range over the same territory; at most, one can expose them by defending the equally valid claim of the weaker party, the advocate of freedom, against the apparently stronger claim of the dogmatist. The basis for this peculiar judgement would thus appear to be that the conflict of mental faculties – indeed, the very sickness of the distracted subject – may yet be conducive to the health of the soul.

For Lyotard the kind of critical judgement exercised by the philosopher is reflective rather than determinate, aesthetic rather than teleological. It is not restricted to any given locale (or discursive regime) but ranges over an entire 'archipelago'. Nor is it guided in advance by any theoretical or practical notion of finality. What guide this judgement are aesthetic considerations pertaining to the integrity of a whole whose parts achieve harmonious equilibrium only through conflict. This is not a judgement of beauty in Kant's sense, but a judgement of the sublime. Whereas judgements of beauty reflect the imagination's success in discovering symbols which represent ideas of reason and attest to the unity of faculties – the unity of the cognitive and the practical in the supersensible Idea of nature being a case in point – judgements of the sublime articulate just the opposite – the incommensurability of imagination and understanding, the presentation of the unpresentable. Sublime for Kant are those experiences of formlessness, boundlessness and lack of finality such as political revolutions, which paradoxically arouse enthusiasm in us because they manage in spite of themselves to signal the finality and community they empirically deny.[42] Sublime, too, is the lack of finality evident in the *différend* since it symbolizes a community in which conflict is the basis for integrity, harmony and justice. Lyotard's philosophy therefore testifies to a justice of judgement rather than of action and representation. As he puts it, 'politics cannot have for its stake the good, but would have to have the least bad'.[43] By contrast, justice demands only that one judge without prescribing, that one listen for the silences that betoken *différends* so as finally to let the suppressed voice find its proper idiom.[44]

Lyotard's refusal to grant judgement any prescriptive force follows from the postmodern standpoint he shares with Arendt. If Arendt and Lyotard do not exactly repudiate the finality of judgement, they certainly deny it any determinate content. In the absence of any final verdicts we are left with little consolation but the dignity that comes from judging responsibly. Arendt, of course, found hope in a purely formal idea of community – one, she believed, that might serve to regulate our search for mutual understanding and reconciliation. Although Lyotard also embraces a formal ideal of 'community' – he, like Arendt, has long since abandoned the quest for global narratives in favour of recounting the *petits récits* of localizable collectivities – he more than she has been attuned to the pessimistic implications of the current crisis. Having resigned himself to the end of community *as a locus of consensus*, he urges acceptance of the sublimely indeterminate, yet painful, spectacle of never-ending conflict, disruption and (it would seem) injustice. This solution seems paradoxical in light of Lyotard's insistence on politicizing art and philosophy; for if ideas of community and justice still find a niche in his philosophy it is in the depoliticized sense of a healthy equilibrium of heterogeneous discourses composed of discontinuous phrases – a justice, if you will, of mutually cancelling injustices. Once the sundering of the community of reason is accomplished, however, philosophical judgement is left curiously suspended in an oceanic void. Due to its extreme discrimination, judgement has deprived itself of any determinate ground on which to discriminate, thereby perhaps explaining Lyotard's curious opinion that the only appropriate response to linguistic fragmentation is silence. At least Arendt continued to regard the function of judgement as in some sense preserving a space for the disclosure of community and world. Lyotard's rejection of the ontological no less than the practical role of judgement, on the contrary, raises doubts about the normative basis underlying his own critical judgement.[45]

Viewed in this light, Nancy's critique of Lyotard is decisive:

> [Lyotard] posits 'passages between "areas" of legitimacy' such as 'language (which, if you will, is Being without illusion) *in process (en train)* of establishing diverse families of legitimacy, critical language, without rules.' Language – that is to say, if I understand correctly, the difference either of/between phrases – is defined 'if you will' as 'Being without illusion.' That is to say that illusion is to speak of Being, but that speaking *is* Being 'without illusion'. . . . It is in process, it hasn't finished or begun, but it is in process *à la place*. What is this place? Lyotard would doubtless say that this question is illegitimate. Let's say that he is right. But what is it to be right? Ultimately it is not a 'play of phrases' which decides what is right. . . . If it is not 'Being' it is at least that which

happens to it, in fact the truth of an experience, the judgment of a (hi)story. It is not 'phrases' that are 'right'. . . . Truth is not a phrase – and yet truth happens.[46]

In situating this difficult passage one must bear in mind Lyotard's insistence on the contextuality of all judgement. This would perhaps explain the inconsistency of many of his own judgements in the Thébaud interview about the rightful boundaries separating moral and scientific discourse. Depending on the context of his own reasoning, Lyotard argued both that prescription should be left out of science and that scientific discourse is and even should be impure and undecided. That the logical status of a scientific law or a rule of language hovers somewhere between the prescriptive and the descriptive is something to be at once praised as 'paralogical' and condemned as 'terroristic'. The resulting lack of centredness and discrimination conveys precisely the impression of sophistry Lyotard seeks so assiduously to cultivate. Nancy's remark, I think, can be understood as a response to the indeterminacy and ungroundedness of this situation. Accepting much of Lyotard's thesis concerning the postmodern condition, Nancy still prefers to read Kant through the eyes of Arendt and Heidegger. Judgement is not an arbitrary game of reversal, but presupposes some relationship to the truth, however this is interpreted. Judging discloses Being – discriminates and brings to light what there is. At the same time, it remains firmly embedded in a form of life, or mode of being, that presupposes a deeper, pre-thematic understanding of a global nexus of meaningful relationships comprising the always implicit background against which one acts and experiences. This disclosure (or 'truth' as Heidegger would say) is already centred (enclosed or located) within a linguistically determined horizon of possible meaning – what Gadamer would call the 'effective history' of past precedent (tradition as a repository of possibilities) – and for that reason must be distinguished from the sort of cognitive truth expressed in propositional or categorical judgements. Kant, too, emphasized the centrality of judgement in bringing about the synthesis of intuition and concept necessary for the possibility of experience, but by this he meant a categorial determination. For Nancy, on the contrary, this synthesis presupposes a deeper disclosure of world, self and community involving reflective judgement, or the interpretative creation or discovery of new modes of action, feeling and cognition. Though reflective judgement encompasses and even incorporates the differential structure of language encapsulated in the notion of the *différend*, it does not dissolve into 'a play of phrases'. For prior to all decentralization Judgement is determined pre-categorically by the web of meanings comprising an ontological pre-understanding. If this is so, then the roots of reason reach further down into the ground than its discursive fragmentation would indicate. Can we accept the finality of this judgement? We can, I believe, so long as we remember that even in our postmodern condition – a condition in which tradition, now fragmented, has lost much of its authority – the indeterminacy of final ends and the determinacy of finite purposes, the aesthetics and pragmatics of judgement, are never absolutely opposed, but remain aspects of one and the same Being.

NOTES

Originally printed in *Review of Metaphysics* 42 (September 1988), pp. 51–77. Copyright © 1988 by the *Review of Metaphysics*.

1 Walter Benjamin, 'Theses on the philosophy of history', in *Illuminations*, ed. Hannah Arendt, trans. H. Zohn, New York, Harcourt, Brace, & World 1968, p. 256.

2 Immanuel Kant, *Critique of Judgement*, trans. J. H. Bernard, London, Macmillan 1951, p. 15. Hereafter abbreviated as *CJ*.

3 Aside from occasional references to judgement in Kant's *Logic*, his essay 'Theory and practice', and his treatise, *Education*, a more detailed discussion of this faculty and its relationship to taste can be found in *Anthropology from a Pragmatic Point of View*.

4 Arendt, 'Understanding and politics', *Partisan Review* 20 (1953), p. 385. The reader is urged to consult Ronald Beiner, 'Interpretative essay' in Arendt, *Lectures on Kant's Political Philosophy*, ed. Ronald Beiner, Chicago, University of Chicago Press 1982.

5 Arendt, 'The crisis in culture', in *Between Past and Future*, New York, Viking Press 1980, p. 218.

6 ibid., p. 199.

7 Arendt (1953), op. cit., p. 379.

8 Arendt, 'Personal responsibility under dictatorship', *The Listener*, 6 August 1964, pp. 185–7.

9 Arendt, *Eichmann in Jerusalem: A Report on the Banality of Evil*, New York, Viking Press 1965, pp. 295–6.

10 Arendt, 'Basic moral propositions' (course given at the University of Chicago, seventeenth session), Hannah Arendt Papers, Library of Congress, Container 41, p. 024560. Cited by Beiner in Arendt op. cit., p. 112.

11 Arendt op. cit., p. 391.

12 Arendt, *Thinking*, vol. 1 of *The Life of the Mind*, ed. Mary McCarthy, New York, Harcourt, Brace, Jovanovich 1978, p. 193.

13 Arendt's claim that the secular orders founded by the framers of the

DAVID INGRAM

Declaration of Independence and the Declaration of the Rights of Man required legitimation *vis-à-vis* the civil ideals of classical antiquity lends credence to the view that the modern age is a continuation of the past by other means. This secularization thesis, which denies modernity any claim to legitimacy other than that bestowed upon it in virtue of its substantial identity with the paganism of antiquity and the Christianity of the Middle Ages, would appear to contradict Arendt's contention that the modern world constitutes a radical break with the past. However, as Hans Blumenberg notes, Arendt correctly saw that the worldliness of the modern age is no more a simple repetition of pagan antiquity than is the unworldliness of the scientific demythologization of nature a simple repetition of the otherworldliness of the Middle Ages. See Arendt, *On Revolution*, New York, Viking Press 1962, pp. 195–215; *The Human Condition*, Chicago, University of Chicago Press 1958, p. 320; and Hans Blumenberg, *The Legitimacy of the Modern Age*, trans. Robert M. Wallace, Cambridge, Mass., MIT Press 1983, pp. 8–9.

14 Frederick Nietzsche, *Thus Spoke Zarathustra*, in *The Portable Nietzsche*, trans. and ed. Walter Kaufmann, New York, Viking Press 1968, p. 251.

15 Arendt, *Willing*, vol. 2 of *The Life of the Mind*, op. cit., p. 170.

16 Kant, 'Theory and practice', in *Kant's Political Writings*, ed. H. Reiss, trans. H. B. Nisbet, Cambridge, Cambridge University Press 1971, p. 91.

17 Kant, 'An old question raised again: Is the human race constantly progressing?' part 2 of 'The strife of the faculties', in *On History*, ed. Lewis White Beck, Indianapolis, Bobbs-Merrill 1963, p. 144. For a more detailed account of Kant's condemnation of revolution in general and the French Revolution in particular, see Kant, *The Metaphysical Elements of Justice*, trans. John Ladd, Indianapolis, Bobbs-Merrill 1965, pp. 84–9, 113–14.

18 Arendt (1982), op. cit., pp. 18, 31.

19 Kant (1963), op. cit., p. 143.

20 Arendt (1982), op. cit., pp. 66–7.

21 Kant, 'Perpetual peace' (1963), op. cit., pp. 129–30.

22 Arendt (1982), op. cit., p. 19.

23 Kant, 'Perpetual peace' (1963), op. cit., p. 119.

24 Arendt (1953), op. cit., p. 392.

25 Arendt, *Thinking* (1978), op. cit., pp. 192–3.

26 Arendt (1980), op. cit., p. 210.

27 Cf. Beiner, 'Interpretive essay' (1982), op. cit., p. 111; and Ernst Vollrath, 'Hannah Arendt and the method of political thinking', *Social Research* 44 (1977), pp. 163–4.

28 Arendt (1982), op. cit., pp. 74–5. Cf. Kant, 'Was heißt: sich im Denken orientieren?' in *Gesammelte Schriften*, Prussian Academy edition, Berlin, Reimer & de Gruyter 1910–66, vol. 8, pp. 131–47. Cf. Kant, *On History* (1963), op. cit., pp. 89, 103.

29 Arendt (1980), op. cit., p. 221.

30 Aristotle, *Nicomachean Ethics* 6.2–4, 7–9.

31 Arendt (1980), op. cit., pp. 220–1. Substantive considerations, however, do enter into the account of judgement and social taste presented in

142

Kant's *Anthropology*. There, judgement ('the faculty of discovering the particular so far as it is an instance of a rule') is similar to Aristotle's golden mean in that it involves correct understanding, which 'maintains the properness of concepts necessary for the purpose for which they are used' (Kant, *Anthropology*, op. cit., p. 92). Such discrimination 'cannot be taught, but only exercised', and 'does not come for years' (ibid., p. 93). Elsewhere, Kant talks about the 'goodness of soul . . . around which the judgment of taste assembles all its judgments' as the 'pure form under which all purposes must be united'. But 'greatness of soul and strength of soul relate to the matter (the tools for certain purposes)' (ibid., p. 144). Finally, Kant remarks that 'to be well-mannered, proper, polite, and polished (by disposing of crudeness)' is a condition of taste, albeit a negative one (ibid., p. 147).

32 Echoing Habermas's criticism of Arendt's contention that 'practice rests on opinions that cannot be true or false in the strict sense' (Jürgen Habermas, 'Hannah Arendt's communicative concept of power', *Social Research* 44 (1977), p. 22), Beiner remarks that 'it is not clear how we could make sense of opinions that did not involve any cognitive claims . . . or why we should be expected to take seriously opinions that assert no claims to truth (or do not at least claim more truth than is claimed by available alternative opinions)' ('Interpretive essay', op. cit., p. 137). Interestingly, in her essay, 'What is freedom', Arendt followed Kant very closely in speaking of 'the judgment *of the intellect* which precedes action' (*Between Past and Future*, op. cit., p. 156 – emphasis added). However, in her unpublished lectures delivered in 1965 and 1966 she reversed herself, identifying judgement with the 'arbitrating function' of the will. It was only after expressing doubts about the status of judgement that she eventually aligned it with the non-cognitive *vita contemplativa*.

33 See Hans-Georg Gadamer, *Wahrheit und Methode*, Tübingen, J. C. B. Mohr 1960, pp. 39–77. For further discussion of the relevance of phronesis to the problem of hermeneutic application see pp. 295–307; and David Ingram, 'Hermeneutics and truth', *Journal of the British Society for Phenomenology* 15 (January 1984), pp. 62–78.

34 See David Ingram, 'Legitimacy and the postmodern condition: the political thought of Jean-François Lyotard', *Praxis International* 4 (3) (October 1987), pp. 286–305. See also Lyotard, *The Postmodern Condition: A Report on Knowledge*, trans. G. Bennington and B. Massumi, Minneapolis, University of Minnesota Press 1984; and Lyotard and Jean-Loup Thébaud, *Au juste*, Paris, Christian Bourgeois 1979, p. 188.

35 Lyotard (1984), op. cit., p. 20.

36 ibid., pp. 65–7.

37 Lyotard and Thébaud (1979), op. cit., pp. 52–3. Emphasis added.

38 ibid., pp. 146–53.

39 Jean-Luc Nancy, 'Dies Irae', in *La Faculté de juger*, Paris, Les Editions de Minuit 1985, pp. 13–14.

40 Lyotard, *Le Différend*, Paris, Les Editions de Minuit 1983, pp. 24–5.

41 ibid., p. 190.

42 Lyotard (1983), op. cit., pp. 240–3.

43 ibid., p. 203.

44 ibid., p. 30.

45 Habermas also has difficulty accounting for the normative basis of judgement, though for somewhat different reasons. He is inclined to distinguish judgement from practical reason, the application of general norms (phronesis), from their discursive justification. Although his understanding of judgement is informed by Gadamer's hermeneutics, which invests phronesis with a certain reflexivity and dialogical openness, he is not willing to see in it a different, perhaps aesthetic, conception of rationality at work. The notion of aesthetic rationality in Habermas's philosophy is unclear, but some of his recent essays have alluded to a kind of artistic rationality and 'truth' which would be holistic and prediscursive, implying more than an ideal speech situation. See Habermas, 'Questions and counterquestions', in *Moralbewußtsein und kommunikatives Handeln*, Frankfurt, Suhrkamp 1983, pp. 53–125; R. J. Bernstein (ed.), *Habermas and Modernity*, Cambridge, Mass., MIT Press 1985; and David Ingram, *Habermas and the Dialectic of Reason*, New Haven, Yale University Press 1987, pp. 101–3, 177–88.

46 Jean-Luc Nancy, *L'Imperatif categorique*, Paris, Flammarion 1983, p. 60.

7

'CES PETITS *DIFFÉRENDS*': LYOTARD AND HORACE

Geoffrey Bennington

The 'Horace' in my title might well have been the Quintus Horatius Flaccus of *Ars Poetica* fame, and more specifically of *ut pictura poesis* fame. This would most obviously have provided access to a discussion of *Discours, figure*. For example, Lyotard refers to this statement, or to its presuppositions, in an analysis of the relationship of word and image in the doctrine of the Fathers of the Church:

> A pedagogy which finds its support in the ancient 'Ut pictura poesis' of Horace, of which Plutarch attributes the earliest formulation to Simonides. It is on condition that it speak 'clearly' that painting will be tolerated. This clarity must be taken literally: it is the transparency of signification in the linguistic term . . . The figure thus strictly subjected to writing cannot create an illusion and its opacity cannot therefore capture and divert the movement of adoration. The function of the visible is [here] to signify the invisible.
>
> (*DF* p. 173)

The 'earliest formulation' referred to here returns later in *Discours, figure*, in a discussion of the rhetorical notion of figure:

> The tradition places the starting-point of rhetoric in the following words of Simonides of Ceos: 'Poetry is painting with words'. Painting, poetry and rhetoric are the places where there comes to the surface the figure which the Pythagorean-Platonic city has the pretension of breaking with. In truth, rhetoric and philosophy belong together to the universe of fragmentary discourses born of the breaking of the speech of *aletheia*. Nevertheless Platonism attributes to the figure the function of seducing, i.e. of separating the subject from itself

and getting an ally within the enemy camp; this is evidently
because the figure is the ruse of a force, namely desire.

(*DF* p. 288n6)

Complicated detours would have been necessary in such an account
of 'Lyotard and Horace'; for example, the context of the 'ut pictura
poesis' statement in Horace himself suggests much less than is
usually supposed a *general* analogy of poetry and painting (as arts
of representation), and certainly does not imply the metaphorical
equivalence suggested by Simonides (though some such equivalence
is suggested in other parts of the *Ars Poetica*): here Horace is dealing,
rather, with a particular analogy to do with conditions of reception,
viewing and reading:

> Poetry is like painting. Some attracts you more if you stand
> near, some if you're further off. One picture likes a dark place,
> one will need to be seen in the light, because it's not afraid
> of the critic's sharp judgement. One gives pleasure once, one
> will please you if you look it over ten times.

(ll. 361–5, trans. D. A. Russell)

This question of distance, of finding the right distance, would itself
have to be referred to Lyotard's elaboration of the non-oppositional
relationship of discourse and figure in the early parts of his book,
around questions of depth, designation, perspective, deictics and so
on, in the wake of Merleau-Ponty. Plotting the relationship of this
essentially phenomenological account (which informs the first quotation from *Discours, figure*) with, on the one hand, a *semiology* of
painting and discourse (as formulated most notably in this country
by Norman Bryson, for example), and on the other with Lyotard's
own attempt, in the second part of *Discours, figure* (and visibly so in
the second quotation) to displace phenomenology via an appeal to
a certain psychoanalysis, and, later, to a 'libidinal economy' –
plotting these relationships would be a redoubtable task which I
shall not attempt here. But the idea that the function of the visible
might be to signify or at any rate to allude to the invisible may yet
provide a bridge between Lyotard's 'early' work, and that following
his 'linguistic turn': for example, a 1981 text on the artist Daniel
Buren is entitled 'Faire voir les invisibles, ou: contre le réalisme'
[literally: 'make the invisibles seen, or: against realism'],[1] and this
would of course be consonant with a number of recent formulations

of the task of philosophy *and* art 'présenter qu'il y a de l'imprésent-able'.[2]

So not that Horace, though it might well have been. Nor even, in terms of the possible bridge linking early and late Lyotard, the Horatius from Book 2 of Livy's *History* or from Macaulay's famous and appalling poem from *The Lays of Ancient Rome*, who might defend such a bridge (defend its existence and/or prevent its being crossed). But the question of the bridge would inevitably, given the later Lyotard's insistent readings of Kant, and especially of the third *Critique*, have embroiled me in the 'bridge' which Kant attempts to throw over the 'abyss' between theoretical cognition of nature and practical laws of freedom,[3] a bridge the possibility of which Lyotard would want to interrogate between genres of discourse in general (see for example the 'Notice Kant 3' in *D* pp. 189–96). In a complex way I could scarcely unpack, it seems to me that both Kant *and* Lyotard are in some sense Horatius, defending both the possibility and impassibility of such a bridge: as Lyotard says in his analysis of the sublime, the 'passage' of the abyss becomes blocked in an agitation over the abyss (*D* p. 240) – the bridge is neither crossed nor not crossed, defended, *défendu* in both senses. And I could scarcely have discussed this Horatius without looking at Heidegger's comment, in 'Building, dwelling, thinking', that 'the bridge does not just connect banks that are already there. The banks emerge as banks only as the bridge crosses the stream',[4] and at Derrida's analyses in *La Vérité en peinture* of the same passage in Kant, and notably the following statement:

> The bridge is not *an* analogy. The recourse to analogy, the concept and effect of analogy are or make *the bridge* itself – both in the [third] *Critique* and in all the powerful tradition to which it still belongs. The analogy of the abyss and the bridge over the abyss is an analogy which says that there must surely be an analogy between two absolutely heterogeneous worlds, a third term to cross the abyss, to heal over the gaping wound and think the gap. In a word, a *symbol*. The bridge is a symbol, passing from one bank to the other, and the symbol is a bridge.
>
> The abyss calls for analogy – the active recourse of the whole *Critique* – but analogy plunges endlessly into the abyss as soon as a certain art is needed to describe analogically the play of analogy.[5]

But such an approach would scarcely be possible without some attempt to unravel the difficult issues of Lyotard's general relationship to Heidegger on the one hand and to Derrida on the other: this would also involve building and/or defending bridges, and I fear that the preliminary surveys are as yet not really complete.

Neither of these two possible Horaces or Horatii, then, but a third Roman Horatius, or rather *the* third Horatius, the one who survives and avenges his two brothers, killing all three Curiatii, thus deciding the war between Rome and Alba Longa, as first recounted in Book 1 of Livy's History. (David's famous painting of the three brothers' oath before the combat is, incidentally, the subject of an analysis by Bryson.[6]) The dispute between the two cities is the apparent result of border-raids by both sides, and the theft of cattle from each other. The dispute has not been settled by litigation, and the declaration of war by Rome answers the Alban leader's refusal to return the stolen goods. This failure of litigation does not of course automatically qualify the dispute as a *différend* in Lyotard's terms, and I shall return to this question in due course. There is in any case a strong suggestion in Livy that the war is a result in the first instance, not of a simple matter of cattle-stealing, but of a renewal of Rome's conquering destiny by the new king, Tullus Hostilius: such a destiny has been promised to Rome at least since the death of its founder, Romulus, and Livy suggests that Tullus's 'one object was to find cause for renewed military adventure',[7] after the peaceful reign of Numa Pompilius, a man who had sought to give Rome an essentially religious unity, and who had, says Livy, 'a great reputation . . . for justice and piety' (p. 52). (This conjunction would immediately arouse Lyotard's suspicion, given that at least since *Instructions païennes* of 1977, he has been explicitly seeking for 'justice in impiety' (*IP* p. 11).)

But whatever cause is assigned to the war, its status is complicated by the fact that both cities come from a common mythical root, the Trojan refugees led by Aeneas: the Trojans had settled in Lavinium, Lavinians had settled Alba, and it was from Alba that Romulus and Remus set out to found Rome. Romulus's act of fratricide at the foundation of Rome is set by Livy in a quasi-causal chain of violence, involving usurpation, murder and rape (this rape of a Vestal Virgin, legendarily performed by the god Mars, leads to the birth of Romulus and Remus). Alba and Rome are successive products of this violent genealogy, and Livy says that 'war between them would be like father against son' (p. 57).

It is not Livy's account that interests me primarily, however, but that presented by Corneille's play *Horace* (1640). Pierre Corneille would also allow a number of trajectories or passages through Lyotard's work. In *Discours, figure*, for example, Lyotard juxtaposes a quotation from Corneille's earlier play *Le Cid* (1636) with one from e. e. cummings, to suggest that both texts are equally 'poetic' in their transgression of certain discursive rules. Lyotard goes on to suggest that this common 'poetic' quality implies a break (in Corneille as much as cummings) with the discourse of communication, but that the poetic function in the two cases is somewhat different:

> [The poetic function] today is critical; it used to be integrative, but even then, this integration of the collectivity in itself took place in a register different from that of the profane language of communication. It is individuals who communicate with each other, and the very category of communication can only become predominant in a society in which the crisis of institutions produces isolated groups or individuals who attempt to establish social links on a 'horizontal' contractual basis. The integrative function of poetic discourse presupposes, on the contrary, a coherent system of institutions culminating in a myth of origin, to which the poem, but also dance or the plastic arts or war, ceaselessly refer as their common meaning.
>
> (*DF* pp. 320–1)

And in the wake of this notion of an integrative poetic function, Corneille reappears in *Au juste* as Lyotard's example of 'classical' writing, defined in pragmatic terms as a set-up in which 'the author is able to write while simultaneously placing himself in the position of the reader' (*AJ* p. 21; *JG* p. 9, trans. mod.), as opposed to the modern writer who does not know for whom he or she writes, and who sends out books like bottles thrown into the sea, in search of their addressee.

But nowhere, I think, does Lyotard quote or discuss the statement from *Horace* which provides my title (although one other line from the play is quoted in *Le Différend*, and will reappear here in due course): Curiace, one of the three brothers who will be opposed to the Horatii, is recounting how the two armies were prevented from engaging in a full-scale final battle by a harangue from the Alban leader. The burden of this harangue is to do precisely with the

common genealogy of Rome and Alba which I have pointed out in
Livy:

> Souffrons que la raison éclaire enfin nos âmes:
> Nous sommes vos voisins, nos filles sont vos femmes,
> Et l'hymen nous a joints par tant et tant de noeuds,
> Qu'il est peu de nos fils qui ne soient vos neveux;
> Nous ne sommes qu'un sang et qu'un peuple en deux villes:
> Pourquoi nous déchirer par des guerres civiles,
> Où la mort des vaincus affaiblit les vainqueurs,
> Et le plus beau triomphe est arrosé de pleurs?
> Nos ennemis communs attendent avec joie
> Qu'un des partis défait leur donne l'autre en proie,
> Lassé, demi-rompu, vainqueur, mais, pour tout fruit,
> Dénué d'un secours par lui-même détruit.
> Ils ont assez longtemps joui de nos divorces;
> Contre eux dorénavant joignons toutes nos forces,
> *Et noyons dans l'oubli ces petits différends*
> *Qui de si bons guerriers font de mauvais parents.*
> Que si l'ambition de commander aux autres
> Fait marcher aujourd'hui vos troupes et les nôtres,
> Pourvu qu'à moins de sang nous voulions l'apaiser,
> Elle nous unira, loin de nous diviser.

> [At last let reason light our souls:
> We are your neighbours, our daughters are your wives,
> And hymen has joined us by so many bonds
> That few of your sons are not also your nephews;
> We are but one blood, one people in two cities,
> Why tear ourselves apart in civil wars
> In which the loser's death weakens the victor
> And the finest triumph is watered with tears?
> Our common enemies wait with joy
> For one of the parties, defeated, to offer them the other as
>   their prey –
> Fatigued, half-broken, victorious: but for sole reward
> Deprived of the help it has itself destroyed.
> Long enough have they enjoyed our divorce;
> Henceforth let us join against them our force,
> *And let us drown in oblivion these little* différends
> *Which make such bad relatives of such good warriors.*
> If the ambition of commanding others

Today makes your troops march, and ours,
So long as we appease it with lesser spill of blood,
That ambition will unite far more than divide us.]

(ll. 287–306; my translation and emphasis)

And this leads to the proposal that the particular *différend* (never specified by Corneille) be settled by the combat of three champions from either side – which three champions are duly chosen as the Horatii and the Curiatii.

I have suggested that failure of litigation does not necessarily lead to *différend*, and in Lyotard's terms the particular *'petit différend'* involved here would seem not to deserve its name. In Lyotard's terms, a *différend* is 'a case of conflict between (at least) two parties that could not be resolved equitably for lack of a rule applicable to the two modes of argumentation' (*D* p. 9). Although, accepting Livy's account, the dispute in question here is to do with the very border-regions or *pagus* from which, in both *Instructions païennes* and *Au juste* (*IP* pp. 42–3; *AJ* pp. 74–5 [*JG* p. 38]), Lyotard derives his notion of the 'pagan', and which returns in *Le Différend* itself as a privileged site (if not the *necessary* site) of *différends* (*D* §218), it would seem that the issue in question here is essentially a litigation: if the dispute in question is to do with stolen cattle, then both sides use commensurable argumentation in requesting the return of their property. And if this be taken as a mere pretext for war, and something like the 'ambition of commanding others' referred to by the Alban leader be seen as the cause of the dispute, then we should still apparently be dealing with litigation rather than *différend*: acting out of imperial ambition, both sides are attempting to impose on the other a *name* (Rome, Alba) and therefore a *narrative* – the 'myth of origin' (and genealogy of heroes) recounted by Livy and referred to by Lyotard in the reference to Corneille just quoted from *Discours, figure*.[8] In so far as both sides are proposing sentences of the narrative genre, then the dispute is not a *différend* (and I wonder whether war could ever be a *différend* in Lyotard's terms: I suspect that in *Au juste* at least, a proportional analogy suggests that war is to terror as litigation is to *différend* – but the fact that the Alban leader describes this as 'civil war' might complicate the issue, especially in view of Lyotard's image of a civil war of language against 'itself' (*D* §201; see too §§188, 190 and 231): this image being justified by the location of the *différend* as a general question of the relationship of genres).

151

This type of set-up, involving the imposition of name and narrative, which is, perhaps, that of imperialism in general, is not, in Livy's account, to be thought of as something Rome got into at a certain point of its history, but as something which constituted Rome from its very beginning: Romulus simply enclosed a certain area of ground and, following in this the standard practice of antiquity according to Livy, 'shark[ed] up a lot of homeless and destitute folk and pretend[ed] that they were "born of the earth" to be his progeny' (p. 42) – this would be, via the imposition of a name ('Romans'), the constitution of a *Volk* and a *Heim* from the *pagus* (see *D* §218). But Rome is not simply one example of this structure: it is *the* example – Lyotard analyses this set-up, in one of his oddest texts, *Le Mur du pacifique*, as a fundamentally Roman set-up which has simply shifted its capital further and further west, at least as far as Washington and maybe to Los Angeles, where it meets the 'wall of the pacific' and stops in this absolute west which can go no further without becoming the east. (This impossible line of separation between east and west gives its title to an essay by Lyotard on the Japanese-American painter Arakawa, 'Longitude 180° W or E'.)[9] (In *Le Différend* itself, Rome returns, again as more than just an example, in the chapter on names and referents, as a persistent and rather bizarre test case for the analysis of 'reality' (*D* §§58, 59, 65, 66, 67, 68) – a little later we shall see why it might be possible to refer to Lyotard's whole philosophy as in some sense a philosophy of Rome, or a Roman philosophy.) In the case before us, however, Rome, which is born of the violent enclosure of a *pagus*, is attempting to annex another *Heim* or *Volk* in order to impose its own name and narrative on a rival name and narrative (that of the Albans). In *Le Différend*, this type of situation, in which the persistence of national worlds of names is seen to block movements of universalization of all sorts (including that of Socialist Internationalism) is analysed precisely *not* as a *différend*. A *différend* requires the attempt by one genre (be it cognitive, performative, economic) to impose its hegemony on another genre (be it ethical or speculative), to enforce judgement of cases pertaining to one genre in terms of another. In the type of conflict we are examining, however, the genres in conflict are the same on both sides (narrative and nominative giving auto-nomination): the conflict is indeed a litigation, but an exacerbated type of litigation not easily to be dismissed – the point is that there is no tribunal which could settle the dispute *as* litigation: unless one posits a tribunal of world history, a hypothesis Lyotard believes to be untenable (see *D* §227). (And this possibility of an exacerbated litigation is matched by that of an exacerbated *différend*, in which no tribunal could even pretend to settle that *différend* as though it were a matter for litigation (see *D* §160): Lyotard never really thematizes or classifies these situations in formal terms, but we shall see that this possible absence of the tribunal is not trivial, nor simply a contingent possibility.)

This exacerbation of litigation takes a curious turn in the case with which we are concerned: in so far as Rome and Alba belong to the same genealogy, then they essentially propose the same narrative of origins – if the Alban leader can claim that they are really one blood and one people, then in a sense they have the same name, or the difference between their two names is a sort of accident or catastrophe. This is why he can suggest that they share an essential identity, defined by their opposition to 'common enemies' – in so far as the outcome of the battle between them will be that one absorbs the other and re-establishes their nominal identity, then this will restore a unity accidentally broken: no need for a lot of blood to be spilt, and the blood that is split will be more that of blood-brotherhood than hatred, integrative rather than divisive. (The logic of his harangue is exactly that which informs the 'no enemies on the Left' argument around political differences, and which consistently identifies a 'real enemy' elsewhere in order to put an end to 'civil war' among natural allies. This masking of possible *différends* in the interests of establishing unity is of course suspect in Lyotard's terms.)

If Rome's battle against Alba is, as Livy suggests, that of son against father, then we could imagine an essentially Oedipal reading of the conflict, but also be at something of a loss to understand how the change of name came about. But in Corneille's presentation, Alba is not Rome's father but its mother, and this complicates any such analysis. In the opening scene of the play, Sabine, wife of the Horace who will emerge victorious in the name of Rome, but herself of Alban origin, makes this very clear: she readily accepts that Rome, in its infancy, can consolidate its power only by war, and welcomes the gods' promise that Rome will conquer the earth, beyond even the Latin region here in question; 'But', she adds, apostrophizing Rome,

> . . . respecte une ville à qui tu dois Romule.
> Ingrate, souviens-toi que du sang de ses rois

Tu tiens ton nom, tes murs, et tes premières lois.
Albe est ton origine; arrête, et considère
Que tu portes le fer dans le sein de ta mère

[. . . respect a city to whom you owe Romulus,
Ungrateful [*ingrate*: Rome is feminine], remember that from
   the blood of its [i.e. Alban] Kings
You take your name, your walls, and your first laws.
Alba is your origin; stop and consider
That you are plunging your sword into your mother's breast].

(ll. 52–60)

This initial familial complication is relentlessly increased by the
way Corneille determines the relationships of the major characters.
For Sabine is not only an Alban become Roman through marriage
to Horace, she is also the sister of the three Curiatii that same
Horace will eventually kill. The play opens on the impossible situation this creates: Sabine is caught in a sort of double-bind where
she can only fear whatever results from the confrontation, and
produces elegantly balanced lines such as 'Je crains notre victoire
autant que notre perte' [I fear our victory as much as our defeat]
(l. 32), or 'Je ne suis point pour Albe, et ne suis plus pour Rome'
[I am not for Alba, and no longer for Rome] (l. 88).

Sabine's dilemma is produced by a change of name: she was
Alban, but is now Roman; she was a Curiatius, now a Horace. Her
appeal to Rome to remember its origin in Alba doubles her own
memory of her own over-written origin: 'Albe, où j'ai commencé de
respirer le jour,/Albe, mon cher pays, et mon premier amour' [Alba,
where I first began to breathe the day/Alba, my dear country and
my first love] (ll. 29–30). In Lyotardian terms, Sabine would be
described as the referent of a sentence (or sequence of sentences)
of the matrimonial genre, which positions as its sender her Alban
family (and specifically the father of that family, as what determines
its name) and as its addressee her Roman family, and specifically
Horace (who shares his name not only with his two brothers, but
also with his father). The meaning of such a sentence is open to
debate, of course, but part of that meaning is that the referent of
the sentence changes name and in principle forgets that of the
sender in favour of that of the addressee. Such at least is the
interpretation of Horace himself, and, more importantly, of his
sister Camille, who says that Sabine need only fear Horace's death,
and not that of her Alban brothers, for her attachment to her

154

brothers is cancelled by marriage; 'pour suivre un mari l'on quitte ses parents' [to follow a husband one leaves one's parents] (l. 886). This explication comes in the middle of a curious scene in which Sabine and Camille are arguing about which of them is in the worse situation: for Camille is not only Horace's sister, she is also to be married to one of the three Curiatii. She is, as it were, the promised referent of a future matrimonial sentence: or, perhaps, stranded between sender and addressee, between Rome and Alba, between Horatii and Curiatii.

The judgement to be made of this situation can be agonistically debated: for example, Julie, a confidant figure, early in the play suggests quite plainly to Camille that it is possible to change one's lover (in the sense of fiancé), but not one's husband, and that Camille need only forget Curiace in favour of a perfectly acceptable match in Valère, a Roman (ll. 145–50). Camille, against such a view, suggests that on the contrary she is caught in an impossible suspension between departure and arrival: following the rules of the matrimonial genre, which we can now analyse further as involving a sentence which is a promise and the matrimonial sentence proper which fulfils that promise, she is pulled forward towards the second sentence (which the genre tends to propose as inevitable or natural), only to discover the truth of one of Lyotard's fundamental tenets, namely that necessity is only *that* a second sentence will arrive, but *what* sentence will arrive is a contingency (see *D* §40). In this sense, in so far as the most general sense of the *différend* is a situation which holds between sentences, on the occasion of the slightest 'enchaînement' or linking, in so far as incommensurable genres are always in conflict over the sentence which actually arrives, then Camille is 'in' the *différend* more radically than anyone, in the 'ontological' position of waiting for the event to come, for the 'Arrive-t-il?' (see *D* §110): living respect for the event as intolerable anguish. (This would perhaps be the point at which to explore the essential differences between the type of reading sketched here and that offered from a dialectical-existential perspective by Serge Doubrovsky, to whose *Corneille ou la dialectique du héros* I am none the less indebted, as is any reader of Corneille today.)[10]

The relationship between Alba and Rome is, then, analogically one of genealogy (father and son for Livy, mother and daughter for Corneille), and really, one of intermarriage, the 'exchange of women'. We might tentatively formulate the *différend* between the two cities as a product of the *différend* between this marital economy and this genealogical analogy, between a narrative of origins and an economy of exchange. But such a *différend* cannot simply be located *between* Rome and Alba: it must affect each from within. And in so far as the economy is essentially to do with the exchange of women by their fathers, then it is not surprising that women (and specifically Camille, caught in mid-exchange) should be, more than the male characters, the privileged witnesses to the *différend* staged by the play.

In Lyotard's terms, a *différend* is signalled by silence and/or sentiment, a frustration of language trying to phrase something in the absence of the means to do so (see *D* §23). Sabine and Camille bear witness to that sentiment, in the impossibility in which they are placed of situating themselves as senders of possible sentences. Their language is therefore 'sentimental': Sabine at several points asking to die, in view of an obligation to choose where choice is impossible; Camille alternating between hope and despair. But if, as Lyotard also suggests, a *différend* is always a call to phrasing, to the search for an idiom in which to phrase the (as yet) unsayable or to present the (as yet) unpresentable, then Camille also provides an example to support this. The language with which she is provided to phrase her situation is the male language of family names and city-names: the language of the genealogical narrative. Horace and Curiace both produce sentences belonging to this language, finalized by the obligation to immortalize the city-name and through it the family name. Appealing to the operator of the 'belle mort', extensively analysed by Lyotard in the context of narrative legitimation in *Le Différend* ('Notice Platon' p. 40; §156), whereby the glorious death of the individual is sublated into the story of the name (and the pronoun 'we' (Horatii, Romans) who call ourselves, each other and the dead heroes by that name), both Horace and Curiace know how to behave. Virtue and glory consist 'in dying the 'belle mort' for the furtherance of the name and the narrative.

Horace explains that in itself there is nothing very extraordinary about this; thousands have died in this way and thousands would want to (ll. 440–1). In the present situation, however, Horace will be fighting his brother-in-law to be, whom he loves; not just anybody, but 'un autre soi-même' (l. 444), and this makes the situation special: not at all regrettably, for Horace. If the law of the 'belle mort' prescribes a rigorous hierarchy of generic ends, and if it places the name of the state above that of the family and *a fortiori* of the individual, then the best (because most testing) situation will clearly be that in which the claims of the subordinated genres are the hardest to overcome. Horace wants to immortalize his own name, that of his family and that of the state: this is done by attempting to sacrifice the first two names to the last; paradoxically, this preserves the two sacrificed names all the better. ('It is true that our names can never die', agrees Curiace (l. 453).) In so far as Rome *names* Horace as its champion (and it is essentially unimportant here that Rome names three Horaces: the other two never appear in the play, and have a functional importance only when an incomplete report of the combat suggests that they both died nobly (within the economy of the 'belle mort') whereas Horace fled ignobly; the other two Curiatii are even less important), he *becomes* Rome and must forget all else – the harder this is to achieve, the greater the virtue; in normal battle one does not know one's adversary as an individual name: knowing and loving Curiace, it is all the more heroic for Horace to be able to say to him, 'Alba has named you, I no longer know you' (l. 502). And in so far as Curiace is none the less another self for Horace, it follows that he no longer knows himself, *already* dying with the promise of his name's returning as immortal through the logic of the *belle mort*. The name thrives on the death of its bearer. Horace has to this extent *already* won his battle with Curiace, who says quite consistently, 'I do still know you, and that's what kills me' (l. 503). This does not in fact prevent Curiace from going to fight, and for both sides to insist on fighting even when the armies they represent want to stop the combat. The complexity here suggests that both Horace and Curiace want their own death, even in the attempt to kill each other.

Lyotard's analysis of the logic of the *belle mort* suggests that it stifles the *différend*: if the *différend* is indeed signalled by sentiment, then it is quite accurate for Horace to suggest that acceptance of the 'belle mort' prescribed by Rome for the preservation of its name 'Ought to stifle in us all other sentiments' (l. 494). But if the stifling of the *différend* in the constitution of identity under the name of *Volk* and *Heim* entails *différends* in the *pagus*, on the borders, then it is also no surprise that the *différend* suppressed by Horace should reappear with Camille, the character we have identified as being constitutively placed in that region. According to the imperial genre (name, narrative, *belle mort*), Camille is enjoined by Horace, before the combat, to receive the victor, whether it be himself or Curiace, in all his proven virtue: neither should be reproached with the

other's death. Such behaviour is also recommended after the battle
by her father (le vieil Horace), and demanded by Horace again
when he returns in triumph. Against this genre, Camille reacts by
a systematic and perfectly consequent repudiation of names.
Already in Act I she has described Curiace as 'mon plus unique
bien' ([my most *unique* good] – Doubrovsky stresses the importance
of this: a Lyotardian transcription would suggest that this value of
the unique would demand an *absolute* propriety in naming which
family names do not respect),[11] and hastens, when Curiace arrives
in the space between the Alban leader's harangue and the selection
of the champions, to assume that this arrival means that he has
fled the battle, refusing to fight under the name of Alba, and subord-
inating his *renommée*, his renown (almost, literally, his re-naming as
the absolute representative of a collective name) to the particularity
of his love for Camille – only to find that when chosen, Curiace,
although admitting the attraction of obscurity over *renommée*,
announces that 'Avant d'être à vous je suis à mon pays' [Before
belonging to you I belong to my country] (l. 562), and that the
names of the cities take precedence over relation-names such as
'brother-in-law' and 'sister' (referring to Horace and Sabine), and
even that of 'fiancé'. Curiace is well aware of the threat to names
posed by love (in the state of suspension before marriage, as
we have seen for Camille), saying to Camille, 'Plus je suis votre
amant, moins je suis Curiace' [the more I am your lover, the less
am I Curiace] (l. 584). After Curiace's death, Camille violently
denounces the violence of a paternal name which makes of her a
Horace, forbidding even her grief for Curiace, and says, 'un véri-
table amour brave la main des Parques,/Et ne prend point de lois
de ces cruels tyrans/ Qu'un astre injurieux nous donne pour parents' [A true love does not take its laws from those cruel tyrants/
That an injurious star gives us as parents] (ll. 1197–8). (This would
need to be placed against her earlier argument with Sabine, in
which the impossibility of her position is stressed in terms of the
importance of paternal recognition of the object of love, that recognition turning love as 'tyrant' into love as 'legitimate king' (l. 922).)
Confronting the victorious and proud Horace, who is scandalized
to find Curiace's 'name on [her] lips' (or, more literally, in her
mouth), Camille denies her relationship as sister to Horace, and
defines herself solely as a lover – and admonished by Horace in the
name of Rome, she unleashes a famous imprecation (the first line

of which is quoted by Lyotard as an example of a possible *enchaîne-ment* onto the name of Rome (*D* §67)):

> Rome, l'unique objet de mon ressentiment!
> Rome, à qui vient ton bras d'immoler mon amant!
> Rome, qui t'a vu naître, et que ton cœur adore!
> Rome, enfin, que je hais parce qu'elle t'honore!
>
> [Rome, sole object of my resentment!
> Rome, to whom your arm has just sacrificed my lover!
> Rome, which saw you born and which your heart adores!
> Rome, which I hate because she honours you!]

(ll. 1301–4)

And goes on to look forward to the destruction of Rome and the last Roman – the extinction of the name, at which she could 'die of pleasure' (l. 1318), in a sort of paroxysm of *jouissance* in anonymity which would be a generalized figure of the anonymity implied by her love for Curiace, as refusal of his name.

Horace kills her on the spot. This too is a sentimental sentence which attests to the *différend* in the attempt to suppress it: for this killing cannot be integrated into the blood-and-name economy of the *belle mort* which determined the main combat. Horace himself attempts to legitimate his act in terms of an erasure of names:

> Ne me dis point qu'elle est et mon sang et ma sœur.
> Mon père ne peut plus l'avouer pour sa fille:
> Qui maudit son pays renonce à sa famille;
> Des noms si pleins d'amour ne lui sont plus permis;
> De ses plus chers parents il fait ses ennemis;
> Le sang même les arme en haine de son crime.
> La plus prompte vengeance en est plus légitime;
> Et ce souhait impie, encore qu'impuissant,
> Est un monstre qu'il faut étouffer en naissant.
>
> [Do not tell me that she is my blood and my sister.
> My father can no longer recognize her as his daughter:
> Whoever curses his country renounces his family;
> Names so full of love are no longer allowed him;
> He makes enemies of his dearest parents;
> Blood itself arms them in hatred against his crime.
> The speediest revenge is the most legitimate;

159

And this impious, though impotent wish [i.e. Camille's wish
   that Rome be destroyed]
. Is a monster which must be stifled at birth.]

                         (ll. 1326–34)

And when Sabine, his wife, suggests he might kill her too, for her
'crimes' and 'miseries' are equal to Camille's, Horace again appeals
to the name: 'Rends-toi digne du nom de ma chaste moitié'
[literally: 'Make yourself worthy of the name of my chaste half']
(l. 1349), and prescribes the stifling of sentiment the right to which
Sabine demands for herself. (Lyotard would no doubt find too
'anthropocentric' her description of the right to sentiment as
'human', as opposed to the 'inhumanity' or barbarity of Roman
virtue.)

But the manifest sentimentality of Horace's killing of his sister
cannot be so rapidly absorbed, and the whole of the last act of the
play is taken up with the attempt to negotiate it. This act is the
scene of judgement demanded by the *différend*. For Horace's action
reveals the *différends* which, under the name of 'Rome', had in
principle been controlled in an economy regulating the generic
claims of love, individual renown, family ties and public duty.
Camille is the sign of the possibility of the *différend* between all of
these orders: by killing her (rather than simply ordering her silence
as he does with Sabine), Horace spectacularizes the possibility of
the *différend* in a way which might in principle fulfil Camille's curse
and bring about the destruction of Rome. For as Valère, speaking
to the King on behalf of 'all good people' (l. 1482) points out, the
sentiment signalled by Camille is generalized, precisely because of
the shared family ties of Rome and Alba – everyone has lost a
relative in the war with Alba, and if Horace's triumph (in which,
as I suggested, he momentarily *becomes* Rome) legitimates his sup-
pressing of that sentiment, then 'Faisant triompher Rome, il se l'est
asservie;/ Il a sur nous un droit et de mort et de vie;/Et nos jours
criminels ne pourront plus durer/Qu'autant qu'à sa clémence il
plaira l'endurer' [In making Rome triumph, he has enslaved it to
himself;/He has the right of life and death over us;/and our criminal
existence can persist/Only so long as his clemency is pleased to
endure it] (ll. 1507–10). If Horace is Rome and demands that the
différend be suppressed, then he will in principle soon be the only
Roman left, in so far as Rome is shot through with that *différend*:
again the demands of the name will prescribe the death of its

bearers, and Valère demands that Horace himself be executed to put an end to this possibility of terror.

But if the demands of the name prescribe in some sense the death of the bearer of the name, then it comes as no surprise that Horace himself wants to die too: precisely to preserve the honour of his name. His heroic action against the three Curiatii seemed to depend on a rigorous subordination of his own name and his family name to the name of Rome: but the very heroism of his action returns him to his own name and its immortality in glory – this can only be preserved by death, for the chance to live up to the reputation created by his act will hardly be guaranteed: Horace fears that he can hardly be a hero every day. Horace's father, however, is dissatisfied with both of these arguments, and suggests (1) that Horace was justified in killing Camille in that she had cursed Rome, and that in any case it was an impulsive action and as such not a crime; (2) that no one need fear his extending such action to the Romans in general in that this was in fact a family matter – Camille's curse, though a crime against Rome, was none the less essentially a slur on the name of her family, and had to be dealt with as such; (3) that the Romans would never tolerate the execution of the man to whom they owe their name:

> Romains, souffrirez-vous qu'on vous immole un homme
> Sans qui Rome aujourd'hui cesserait d'être Rome,
> Et qu'un Romain s'efforce à tacher le renom
> D'un guerrier à qui tous doivent un si beau nom?

> [Romans, will you tolerate the execution of a man
> Without whom Rome would today cease being Rome,
> And that a Roman try to stain the renown
> Of a warrior to whom all owe such a fine name?]

> (ll. 1683–6)

(this argument is backed up by the idea that it would be impossible to find a suitable *place* for the execution: neither within the walls which only stand, nominally speaking, because of Horace, nor outside, on the scene of his action); (4) that he, the father, has lost three of his four children already that day, and maybe that's enough. Where Valère claims to speak for all good people, Horace *père* asserts that 'All of Rome has spoken through my mouth' (l. 1728).

This juridical dispute must be settled: unlike the litigation between Rome and Alba, which could not be presented to a tribunal, here there is a judge in the form of the king, Tullus, who has promised to provide justice (and implied that this is essentially what a king is for) (ll. 1476–80). Tullus rapidly determines what the issue is: Horace's suicidal urge is not considered, nor are the father's attempts to argue about impulsiveness and family questions. In terms of the law applicable to this case, Horace should die: no question about this. Horace's action is in this sense the object of a litigation – it has broken particular generic rules which can be reimposed. But here the position of the tribunal is complicated by the argument around the name of Rome. Without Horace, the tribunal would not exist because Rome would not exist – it would have become Alba. Although Horace's crime is 'great, enormous, inexcusable' (1. 1740), it was carried out by the same man, the same case, which has allowed there to be a tribunal, a king, and justice, under the name of Rome. 'Without [Horace] I would obey where now I give the law,/And I would be subject where I am King twice over [i.e. of both Rome and Alba]' (ll. 1745–6). There would be no law without the perpetrator of the case currently before the law. Tullus concludes that Horace's action places him above the law, and prescribes, from his position as distributor of the law, that that law be silent. Horace's being above the law places him before the law, as what makes the exercise of the law possible. The 'crime' can then, reasonably enough, be assimilated to the originary crime on which Rome was founded, namely the murder of Remus by Romulus: this originary (but already and now again repeated) violence must be dissimulated, as it is the condition of the name of Rome:

> que Rome dissimule
> Ce que dès sa naissance elle vit en Romule;
> Elle peut bien souffrir en son libérateur
> Ce qu'elle a bien souffert en son premier auteur.

> [let Rome dissimulate
> What at its birth it saw in Romulus;
> She can certainly tolerate in her liberator
> What she tolerated in her first author.]
>
> (ll. 1755–8)

How to judge? Lyotard used to define as 'pagan' a situation in which the obligation to judge went along with the absence of criteria according to which to judge. The critical judge, in Lyotard's transcription of Kant, has no code of law or body of jurisprudence to determine the judgement (see *E* pp. 17–18). The law for the case must be found, invented. But if the judge has no law at hand, it would seem that the possibility of judging is given, in the name of Reason: our task in this book (that of 'Judging Lyotard') puts us in the situation of having to judge the case which thus prescribes judgement without grounding its possibility: we therefore repeat the presupposition of judgement in the attempt to judge it. The name 'Rome' names an example (which cannot be just an example) of this situation. Rome is instituted in violence, out of the *pagus*, and this violence returns to question the institution as it defends it. In a brilliant article called 'Lapsus Judicii', Jean-Luc Nancy, wondering what happens when philosophy determines itself as essentially juridical, suggests that Rome (as opposed to Athens) names this very situation. The question of the juridicalization of philosophy is then, says Nancy, 'double and doubly heterogeneous': 'If philosophy is Greek, this is the *Latin* question of philosophy; if Rome is the dissolution of philosophy, it is the *philosophical* question of Rome.'[12] If, for Nancy, Kant is a repetition of that 'Roman' moment, then Lyotard is another, displaced, repetition of Kant's repetition.

In Nancy's reading, the oddness of the juridical is that it must take into account a sort of necessity of the accidental (in the form of the case, the event): he goes on to elaborate this question in terms of an essential fictional or fictioning activity of the law in its constitutively impossible drive to predict the case, the accident, which cannot be predicted as such. The law has an essential relation to the accidental. And, more crucially, at some point the law must attempt to take *itself* as a case and fictionalize its own institution or origin, stating the law of the law (as case). In the case of *Horace*, the law cannot take his act as a case, in that it precedes the possibility of the activity of the law in general: whether this be figured in terms of fratricide or not, it is clearly a situation of violence, if only in that it falls outside the law as the very possibility of its jurisdiction. In the paradoxical terms which Lyotard finds in any attempt to derive or legitimate authority (see *D* §203), the tribunal can only, as Nancy suggests, produce simultaneously a sentence or a judgement and the very institution of the law which allows that judgement to be made. To do so it has to absolve the violence which presides over that institution, and in so doing do violence to the justice made possible by that violence: this is Tullus's command to *forget* the founding fratricide and its repetition. This violent secondary attempt to erase the primary violence can presumably be repeated indefinitely as Rome pursues its imperial adventure.

Can this be thought of in Lyotard's terms? For him, critical activity is essentially an activity of judgement, respecting the case in its singularity, finding the appropriate rule always only after the event. This peculiar temporality, much more than any periodizing hypothesis, is in fact what constitutes the postmodern (which is anything but a question of dating).[13] But what happens when the judgement that judgement is what we must do is *itself* up for judgement? How do we judge, for example, the judgement that philosophy is the discourse that has as its stake the discovery of its rule (see *D* p. 12)? Or the judgement that the 'object' of philosophy is a sentence, because a sentence is indubitable (see *D* §94)? Lyotard would say, I think, that these questions are *already* philosophy in search of its rule. Nancy would argue that they imply that Lyotard cannot dissolve the question of being into sentences, in so far as any sentence presupposes this moment of pre-judgement, which Nancy, if I understand him aright, calls Being. Lyotard retorts, in a note on Nancy's article (*E* p. 17n3), that this appeal to Being, along with its corollary in the notion of fictionalizing, is to return to a problematic of origins (and, eventually, subjects) which we are better without – and this judgement of what is 'better' would argue from historico-political names such as 'Rome' and, more urgently, 'Auschwitz': but can perhaps do so only by prejudging judgement in the presentation of particular cases which violently demand judgement before there is time to judge. (The form of this problem seems to be linked to what can appear to be a persistent equivocation in Lyotard's recent thought between apparently transcendental claims and the use of historico-political names in the refutation of rival claims. This situation, which would demand new formulations of the relationship between philosophy and the historico-political, is perhaps programmed by the location of a logic of presentation which holds for sentences in general within a discourse which argues that there are no sentences in general, but only particular sentences, now.)

This 'pre-', this 'before' (which would have to be read with Derrida's notion of the trace, and its implication of an 'absolute past') is clearly complex, to say the least. In their opening address to the 'Centre de recherches philosophiques sur le politique' in Paris in 1980, Nancy and Lacoue-Labarthe name this 'pre-', 'provisionally and over-simplyfyingly,' *la mère*, 'the mother'[14] (Alba, then, in Corneille's terms: Rome's mother). Lyotard explicitly disagrees with this nomination, and proposes to think this 'pre-' analogically as *la mer*, the sea, the milieu of the dispersion of regimes and genres of discourse, the place of attempted bridge-building and passages (*E* p. 111). I do not know precisely the reason for Lyotard's objection: 'mother' can scarcely be criticized for being 'anthropocentric' in so far as it too can only be an analogical presentation – and is clearly neither simply empirical nor psychoanalytic in that we would have to presuppose the sense of this 'mother' in order to understand empirical and psychoanalytic notions of 'mother'. Is Lyotard, in the never-quite-instituted institution of philosophy as juridical and Roman, as refusal of the pre-eminence of the question of Being, in fact repeating the analogical violence of Rome towards its 'mother'? Is this a *différend* before the *différend* as described by Lyotard? Is this the possibility which allows for the exacerbated forms of litigation and *différend* which I chided Lyotard for not classifying and thematizing? Would this question, which I cannot presume to answer here, send us back to the first Horace's appearance in *Discours, figure*, to the postulation of the *figure-matrice* as the essentially invisible to be made visible, a sort of 'initial violence' of discourse and figure (*DF* p. 270), a sort of originary institution and transgression (institution as transgression, transgression as institution: this is, I think, exactly the sense of what Lyotard later calls, much more laconically, but perhaps more problematically, 'experimentation')? This moment is not a possible object of knowledge or judgement, but it is what, in *Discours, figure*, Lyotard calls the truth (see for example *DF* p. 17). Truth before any tribunal or judgement, before the determination of genres and regimes, before even the indubitability of a sentence.

In *Horace*, this 'truth' is ultimately referred to the gods, and will be dealt with by the priests, the *pontifices*, the bridge-builders (1. 1773). Lyotard's effort, in its impiety, will have been to prevent the building of *that* bridge. The question left open here, in its enormity, would be whether Being (however named) can be respected by a *judex* who does not need to refer to a *pontifex* to absorb that initial violence: and if so, how.

NOTES

1 J.-F. Lyotard, 'Faire voir les invisibles, ou contre le réalisme', in B. Buchloh (ed.), *Daniel Buren: Les Couleurs, Sculptures; Les Formes, Peintures*, Paris, Centre National d'art et de culture Georges Pompidou 1981, pp. 26–38.

2 This strictly speaking ungrammatical formulation appears for example in 'Réponse à la question: qu'est-ce que le postmoderne?' (*PE* pp. 13–34, at p. 27): Régis Durand translates this as 'to present the fact that the unpresentable exists' (*PMC* p. 78) – but the unpresentable is not a fact and does not exist. The more literal translation: 'to present that there is (some) unpresentable' has its own disadvantages, however.

3 Kant, *The Critique of Judgement*, Introduction, §IX, trans. James Creed Meredith, Oxford, Oxford University Press 1928, pp. 36–7.

4 Heidegger, 'Building, dwelling, thinking', trans. Albert Hofstadter, in *Martin Heidegger: Basic Writings*, ed. D. F. Krell, London, Routledge & Kegan Paul 1977, pp. 323–39, at p. 330.

5 J. Derrida, *La Vérité en peinture*, Paris, Flammarion 1978, p. 43; *The Truth in Painting*, trans. Geoff Bennington and Ian McLeod, Chicago, University of Chicago Press 1987, p. 36.

6 Norman Bryson, 'David's *Oath of the Horatii* and the question of "influence" ', *French Studies* 37(4) (1983), pp. 404–25.

7 Livy, *The Early History of Rome*, trans. A. de Sélincourt, Harmondsworth, Penguin Books 1960, p. 57. Further references to Livy will be to this edition and will be given in the text.

8 In that analysis of the 'integrative function', the 'myth of origin' referred to could of course have been, for Corneille, only analogically the myth of the foundation of Rome. I shall be ignoring this obvious fact, which does, however, relate to difficult questions around Lyotard's notion of *genre*: clearly the way the sentences are linked together in Corneille's *Horace* would have to be described by Lyotard as obeying the rules of the tragic genre: but, equally clearly, crucial sub-sequences of sentences are *also* linked according to the rules of other genres, as I shall attempt to illustrate. It is not clear to me how to describe this multiple generic status of certain sentences or linkages which is clearly constitutive of much of what we call literature, and this question around the far from simple relationships between discursive genres and literary genres is perhaps, for me, the point of greatest difficulty in Lyotard's recent work.

9 J.-F. Lyotard, 'Longitude 180° W or E', in *Arakawa: Padiglione d'arte contemporanea*, Mailand, Edizione Nava Milano 1984.

10 Serge Doubrovsky, *Corneille ou la dialectique du héros*, Paris, Gallimard 1963. I cannot here attempt to specify the differences with Doubrovsky's powerful reading of the play: perhaps the nexus of these differences is that whereas Doubrovsky tends to treat characters as subjects, I try to treat them as supports for proper names.

11 Any such absolute propriety is of course illusory. See for example Derrida's discussion of Lévi-Strauss in *De la grammatologie*, Paris, Minuit 1967, p. 164: 'There was indeed a first violence in naming. Naming . . .

such is the originary violence of language which consists in inscribing in a difference, in classifying, in suspending the absolute vocative' (*Of Grammatology*, trans. G. C. Spivak, Baltimore, Johns Hopkins University Press 1976, p. 112 (trans. mod.)).

12 Jean-Luc Nancy, 'Lapsus Judicii', in *L'Impératif catégorique*, Paris, Flammarion 1983, pp. 35–60, at p. 36. Lyotard's brief response to an earlier publication of Nancy's article can be found in *E* pp. 17–18n3, and Nancy's reply appears at the end of the version to which I refer.

13 'Postmodern is not to be taken in a periodizing sense' (*AJ* p. 34; *JG* p. 16).

14 P. Lacoue-Labarthe and J.-L. Nancy, 'Ouverture', in *Rejouer le politique*, ed. P. Lacoue-Labarthe and J.-L. Nancy, Paris, Galilée 1981, pp. 11–28, at p. 26.

8

PAGANS, PERVERTS OR PRIMITIVES? EXPERIMENTAL JUSTICE IN THE EMPIRE OF CAPITAL

Bill Readings

In characterizing Lyotard's work as providing 'a rationale for lying back and enjoying late capitalism', Alex Callinicos speaks for a number of critical sociologists and Marxist cultural analysts.[1] Horrified by the prospect of a paganism that leaves him nothing to believe in and everything yet to be done, Callinicos concludes that the benefit one draws as a reader of Lyotard is the indulgence of perversions; simply that one 'may now sample the benefits of commodity fetishism without a twinge of guilt'.[2] Paganism, it seems, is the old spectre of *fin de siècle* perversion and decadence. I want to argue that Lyotard's rethinking of philosophy as a process of experimental or pagan judgement allows the question of justice to be kept alive in late capitalism. Just as paganism is not merely decadent perversion, it is not the return to primitive mysticism that Habermas claims.[3] Lyotard's insistence on the radical heterogeneity of language games provides a series of hints as to the stakes in the complete 'overhaul' of 'the meaning of the world "politician"' for which he calls in *Just Gaming*.[4]

The case requiring the exercise of experimental or pagan judgement that will be examined concerns the relation between Australia (a modern republican nation-state, officially dedicated to the Idea of humanity) and the indigenous people of the Australian continent. A brief excursus, beside marking this essay as resolutely occasional, may allow us to establish the relevance of this marginal case, at the edge of the Western Empire, to the contemporary framework of political dispute.[5] The tensions attendant on the collapse of the Soviet empire in 1989 seem to me to have less to do with the social impact of rampant acquisition of consumer durables than with newly emergent nationalisms rejecting the claim of the Soviet government that Marxist doctrine speaks for universal human nature. A series of conflicts over the extent of federalism also marks the politics of the United States, the European Economic Community and India. These struggles do not have any common political agenda, nor do they translate simply into political calculations of progressive and reactionary. Thus, for example, the United States federal government at times protects minority rights against recalcitrant local practices of discrimination in a classic paradigm of Enlightenment, at times suppresses diversity in the name of universal citizenship. The dispute common to these problems is the clash between the metanarrative of a unitary state claiming to embody universal values and more fragmentary or explicitly local communities or minoritarian groups, groups which may seem either reactionary or progressive. The central state imposes a notion of abstract citizenship in the name of a narrative of the progressive realization of national (and ultimately, supra-national or human) destiny, erasing the specificity of local practices.

Such oppositions between the totalizing and the minoritarian raise a problem for the social critic: if justice is an abstract universal, how can it reside with the explicitly local?[6] Traditional political discourse suggests that social justice is an abstract model, a set of criteria in terms of which each case can be judged. As Lyotard puts it in *Just Gaming*:

> there is a type of discourse that somehow dominates the social practice of justice and that subordinates it to itself. This type of discourse is common to an entire political tradition (that includes Marx as well), in which it is presupposed that if the denotation of the discourse that describes social justice is correct, that is, if this discourse is true, then the social practice can be just insofar as it respects the distribution implied in the discourse.
>
> *(JG* p. 20)

Tactically, one may at times support the centre against the margins (over civil rights in the USA) or the margins against the centre (resisting forced sterilization in India). One may criticize the Soviet Union in terms of Marxism, or the USA for failing to live up to the condition of republican democracy. None the less, a model of universal justice conventionally grounds our arbitration of these disputes; one defends the minority against the totality only in the name of a higher totality, such as universal human rights. What is common to American liberal republicanism, European social democracy, Indian socialism and Soviet communism is an understanding of the nature of human society in terms of universal abstraction. In this sense, they all share a common 'modernity', proposing a metanarrative of emancipation. As Lyotard characterizes the stories in *Le Postmoderne expliqué aux enfants*, Marxism will reveal the proletariat as universal subject of history, democracy will reveal human nature as the people become the subject of a universal history of humanity, the creation of wealth will free mankind from poverty through the technological breakthroughs of free-market capitalism or the redistributive policies of state socialism.[7]

Lyotard's paganism consists in refusing to counter the evident repressive force of these metanarratives (the imperialism of modernity) with another, purer metanarrative, a new model. Lyotard's point is that such a model would itself be an imperializing abstraction, that 'the question of justice for a society cannot be resolved in terms of models' (*JG* p. 25). The claim to legitimate a prescriptive politics by appeal to a literally describable model of universal justice necessarily totalizes one narrative of the state of things and victimizes those excluded from political performativity. Lyotard redescribes justice as the task of responding to what he calls *différends*, points at which the framework of political representation (what counts as 'political discourse') performs a victimization ('a damage [*dommage*] accompanied by loss of the means to prove the damage').[8] The aim of this brief survey is to point out that *différends* occur marginally and occasionally because they are marginal to our ways of thinking about social justice, rather than because they are uncommon. *Différends* are singular, but they are not rare. If a *différend* is 'a case of conflict between (at least) two parties that cannot be equitably resolved for lack of a rule of judgement applicable to both arguments' (*TD* p. xi), the metalanguages of our modernity consistently propose a universal rule of justice or equity that silences any argument structured on other principles, any heterogeneous language game.

The structural implication of such victimization with the category of knowledge itself in the post-Enlightenment west is amply evidenced in the history of anthropological treatment of the Aborigine. Kenelm Burridge's *Encountering Aborigines* offers a straightforward example of the conceptual imperialism that dogs even the most well-meaning and tolerationist attempt to think about Aboriginal

culture within the terms of universal humanity. Using the Australian Aborigine as a test case for the history of anthropology itself,
Burridge eschews the imperialist myths of primitivism that animated the first anthropological studies of the Aborigine. His insistence on 'the reach into otherness' demands that we must learn
from the Aborigines just (or almost) as much as they from us
and he explicitly links the epistemological assurance of western
modernity (the assurance that makes other cultures merely objects
of study and the western man of science into an 'impersonal'
observer) to the road to Dachau.[9] Yet Burridge singularly fails to
perceive that his notion of common humanity is itself a product of
that very epistemological arrogance that the Enlightenment celebrated, that the notion of a 'common heritage' that 'we and they'
might 'come in time to share' is very much *our* notion.[10] In his
concluding sentence, Burridge remains an imperialist when he fails
to recognize that 'history' is an entirely western term, that it still
spells extinction for the Aborigine:

> as Aboriginal cultures melt into history, Aborigines have to
> explain themselves not only to themselves but to those others
> in the differentiated community they are joining.[11]

As we shall see, it is very little by way of differentiation if Aborigines
are only permitted to be different provided that they give evidence
before the imperial tribunal of world history. The argument of this
essay will be that universal history is not the ground of global
community but of victimization and terror, in so far as aboriginal
otherness is admitted only with the proviso that the rules of evidence of
western rationality and the temporality of western historicism prevail.

Thus, in turning to Australian Aborigines in order to illustrate
the pagan justice called for in Lyotard's writings I am not proposing
that the Aborigines offer an identity like ours, and thence a model
of paganism that we might apply universally. Rather, the *différend*
between Aborigines and the liberal capitalist democracy of the
Commonwealth of Australia illustrates the injustice. Justice in this
case will not be an abstraction that can reside with one argument
or other; the radical incommensurability between the two kinds of
arguments means that neither can recognize the other as an 'argument' at all. If I am to do justice to this case, a number of caveats
are necessary. First of all, within the terms of western intellectual
rationality, I am not talking about Australian Aborigines at all. I
shall be looking at the *différend* between the Aborigines and the west

as it is witnessed in a film, Herzog's *Where the Green Ants Dream*; this is a fiction of indigenous Australia, which I hope to use by analogy to Barthes's 'fictional Japan' in *Empire of Signs* – as much of Aboriginal life as a westerner can see.[12] As such, I can claim no more than to 'write the history of our own obscurity – manifest the density of our narcissism'.[13] That is to say, these are not 'real' Aborigines, an authentic other (another identity) to western culture into which westerners can transplant themselves empathically. Rather than an alternative organic community these Aborigines (who do not *belong* to either myself or to Werner Herzog) appear to us as pagans, or what Lyotard has elsewhere called 'the jews', an other to western modernity that haunts its margins.[14]

Paganism does not lie in a celebration of Aboriginal rootedness but in the fact that, whatever it is, the Aborigines' 'authenticity' or 'identity' is radically inaccessible to us. Keep the question open, imagine that I make no negative value judgement in saying, as I shall have to later in this paper, that Aborigines are not 'human', because by considering them 'human' (exemplars of an abstract nature that we share) we victimize them, make them more like us than they are. Their identity remains radically untranslatable, heterogeneous to western modernist rationality.[15] And yet it remains. It remains as that otherness which western modernity must annihilate, whether by murder or assimilation, in realizing its own universal dream. It remains in that the very energy required for its extinction bears mute witness to a non-identity, to the imperialist terror inherent in western notions of justice and humanity as universal abstractions. It remains as the encounter that Herzog's film evokes, an encounter which lacks a language that might phrase it adequately, an encounter in which language *encounters* silence rather than silence being simply language's absence (or vice versa).

Herzog's film centres on the dispute between an Aboriginal group and a mining corporation (Ayers Mining). It takes place at the edge of Empire, in the Australian desert, on a site which is at the same time central to the political struggles currently animating the west: the rights of indigenous peoples in the wake of Empire. In the course of the film a radical aporia in legal arbitration appears as a structural necessity of the modernist insistence on the representability of the human and the possibility of universal justice.

In Herzog's treatment of the Aboriginal in the face of the law, injustice is shown to reside not in accidents or errors of the political or legal representation of rights nor in a particular structure of political or legal representation but in the exclusive rule of representation itself. *Where the Green Ants Dream* shows that ethical responsibility demands a quasi-aesthetic experimentation if justice is to be done to an Aboriginal claim that can only be evoked as irrepresentable. The film, that is, simply does not make sense, if sense is delimited by considerations of representability (*Rücksicht auf Darstellbarkeit*, in Freud's term). And it is only by not making sense, by evoking what we may call the 'strange beauty' of the Aboriginal, that a sense of the injustice that is being done to the indigene can be preserved.[16] Doing justice is a matter of experimentation rather than of correspondence to models. The quasi-aesthetic strategies that evoke this aporia in the political representation of justice will be explored in order then to argue for a refiguration of the political, specifically one that rejects the universality of the human as a category. This is something rather more unimaginable than the orthodox post-Althusserian attack on humanism, where 'subject' reinscribes the very categorical universality that is denied to the liberal concept of 'human nature'.[17]

Before discussing the film in detail, I want to establish in some specificity the discursive co-ordinates of the modern state, which always aspires to empire by virtue of its claim to embody the universal will of human nature in speaking with a republican 'we'. Lyotard argues in *The Differend* that the notion of universal human nature, and the attendant imperialism (external and internal) of the modern nation-state, proceed from the representational structure of the republican 'we'. *Where the Green Ants Dream* is set in contemporary Australia, an effectively republican commonwealth. Whatever its *de jure* relation to the English crown and the historical traditions of British imperialist expansion, Australia has a long history of genocide that parallels treatment of indigenous peoples in the United States. The continued existence of the immigrant Australian Commonwealth after the dissolution of the British Empire means that Australia finds its rationale as a modern state in the Republican tradition, by analogy with France or the United States. As Lyotard points out in *The Differend*, the idea of the modern democratic republic is that of a people that becomes a people by saying 'we, the people', rather than by living together, or living in any one place, for a long time: 'In a republic, the pronoun of the first-person plural is in effect the linchpin of/for the discourse of authorization.'[18] In the notice entitled 'Declaration of 1789', Lyotard points out the links between the republican 'we' and the notion of universal humanity, 'the Idea of man'.[19] As he puts it, 'After 1789, international wars are also civil wars'.[20] Lyotard's analysis of the republican 'we' in *The Differend* focuses on France, but its contours apply to the modern western democracy, be it Europe, the United States, or Australia.

The claim of universal humanity inherent in the republican 'we' underpins the apparent paradox that a nation like the United States, dedicated to the inalienable rights of man, should be hostage to racism, sexism and homophobia, with a long history of genocide waged against Native Americans. American hatred of difference and fear of the other is so persistent and complex precisely because Americans believe themselves to be human. Theirs is not a tolerance of difference, but of identity, of the identity of an abstract human nature. Or, to put it less provocatively, they believe that they can say 'we', and that their 'we' will stand for humanity, that it can mean 'we humans'. The Republic declares itself to be the citadel of freedom and religious tolerance freed from monarchical oppression. The United States stands today indicted of enormous crimes of intolerance towards other cultures both internally and externally, from the repression of African-Americans and the near-extermination of the indigenous peoples of central North America through to at least the Vietnam War. How can the citadel of freedom have been built with the stones of oppression and imperialism, cemented with the blood of victims rather than of martyrs? This is no accident. It has to do with the way the Republic says 'we', from its inception in the phrase 'we, the people'. That 'we' has the effect of never allowing the question 'Who are we to speak?' to arise. The American 'we' is inherently integrationist – which is why anyone can become an American, why all Americans (and Australians) are essentially immigrants. This is why fantasies of space travel such as *Star Trek* are so compelling: the site in which the modern state elaborates the understanding of the human subject as essentially immigrant.[21] The Americanness of someone who says 'we' is not grounded in anything outside the act of saying 'we', which makes America a modern country. A republic is not founded in a common tradition but in a common declaration of independence from tradition, something which the facts of colonialism and immigration underline in the United States and Australia even more than in Lyotard's France. So republics do not ask where they have come from (no aristocracy of blood) but where they are going. The republic is the nation that is modern because it is going somewhere, that is headed towards a 'we' that will be the 'we' of humanity itself. Humanity in its essence, freed from any local constraints of class, race, creed, geographic origin. Universal humanity.

Lyotard notes the paradox of the fact that the republican 'we' is self-authorizing in part four of his Notice on the French Declaration of 1789.[22] The same logic applies to the American Declaration of Independence. When we say 'we, the people' in order to found a state, we presuppose the existence of a people who can say 'we', even though it is only the declaration of independence that brings that people into existence as a people capable of saying 'we', a people that understands itself as a community. The founding fathers didn't worry about this logical flaw because they understood this statement as something in the nature of a promise. The American state is dedicated to a proposition that it will be its historical project to bring into being: the proposition of a common humanity, the proposition that there is such a thing as a people out there waiting to come into being. Lyotard's vigilance reminds us that it is very dangerous to assume that we know humanity in advance, that humanity, or tomorrow, belong to us. We are never so terroristic as when destiny seems manifest.

The project of the republican 'we' is to build a consensus that defines its community as that of humanity in its freedom. As Lyotard puts it, the republic asks, 'What must we do to become ourselves', to become a freer, more American, more human society?[23] Our community is established in the suppression of difference and the revelation of the common humanity that underlies our various cultural and racial 'clothes'. The achievement of tolerance will be a consensus, the community of a homogeneous 'we', in which our association is grounded on our common humanity. But the question we don't ask, can't ask, is 'Who are we to speak?'. We cannot enquire into the 'we' that grounds the possibility of our becoming 'ourselves'.

Lyotard argues that the homogenous 'we' is not innocent, but that its union of the 'I' and the 'you' is the domination of the sender or speaker and the suppression of the receiver or hearer. Any culture that doesn't understand itself as a 'self', or as potentially human, is silenced, suppressed. No one can speak to republics unless they understand themselves as a 'we', a people – a different people perhaps, but a people all the same. All the same: a people united by being all the same, being people. As Lyotard reminds us, acts of great terror have been committed not simply in the name of but *as a result of* the presumption of a common, abstract, universal humanity.

Herzog's film is a minute example of the paradigm of such acts of terror, focusing on a small mining station called Mintabe.[24] Hackett, a young white mining engineer, conducts blasting tests for mineral deposits on behalf of the Ayers Mining Company. His tests bring the mining company into conflict with a group of local Aborigines who wish to prevent the blasting or mining lest the 'dreaming' of the green ants be disturbed and the 'universe world' come to an end. The dispute is taken to the Supreme Court, where the Aborigines lose. An extra-legal settlement by Ayers Mining apparently 'pacifies' the Aborigines by giving them a large green ant-like aeroplane (an RAAF Caribou) in which the tribal elder and an alcoholic Aboriginal ex-pilot fly off east in the direction of the annual migration of the green ants, apparently crashing in the mountains. Disgusted by the conduct of the mining company, the engineer Hackett goes off into the bush to live as a kind of hermit. The film does not explain whether or not the world would have ended had not the mimetic sacrifice been made.[25]

Where the Green Ants Dream can therefore be viewed as an attempt to negotiate with the terms of Lyotard's call for a quasi-aesthetic experimentation as the grounds of doing justice: 'let us wage a war on totality; let us be witnesses to the unpresentable; let us activate the differences and save the honor of the name'.[26] The film does not represent an other so much as bear witness to an otherness to representation, a *différend*. The task of witnessing requires, according to Lyotard, a series of paralogical experiments which displace the governing frame of representation. Such experiments are 'pagan' in that they seek to do justice rather than represent the truth in their interventions. If the problem of cultural transformation is that of how the weak can be made strong, paganism resists the Marxist piety which claims that the oppressed are really, truly, strong, and that we need merely to strip away the veils of ideological illusion to reveal the proletariat as historical destiny. There is no true strength to the Aborigines that western discourse can represent, yet a tendency to be exterminated is not the mark of some internal flaw. Paganism does not aim to represent the truth of the Aborigines, to show them as truly strong; rather it employs ruses so that their *weakness* may overcome the strength of their oppressors. I call these ruses, tricks and experiments quasi-aesthetic, following Lyotard's

insistence on the paralogical nature of postmodern aesthetic experimentation (as opposed to modernist aesthetic innovation).[27]

Don't represent the Aborigines; testify to their *différend* with representation as the voicing of an identity. The opening sequence jump
cuts between the diagonal slash of a conveyer belt and that of a
digeridoo, between the booming of a digeridoo and the grinding of
machinery, between the conical pile of the anthill and that of the
slag-heap. All of the film is wagered on the possibility that these
are not differences within a representational frame but marks of a
différend with representation itself.[28] Thus, the opening shot of Mintabe exacerbates the visual effect of heat haze to the point where
the filmic surface seems to buckle. The titles supervene, extended
in the two-dimensional virtual space of 'textuality' (as described by
Lyotard in *Discours, figure*) evoking the incommensurability of this
landscape of the green anthills with the rational discourse that seeks
to map and name it. This incommensurability is that of the *différend*
between the modern republic, founded on the Idea of man, and
the Aborigines. From the strange relation of the Aborigines to
electromagnets to the final sacrifice, the film consistently hints that
the Aborigines are in some sense closer to the ants than to the white
men. In making this comparison I do not mean that ants are or
should be in any way anthropomorphized, or that Aborigines are
animals. Rather, the western inability to consider Aborigines except
as animals or plants marks the obscurity of our pretended 'enlightenment' and the limited 'universality' of the western concept of the
'human'.[29]

The array of white characters in the film embodies a multiplicity
of destinies for modernity. Ferguson, the executive vice-president of
the Ayers Mining Company makes the claim of universalism, that
'what we take out of the ground was meant for everyone'. The
liberal capitalist claim for emancipation by means of the creation
of wealth is backed by a negotiating strategy in which communication and domination are inextricably linked. Ferguson immediately demands 'Who is your spokesman?', insisting that the Aborigines isolate an individual speaking subject authorized to produce
a republican 'we' analogous to that of the white man. When the
Aborigines reply by indicating that they have a group of 'tribal
elders' and 'a giver of song' rather than a single voice, he reminds
them that:

Until today we've lacked a contact, or at least one official

person to address . . . All of us, including you, are subject to
the binding strictures of the Land Rights Act of the Commonwealth of Australia.

This rigid insistence of the universality of the law of the white man,
in this case the law that claims to take note of Aboriginal rights, is
mocked when Ferguson plaintively demands that the Aborigines
produce someone authorized to sign for receipt of the aeroplane.
The Aborigines ignore him, just as they refuse the company's offers.
The litany of negotiation, in which Ferguson progressively raises
the stakes, charts the history of exploitation and assimilation of the
indigenous people. First, in return for the right to mine, the company offers technological toys: a pumping station and a school bus.
Then Ferguson switches to the strategy of assimilation rather than
robbery: a small percentage of profits. His final offer underlines the
link between representation and death for the Aborigines: funding
for an Aboriginal art museum. Kenelm Burridge's 'melting into
history' of the Aborigine appears clearly as an oppressive move,
offering the Aborigines the chance to turn their culture into an
object of western historical representation and a commodity for
exchange among white men.[30]

Hackett, the young geologist, figures the heroic phase of modern
capitalist man, the youthful explorer who conducts tests despite the
initial opposition of the, hidebound traditionalists of the mining
corporation. His general liberalism links the emancipatory or even
rebellious spirit of modernity to imperialist expansion. His main
companion on the site is a supervisor called Cole, who calls Aborigines 'black bastards' and makes Nazi jokes referring to Hackett as
'mein Kapitän' or 'mein Kommandant'. The liberal and the thugg-
ish faces of modernity are accompanied by an old lady, named
Miss Stralow (Australia?), who exhibits a naïve faith in modern
technology's capacity to find her dog, Benjamin Franklin, lost in
the mine workings. Technological invention proves inadequate, and
poor Benjamin Franklin remains 'out in the tunnel, in the darkness',
helpless despite the ingenuity of his namesake's epigones.[31]

In contrast, the Aborigines remain largely silent and impassive.
Most of their statements in the first part of the film are made in
their tribal language and then translated into English. As if to
underline the issue of translation, those who at times act as trans-
lators in turn require their own statements to be translated by
others. Like the green ants, which possess a susceptibility to mag-

netic fields and always align themselves on a north-south axis, the Aborigines seem to possess a peculiar relation to electronics, repeatedly causing elevators and digital watches to malfunction. As is later pointed out in court, their relation to time and number is entirely alien to the abstract enumeration that characterizes western rationality, evidenced in the following dialogue:

Hackett: How long have you been waiting?
Daipu: A little long while.
Hackett: Ten minutes?
Daipu: Yes.
Hackett: One hour?
Daipu: Yes.
Hackett: Since yesterday evening sundown?
Daipu: Yes.

The truth of each response marks a stoic refusal to conceive of time in chronological terms. Each question is answered in response to the immediate situation in which it is posed, rather than according to any commonly held metalanguage of universal temporality.[32] This is paralleled by a relation to space which is not that of the western cartographic tradition, which is not organized by abstract dimensional co-ordinates. Thus the land exists as an apparently random series of sacred sites or dreamings, which mark pathways in an ahistorical temporality.[33] Importantly, however, the film does not mark this alterity as a mystical identity but insists upon its otherness. Thus, the Aboriginal critique of western man appears entirely incongruous in its failure to evoke the organic rootedness that is the usual object of western nostalgia:

You white men are lost. You don't understand the land. Too many silly questions. You have no sense, no purpose, no direction.

The différend, the heterogeneity of Aboriginal to western argument, appears here in the very congruity of this statement with the western criticism of the Aborigines (who at one point steal transmission fluid in order to get high by drinking it). Each side speaks a different language, and the film refuses to identify the Aborigines as simply the inchoate or primitive opposite of the rationality of technological man. They are not an opposite, an other that the west might represent, they are different, irrepresentable.

This différend appears most clearly in the representation of the

Supreme Court hearing in *Where the Green Ants Dream*, on which I want to focus. The plaintiff and the defendant do not merely speak different languages, they participate in utterly incommensurable language games. As Lyotard's analysis of Auschwitz in *The Differend* establishes, the assumption of common humanity and the goal of tolerant consensus, which has universal human understanding as its horizon, grounds the claim of western liberal democracies that all difference can be overcome and that we can understand each other. Thus, if we are truly human, truly tolerant, then everyone may speak and no one will be silenced. Each community may speak a different language but all languages can be translated into each other so that understanding may be reached. The goal of republican tolerance, the tolerance of identity, is to find the universal language, the 'common law' of humanity that will arbitrate all disputes in reference to what is human, to what constitutes human liberation. The variant idioms of plaintiff and defendant will then be translated into this common language, this common law, so that a justice may be done which respects human freedom. Differences arising from cultural diversity are referred to the universal language of human liberty and freedom so that difference may be overcome.

In this case, the judge is a kindly old man who professes himself sympathetic to the Aborigines, and Herzog makes it clear that he is not biased in favour of the mining company. The injustice done to the Aborigines is not the effect of a biased white man's law. Rather, injustice is the effect of the very fairness of the white man's law, its blank, bleached, abstract humanity – its claim to be 'common law'. Common – both traditional and universally reasonable. That is to say, the silencing of the Aboriginal voices is not the product of an external censorship, a repression that we might denounce as unfair. The Aborigines are killed with kindness, by the assumption that they are the same kind of people as the white Australians; they are silenced by the very fact of being let speak.

The question of silencing structures the entire court hearing, as Aborigines are silenced in the very act of being ushered into court to speak. The scene begins with an usher, who calls out for 'silence', so that 'all persons . . . shall be heard'. The possibility of being heard depends on a dismissal of noise, of a certain multiplicity of voices that characterizes Aboriginal tribal discussions. There is only one kind of voice, the 'we' of abstract human nature discovering itself. And the Aborigines do not speak with that unitary 'we'; their resolutely ungrammatical 'we' marks the inception of a multiple patchwork of stories, what Lyotard would call 'little narratives': 'We're going to tell you about the land. The land that we is living on.'

During the court hearing, the Aborigines produce as 'evidence' certain sacred objects. But the sacred objects that will show and prove 'what the land is belong and belong to the land is' can only be recorded as an utter blank: 'wooden object, carved, with marking, the markings indecipherable. The significance of the markings not plain to this court'. Unlike the flag that Governor Phillips erected in 1788 to lay claim to the land at about the same time as the burial of the sacred objects, these markings are untranslatable into any language. They are inhuman, it seems. And their untranslatability is a structural principle: the court must be cleared lest they be seen and the world die (we never see them in the film).

It could be argued, however, that the Aboriginal markings could be translated if only we learnt the language. The heterogeneity of the aboriginal language game is underlined by the appearance of a witness known as 'the mute', Mr Balai-La. Balai-La speaks out of turn, and the judge is bemused because Balai-La was introduced to the court as a mute. He is 'mute' because he is the only one left alive who speaks 'his' language.[34] He doesn't speak any other languages, even if it were not a sin for him to teach the secrets of his tribe's language to a foreigner. He is mute because there is no one left on earth who can understand what he says. And yet we realize that he does speak a language, but one which we will never be able to understand.[35] The mute is the strong figure for the condition of all Aboriginal discourse in the court: the ability to speak is merely a sham. Just because you have a voice doesn't mean you're not mute.

In this dispute 'between (at least) two parties, that cannot be equitably resolved for lack of a rule of judgment applicable to both arguments', whose claim is just?[36] Governor Phillips raised his flag in 1788, around 200 years ago, more or less when the Aboriginal sacred objects were buried. But they weren't buried at the same time, since they weren't buried in the same history. The problem is not just that there are two different histories, one of 'discovery' and one of 'invasion', but that the flag is raised in western historical time and the objects are buried in a time that is not historical in any sense we might recognize. We are dealing with 'unthinkably ancient times' as an anthropologist witness puts it: time which cannot be thought by western science.[37] This is not so much because it is so old as because its cumulation is not organized by counting but by a kind of remaining, as evidenced in the conversation quoted above, so that even to try to write an Aboriginal counter-history would be a kind of imperialism. This radical heterogeneity of languages is replayed not simply in time, but in space as well.

Thus the Solicitor-General, appearing for the mining company, mocks the Aboriginal testimony that delineates territorial space by means of a gesture, or the phrase 'a little long way', asking sarcastically 'Can you please translate that into English?'. The judge's reprimand of this discourtesy does nothing to alter the discounting of the radical heterogeneity of this language game to that of rational evidence. These are not just two different concepts of the 'same' space but understandings of space that are in one case conceptual and in the other not even linked to conceptual abstractions. As the other anthropologist, the white man who dwells beside the Aborigines, points out: there is no abstract enumeration in Aboriginal culture, only the sequence of numbers from one to three followed by 'many'. Yet, he adds, this is not merely incoherent, since a cattleman will know at a glance if one cow is missing from a corral of six hundred or more.

It might seem therefore that Aboriginal evidence is funny. It's not obviously evidence. But common law is flexible: as the judge points out, enough hearsay may 'condense into a palpable truth'. After all, we are all human, and the dignity and eloquence of the judge is exemplary. But what is condensation, here, if not a form of 'abstraction', as Marx analyses it, the point at which sheer quantity is translated into quality, when material becomes commodity, when materials become exchangeable, when they speak the common language of money?[38] This is the structure of evidence in the white man's law, even when it doesn't conform to formal rules. Thus the judge's tolerance extends to admitting that the rough weight of speech acts, 'hearsay', may achieve a mysterious transformation into the supposedly 'universal' language of evidence – 'palpable truth',[39] but only by becoming universally exchangeable, palpable; the tolerance that admits Aboriginal evidence, that lets it speak in court, silences the Aboriginal in its translation. In gaining value as evidence, the Aboriginal voice is abstracted from its locality just as the mining company gives land value in abstracting minerals from their location. In order to become evidence, Aboriginal language must be 'mined'. And of course the voice of the Aborigines is an attempt to speak the land in a way that resists any such mining. As the giver of song introduces the Aboriginal case to the court, 'We're going to tell you about the land . . . the land that we're living on'. The sacred land, where green ants dwell. The green ants cannot emigrate. If the land is not there for them to return to in season, then they cannot return and the world will be destroyed. And the Aborigines 'belong the land' in the same way. Not belong *to* the land: there is no possibility of even a thought of separation or abstraction. They can't be transplanted, immigrate elsewhere. They have no *abstract human nature* that would survive in another place, anywhere else.

How then can this case be resolved? What 'we' can judge it? Each claimant is right in their own terms, and the application of a notion of universal justice, the appeal to an abstract human nature as the ground of a solution, is unjust to the Aborigines, victimizes them. The Aborigines 'belong' (to) a land which cannot be abstracted, transferred, translated (*trans-latio*, lift across, move, transfer); it is not a land *on* which humans live, which they exploit, but a land to which humans and non-humans belong in ways that cannot be mapped conceptually. To put it another way, Aborigines are not candidates for the next casting call on *Star Trek*. Abstraction from the land into a virtual space organized by rational co-ordinates (mapped land, legal property), produces death.[40] How can one (a knowing subject) begin to translate, to transpose and take away into another place, the chiasmatic interpenetration of the Aboriginal task of witnessing to 'What the land is belong, and belong to the land is'? It is a land that cannot be 'mined' for its truth, that is destroyed in being made 'evidence'.

Thus, the injustice that arises is not that of a simple collusion between the language of the mining company and that of the court. The mining company might as well be French, or American, or multinational. Translation would be possible, in principle, between these languages. Injustice in the proceedings of translation comes not from the fact of simply speaking a different language but from the fact that the language of the Aborigines is untranslatable into the language of the court, heterogeneous to the language of common law, of common humanity. An encounter takes place, it happens, but no language is available to phrase it, for the Aboriginal language is insistently local, rooted in the land from which it comes; it cannot become multinational. It cannot, that is, become modern: no one can immigrate into Aboriginal culture. Hence the white man who dwells beside the Aborigines repeatedly remarks that he knows nothing of their culture, insisting that the mining company should go away rather than assimilating to the Aborigines. The vagrant anthropologist who lives at the edge of the bush (or *pagus*), like Hackett who goes to dwell beside him, becomes pagan; he does not become an Aboriginal tribesman.[41]

The Aborigines retain their difference. The pagan tolerance of difference does not mean an identification with the other but an endurance of that unbearable difference without trying to appropriate it. The suggestion that all cultures are fundamentally the same is the trade mark of the imperialism of modernity, which seeks to erase rootedness and difference, to reduce everyone to a blank abstract humanity, a bleached-out indifference. To put it bluntly, saying that we are all just human is an act of imperialism, because it means we are all white under the skin. The last freedom, the power of the enslaved, lies in the refusal to relinquish the experience of difference to the cultural tourism of the oppressor.[42]

Hence Lyotard's paganism is not a politics of despair, though it may reject the confidence of political piety that has traditionally animated Marxism. If this is a loss of confidence, the confidence is that of the imperialist. Rather than a relinquishment of political agency, it is a chance to think liberation otherwise than as an abstraction into ever more splendid (more universal) isolation, a refusal to think freedom as self-domination. Lyotard calls for a rethinking of the notion of community under a horizon of dissensus rather than of consensus, a dissensus distinct from atomistic individualism.[43] The horizon of consensus is the production of a total subject who will serve as the end of narrative, whether 'man' (humanism) or 'the proletariat as subject of history' (Marxism). It aims at the revelation of a total 'we'. To ask, as I have done, 'Who are we to speak?' is not to entrench that 'we' more firmly but to displace it. To say that we speak radically heterogeneous language games (even to 'ourselves') is not a recipe for isolation or solipsism – but a thought of our interaction otherwise than in terms of consensus, unity and self-domination.

What this film portrays is not an incidental act of injustice, a casual imperialism, but the necessary, structurally implicit terror that accompanies the encounter of a people that says 'we' with a community that is not modern, that doesn't think itself as a people. Australia is a republic, however much the Crown is mentioned, and the Aborigines are up against 'common law', not an artificial set of rules, a code, but a law that bases itself in the understanding of a 'reasonable man', in a common humanity. The paradox that arises is that neither side is wrong. There is simply no common humanity between the two sides. Rather, it is unjust to the cultural diversity of the Aborigines to presume that they are human, that the law can understand them. It is unjust to think that they are human. What if thinking diversity lay not in affirming a common humanity, but in actually thinking difference, rather than oscillating between the poles of identity and non-existence? This would mean that doing justice to the difference of the Aborigines lay in westerners recognizing the possibility that their 'we' had nothing in common with them, that differences cannot be overcome either by our uniting with them in common humanity or exterminating them.

Thinking this multiplicity and difference is not a matter of fine-tuning the intersections of race, class and gender in order to liberate a new 'we' but a matter of rethinking what struggle and liberation may have to come to be in the light of the radicality of cultural difference. The acknowledgement of the opposition of the 'we' to cultural diversity means that politics, the play of dispute and difference, *doesn't end* – there is no universal community, no city on a hill. Or as Lyotard puts it in *Just Gaming*, 'there is no just society'.[44] It is very hard to think this, since most politicians simply want to put an end to politics, to argument, to dispute. Lyotard's acknowledgement that politics is everywhere, that 'everything is political if politics is the possibility of the differend on the occasion of the slightest linkage [of phrases]' means that politics is not about getting it right.[45]

'We' have no way of saying who is *right* here, the mining company or the Aborigines. No 'we' can pronounce once and for all on their dispute. All we can do, and it is a very difficult task, is to try to tell another story, after these two, one that doesn't seek to synthesize or assimilate them but to keep dispute and the difference an open question, that avoids the injustice of victimization, that doesn't speak with a 'we'. This does not mean resolving the dispute within the terms of western rationality but preventing its suppression, keeping difference in question. It is the difficult task of opening western language to silence (which is *not* the same thing as giving voices to the silent); it is to recognize that this encounter with the mute voice of the Aboriginal happens, although no translation is possible, although it cannot be spoken in any obvious sense, since language would only kill the silence in speaking (of) it. As Lyotard says, 'Let us . . . activate the differences'.[46] The struggle must go on, in order that the *différend* of the Aboriginal cannot be erased by the pretensions to abstract universality of the white man's discourse. This involves a guerrilla struggle to prevent totalizing abstraction, which is also a struggle in this case to prevent mining. Of course this is not because the Aboriginal land claim is *more true* in any simple sense. One can't clear up the question of who owns the land, since the Aboriginal way would be silenced even granting them ownership in 'our' terms (prepositional 'property'). Here, then, is Lyotard's paganism. It is not that 'we' have to learn to live with cultural difference; rather, an attention to difference, a living in diversity, explodes the indifferent domination exercised by the consensual 'we'. It is important to understand that in making this claim I am not simply providing a recipe for giving up the power and pleasure of the dominating 'we'. I am not romanticizing Aboriginal culture, or saying with Burridge that 'we have much to learn from them'. 'We', in so far as we think ourselves as 'we', cannot learn anything – for to learn in that way would be to perform one more act of cultural 'mining'. Rather, the force of their silent accusation is to make us ask 'Who are we to speak?', to give up the unquestioned assumption of our common humanity and to force us to think community and freedom otherwise. Ceasing to think community in terms of a universal 'we' gives us the chance to relinquish our enslavement to our own power, to transform a culture in which we only feel ourselves to be 'men' in so far as we silence what we cannot understand. bell hooks has pointed out that feminism is not a threat to African-American masculinity, but perhaps the only hope of young black men in an American culture that leads them to murder each other in pursuit of manhood.[47] Likewise, to struggle against ourselves, to attempt to think the multiplicity and diversity of culture without recourse to totalitarian notions of the universal, may be the best hope for avoiding total destruction in a world where the dream of consensus stands revealed as the nightmare of mutual annihilation.

The injustice perpetrated on indigenes is not a racism accidental to modernism which might be prevented by including them within a wider concept of human nature. Rather, the assumption of universal human nature, like all modernist metanarratives, lights the way to terror even as it upholds the torch of human rights. The problem of averting genocide demands a respect for difference, a deconstructive ethics, that is prepared to relinquish the concept of the human, to separate liberty from fraternity. Deconstruction rephrases the political, not by adding race along with gender and class to the categories by which we calculate oppression but by invoking an incalculable difference, an unrepresentable other, in the face of which any claim to community must be staked.

NOTES

1 Alex Callinicos, 'Reactionary postmodernism?', in Roy Boyne and Ali Rattansi (eds), *Postmodernism and Society*, New York, St Martin's Press 1990, p. 114.

2 ibid.

3 Habermas finds poststructuralism to be 'neoconservative' because it wavers between a decadent postmodernity or a primitivist 'return to some form of premodernity' ('Modernity: an incomplete project', in *The Anti-Aesthetic*, ed. Hal Foster, Seattle, Bay Press 1983, p. 8).

4 Jean-François Lyotard and Jean-Loup Thébaud, *Just Gaming*, trans. Wlad Godzich, Minneapolis, Minnesota University Press 1985, p. 55.

5 My usage of the term 'western' is cultural rather than geographical throughout – referring to the rule of European modernism.

6 The Eritreans are a good example of this problem for the Marxist critic. When opposing Haile Selassie, the Eritreans were freedom fighters, upholding the torch of liberty against capitalist monarchy. However, once the Marxist Mengistu regime was established in Ethiopia, the Eritreans became forces of ignorance and superstition, preserving oppressive tribal values against universal human freedom as incarnated in the communist government of Ethiopia. This volte-face is not simply the hypocrisy of *realpolitik*, it is the perfectly logical outcome of the privileging of a universal abstract model of justice. See also Kurdistan.

7 J.-F. Lyotard, *Le Postmoderne expliqué aux enfants*, Paris, Galilée 1986, pp. 53–5.

8 J.-F. Lyotard, *The Differend: Phrases in Dispute*, trans. G. van den Abbeele, Minneapolis, University of Minnesota Press 1988, p. 5.

9 Kenelm Burridge, *Encountering Aborigines*, New York, Pergamon Press 1973, pp. 6, 42.

10 ibid., p. 84.

11 ibid., p. 243.

12 Roland Barthes, *Empire of Signs*, trans. Richard Howard, New York, Hill & Wang 1979. As Barthes puts it (p. 3:)

> Hence Orient and Occident cannot be taken here as 'realities' to be compared and contrasted historically, philosophically, culturally, politically. I am not lovingly gazing toward an Oriental essence – to me the Orient is a matter of indifference, merely providing a reserve of features whose manipulation – whose invented interplay – allows me to 'entertain' the idea of an unheard of symbolic system, one altogether detached from our own. What can be addressed, in the consideration of the Orient, are not other symbols, another metaphysics, another wisdom

(though the latter might appear thoroughly desirable); it is the possibility of a difference . . .

I share Barthes's reserve as to epistemic authority, if not the infelicitous implication that the possibility of difference can be a 'matter of indifference'.

13 ibid., p. 4.
14 See *Heidegger and 'the jews'*, trans. Andreas Michel and Mark Roberts, intro. David Carroll, Minneapolis, University of Minnesota Press 1990. Carroll's introduction offers a helpful statement, as much of a generalization as is possible this side of totalization, of the kind of dispersal and heterogeneity that this lower-case plural word names:

> For Lyotard, justice demands that 'the people' be thought in terms of 'the jews,' that is, in perpetual exodus, both from themselves and from the Law to which they attempt to respond but to which they can never adequately respond. The community of 'the jews' is without a project for its unification (either in terms of a mythical origin or end). 'The jews' are an 'unfashioned,' 'unworked' community, a community without a single foundation or identity, a profoundly heterogeneous linkage of the nonidentical.
>
> (*Htj* p. xxxiii)

Herzog's German origins, and his long interest in the question of empire (*Aguirre, Wrath of God, Fitzcarraldo*) are not coincidental to this analogy; however, we should remember Lyotard's caveat:

> I use quotation marks to avoid confusing these 'jews' with real Jews. What is most real about real Jews is that Europe, in any case, does not know what to do with them: Christians demand their conversion; monarchs expel them; republics assimilate them; Nazis exterminate them. 'The jews' are the object of a dismissal with which Jews, in particular, are afflicted in reality.
>
> (*Htj* p. 3)

15 I risk the pleonasm of 'radically untranslatable' in order to mark the extent to which this is not merely a horizontal difficulty incidental to the translation between languages but also a kind of vertical impossibility of translation analogous to that which governs the (non-)relation between consciousness and the Freudian Unconscious. On the vertical impossibility of translation, see J. Derrida, *Writing and Difference*, trans. Alan Bass, London, Athlone Press 1987, pp. 210–11.
16 I draw the term 'strange beauty' from the lexicon of particle physics.
17 Thus *Reading Capital* replaces the 'young Marx's' humanist contrast of the free producer within a unified community to the alienated subject of capitalism with a distinction between the subject hailed to illusory individuality by ideology and the proletariat as universal subject of history. L. Althusser and E. Balibar, *Reading Capital*, trans. Ben Brewster, London, New Left Books 1970.
18 Lyotard (1988), op. cit., p. 98.

19 ibid., p. 145.

20 ibid., p. 146.

21 *Star Trek: The Next Generation* proves that even Klingons can immigrate (become human), as long as space still provides a trackless waste within which mankind may wander and which it may dominate.

22 Lyotard (1988), op. cit., p. 146.

23 ibid., pp. 147–8.

24 Since the film script is currently unavailable and the videocassette version of the film in the United States does not list the *dramatis personae* on the credits, all my spellings of proper names are approximations.

25 A similar effect, whereby what looks like myth turns out to be at least as 'real' as narrative, occurs at the conclusion of Peter Weir's *The Last Wave* (1977).

26 J.-F. Lyotard, *The Postmodern Condition: A Report on Knowledge*, trans. G. Bennington and B. Massumi, Minneapolis, University of Minnesota Press 1984, p. 82.

27 For a detailed discussion of postmodern experimentation, see chapter 2 of my *Introducing Lyotard: Art and Politics*, London, Routledge 1991.

28 It is worth noting the demand of paralogical experimentation in order to testify to the irrepresentable is a far cry from the more programmatic demands that Lyotard makes in 'Acinema', in *The Lyotard Reader*, ed. Andrew Benjamin, Oxford, Blackwell 1989. There he lays down a set of rules, a model for the destruction of the representational model. As such, 'Acinema' remains a modernist critique of film rather than a postmodern experiment; indeed, in many respects *Where the Green Ants Dream* fails to conform to its requirement of pure seriality of sterile moments of singular jouissance, whilst remaining a singular film.

29 Something of the force of this *différend* might be witnessed by pointing out that in speaking of Aborigines within the terms of western rationality, one turns for example to the language of plants in attempting to indicate their habitat-specific existence.

30 This risk establishes just what the stakes are in my present attempt to write about the Aborigines. The celebration of Aboriginal identity as offering a model of paganism for us would be entirely complicit with this move by the mining company.

31 Herzog gives short shrift to Christianity's claim to be the conscience of capitalist expansion. After an encounter with the deep mystery of the Aboriginal relation to the land, which leads a group to sit in a supermarket on the site where a tree once stood, in order to 'dream' their children, Hackett visits a mission station. There an enthusiastic priest teaches Aborigines to sing Christian songs saying 'I am happy' in English and Aboriginal language. The ludicrous quality of Christianity's claim to be a universal faith is nowhere more apparent than in the contrast between the minister's sweaty enthusiasm and the silent dignity of the Aboriginal 'giver of song'. The minister asks 'Can I help you?'; Hackett simply replies 'No, not really' and walks away.

32 This kind of discursive fragmentation is an example of the constellation of 'little narratives' by which Lyotard characterizes both the postmodern condition and pagan justice.

33 Bruce Chatwin's *The Songlines* Harmondsworth, Penguin 1987, offers a fascinating account of as much of the patchwork of 'dreamings' with which a westerner might come to terms.

34 I place 'his' in quotation marks in order make clear that this instance does not fall foul of Wittgenstein's argument against private languages; it is the language of the victim, not the individual will. Balai-La's words have always already been spoken elsewhere, in a time and place lost to representation. Balai-La thus corresponds to the opening question that *The Differend* poses to referential discourse, alluding to Auschwitz:

> 1 You are informed that human beings endowed with language were placed in a situation such that none of them is now able to tell about it. Most of them disappeared then, and the survivors rarely speak about it.
>
> (p. 3)

35 Nor is this case simply external to us, taking place beyond the margins of our culture, in the nether or outer, savage or primitive world. Freud named this the problem of the Unconscious: a force radically alien to consciousness and yet linked to it, which western rational discourse must seek unsuccessfully to excise.

36 Lyotard (1988), op. cit., p. xi.

37 The court hears from two anthropologists. The expert anthropologist produces a structural description of 'mata/mala' exogamic traditions. Another man, who lives in a shack in the bush, informs the court of the impossibility of understanding the Aborigines in western terms.

38 Karl Marx, *Capital: A Critique of Political Economy*, trans. Ben Fowkes, New York, Vintage Books 1977, vol. 1, book 1, chapters 1–3.

39 The judge refers to legal precedents in Africa and North America where 'Evidence relating to tribal customs and practices, though founded in hearsay, was given in such overwhelming numbers and with such consistency by the tribal witnesses, as to condense into a palpable truth.'

40 Death in a very real sense. Extermination of Aborigines continues today by the apparently 'neutral' act of gaoling them. Aborigines die in gaol not solely because of occasional brutality but because they are marked as individual subjects of the Australian commonwealth, 'free and equal' before the law, abstracted from the land into the virtual space of the legal system.

41 This vagrant anthropologist is thus a kind of 'métèque', the peripatetic foreign teacher with whom Lyotard identifies in *Instructions païennes*, Paris, Galilée 1977, and *Pacific Wall*, trans. Brian Boone, Venice, Los Angeles, Lapis Press 1990. Lyotard explains the distinction between pagan and primitive in *Just Gaming*:

> And then there is a third ordering that is popular, properly pagan, 'peasant' in the sense of pagan (and not the reverse): the people of the *pagus* (who are not the people of the village), who do any telling only inasmuch as it has been told, and under the form of ethnology, of folklore, with the idea that it is a primitive state of discourse from which we have managed

to get out by means of some well-known operations, basically
Platonic ones – I am thinking here of the (unsuccessful)
repression of poets and myths attempted in the Republic.

(p. 38)

The pagan is 'peasant' in the sense that s/he is denigrated with all the
force of the word as an insult in French. Yet s/he is not 'peasant' in
the sense that s/he dwells in an organic or rooted community, a 'village'.

42 By analogy, the feminism that really frightens men is not simply the
feminism that provides a coherent and exhaustive political platform of
articulated demands. It is the feminism that makes its demands felt
without ever giving in to the plea of the anxious patriarchy that Freud
articulated so strongly, 'What do women want?'. The partriarchy wants
to know that answer in order to (i) do away with the woman question
once and for all by giving them what they want – which can't be
everything; (ii) overcome feminism by forcing female desire to articulate
by analogy with the end-directedness of male desire – which is another
way of saying, show that women were men, all along, under the skin.

43 Lyotard (1984), op. cit., p. 81.
44 Lyotard (1985), op. cit., p. 25.
45 Lyotard (1988), op. cit., p. 139.
46 Lyotard (1984), op. cit., p. 82.
47 bell hooks, 'Representations: Feminism and black masculinity', in *Yearning: Race, Gender, and Cultural Politics*, Toronto, Between the Lines Press
1990.

9

LES IMMATÉRIAUX AND THE POSTMODERN SUBLIME

Paul Crowther

. . . one should see the quest for the sublime . . . as one of the prettier unforced blue flowers of bourgeois culture. But this quest is wildly irrelevant to the attempt at communicative consensus which is the vital force which drives that culture.

(Richard Rorty)[1]

In early 1985, J.-F. Lyotard organized an exhibition entitled *Les Immatériaux* at the Centre Georges Pompidou in Paris. The exhibition has, so far, elicited little more than polite non-committal reviews from the English-speaking art world. In this discussion, however, I want to consider some of the critical issues which *Les Immatériaux* raises in relation to postmodern art and postmodern culture generally. Specifically, I hope to pick out its shortcomings, and develop its implications in a direction which points to sublimity's having the kind of significance which Rorty (in the quotation at the head of this chapter) denies.

Let me start with Lyotard's own overall attitude to *Les Immatériaux* – which is that it should be regarded in its totality as an artwork.[2] This would seem, at first sight, to be very much in the vein of 1970s conceptual art, i.e. 'high modernism' (to use a term applied to Lyotard by Fredric Jameson). However, if *Les Immatériaux* relates to modernism it is as its *Götterdammerung*. As Lyotard points out, 'Its purpose is to introduce the visitor into the "dramaturgy" of postmodernism'.[3] Indeed, a publicity leaflet for the exhibition tells us

It's neither pedagogical or demagogical . . . Our objective is to rouse a sensitivity which already exists in all of us, to make one feel the strange in the familiar, and how difficult it is to imagine what's changing.

The basis of this sensitivity arises from the fact that in post-modern times, reality is no longer simply *perceived* in terms of sub-stantive, self-contained material surfaces. It is, rather, *deciphered* as the intersection of various complex levels of meaning. Hence the exhibition is organized on the basis of communication theory's notion of the 'message'. This involves the interplay of five factors: (1) the origin of the message (*maternitié*); (2) the medium of support (*matériau*); (3) the code in which it is inscribed (*matrice*); (4) what is referred to (*matière*); (5) the destination of the message (*matériel*). The many different ways in which each of these five factors is involved in our deciphering of contemporary reality is explored through a physical layout of thirty-one zones (some subdivided) yielding a total of over sixty sites. There is no one route through this labyrinth. Rather, the visitor is free to wander, wearing radio-controlled headphones which offer 'commentaries' in the form of music, poetry, literature, philosophy and other readings, which change as one moves from zone to zone. For the sake of brevity I shall describe only one of the five factors explored through this complex – namely *matériau* (the support of the message). The aspects of *matériau* considered include the human body, sexuality, the human form reproduced on video, maps, the raw materials of industry and new materials used in artistic production. What emerges from these presentations is that the surfaces which support the messages of contemporary life are unstable, elusive and undergoing rapid trans-formations. This is not *just* to say that technoscientific advances are transforming reality but that we are acutely conscious of, and made radically insecure by, them. As Lyotard puts it:

> The word 'human' as substantive adjective, designates an ancient domain of knowledge and intervention which the technosciences now cut across and share; here they discover and elaborate 'immaterials' which are analogous (even if they are in general more complex) to those examined and detected in other fields. The human cortex is 'read' just like an elec-tronic field; through the neurovegetative system humanity affectivity is 'acted' on like a complex chemical organisation . . .
>
> As a result of this, the ideas associated with the one of 'material' [i.e. *matériau*], and which lend support to the immediate apprehension of an identity for Man, are weak-ened.[4]

193

These remarks indicate the very essence of *Les Immatériaux*. Every familiar aspect of reality – even that of the embodied self, now proves to be infinitely analysable and transformable into a web of microscopic and macroscopic processes and relations (i.e. 'immaterials'). Although these 'immaterials' sustain lived-reality, they have hitherto been undiscovered or ignored. With the techno-scientific advances of postmodern times, however, they are thrust to the forefront of our consciousness. It is this awareness of infinite analysability and transformation which *Les Immatériaux* evokes, with startling success.

Now traditionally, an aesthetic sensitivity to infinity (or to the suggestion of it) has been understood in terms of the 'sublime'. This notion can (indeed must) be applied to *Les Immatériaux*, though I shall defer justification of such a claim until the final part of this chapter. Provisionally, however, one might say in relation to *Les Immatériaux*, that our appreciation of infinite analysability or trans-formability does not (as is usually the case with the sublime) arise from an encounter with objects which are, or which suggest, physi-cally overwhelming size or power. Rather it arises when our powers of perception and imagination are overwhelmed by the complexity of those processes and relations which make the surfaces of everyday reality possible, but which normally pass unnoticed or undiscov-ered. The sublime, in other words, arises here from a deconstruction of the familiar into that which normally functions *subliminally*. Our postmodern sensibility can, therefore, be aptly described as 'sublim-icist'. It is interesting, however, that, whilst *Les Immatériaux* itself unmistakably *points* in this sublimicist direction, and whilst the sublime figures crucially in Lyotard's philosophical writings on postmodernism, he does not, nevertheless, explicitly discuss sub-limity in the lengthy catalogue material of *Les Immatériaux*. This is particularly unfortunate, as the problem of the sublime lies, I think, at the heart of several problems and possibilities which the exhi-bition raises. It is to these which I now turn.

First, the question of art. Those works which Lyotard includes in *Les Immatériaux* are either very much in the tradition of avante-garde abstract/conceptual art, e.g. Moholy-Nagy, Flavin, Ryman, Fontana, Malevich, Duchamp, or ones which utilize new 'hi-tech' processes and materials, e.g. Stephen Benton, and Doug Tyler's holograms. What is *not* included are those recent (to use a very misleading label) 'neo-expressionist' works by the likes of Morley, Baselitz, Schnabel or Clemente, and which, of course, are generally regarded as postmodern. In relation to such 'eclectic' works, Lyo-tard has said

> they've lost all sense of what's fundamentally at stake in paint-ing. There's a vague return to a concern with the *enjoyment* experienced by the viewer, they've abandoned the *task* of the artist as it might have been perceived by a Cézanne, a Du-champ, or by any number of others, such as Klee, for instance.[5]

Lyotard's claims here are based on a general theory of the sublime and the postmodern nature of the avante-garde as such. His (rather difficult) argument proceeds broadly as follows. The modernist era dates from the Enlightenment onwards, and in art is characterized by an aesthetic of the sublime. In Lyotard's words,

> 'Modern painters' discovered that they had to represent the existence of that which was not demonstrable if the perspec-tival laws . . . were followed. They set about to revolutionise the supposed visual givens in order to reveal that the field of vision simultaneously conceals and needs the invisible, that it relates therefore not only to the eye, but to the spirit as well.[6]

Hence the modernist painter asks, in effect, the question 'What is painting?'. An experience of this sort of work is sublime – combining pain and pleasure – in the sense that through attempting to present the 'invisible', the painter is striving after something which, in visual terms, is unpresentable. Now the problem which much mod-ernist work is that this rigorous questioning of the nature of painting is not carried through.

> It allows the unpresentable to be put forward only as the missing contents, but the form because of its recognisable consistency continues to offer to the . . . viewer matter for solace and pleasure. Yet these sentiments do not constitute the real sublime sentiment, which is an intrinsic combination of pleasure and pain.[7]

However, there is an alternative to this 'nostalgic' mode of the sublime, and it is found in the work of the authentic avante-garde. In relation to the work of Cézanne, the Delaunays and Mondrian, for example, we are told that

> Their sublime was fundamentally not nostalgic, and tended towards the infinity of plastic experiment rather than towards

the representation of any lost absolute. In this, their work belongs to the contemporary industrial techno-scientific world.[8]

On these terms, then, whereas the modernist painter seeks to suggest the spiritual realm and ends up stopping us short at a consoling, beautiful surface, the avante-garde artist questions painting in a way that disrupts and disturbs, thus suggesting the (visually unpresentable) possibility of painting as infinitely developable. This, allegedly, anticipates the postmodern sensibility which *Les Immatériaux* seeks to evoke. Unfortunately, the difficulties raised by Lyotard's arguments are enormous. I shall confine myself to the following. First, it is extremely ironic that in his book *The Postmodern Condition* Lyotard defines postmodernism as an incredulity towards metanarratives, i.e. towards discourses which seek to legitimize themselves through

> making an explicit appeal to some grand narrative, such as the dialectics of the Spirit, the hermeneutics of meaning, the emancipation of the rational or working subject, or the creation of wealth.[9]

However, Lyotard's account of the triumph of the avante-garde's authentic sublimicism over modernism's nostalgic aesthetic of the sublime is itself very much an emancipatory 'grand narrative'. This means, in other words, that Lyotard's exclusion of 'neo-expressionist' work is, paradoxically enough, based on a persistence of *modernist* attitudes. Now in response to this, Lyotard might argue as follows. The task of *Les Immatériaux* in highlighting a postmodern sensibility is neutral rather than prescriptive – it seeks simply to *evoke* a change in sensibility which has already taken place. If, therefore, avante-garde works are included in the exhibition to the exclusion of others, it is simply because of the *fact* that they anticipate or embody the postmodern sensibility highlighted by *Les Immatériaux* in a way that the other works do not. This neat response, however, would not be consistent with the general high *moral* tenor of Lyotard's writings on art. In relation to those excluded 'neo-expressionist' artists who mix styles, we are told that such 'eclecticism' is 'the corruption of painting's honour'[10] and

> strips artists of their responsibility to the question of the non-demonstrable. That question is, to me, the only one worthy of life's high stakes.[11]

On these terms we must see Lyotard's exclusion of 'eclectic' works as based on the fact that they fail to satisfy the demands of *authentic* painting, i.e. the task of asking the question 'What is painting?'. This would mean that Lyotard's attitude to art in *Les Immatériaux* involves a conflation of two rather different approaches. On the one hand, there is an empirical theory about a changed sensibility founded on technoscientific advance; and, on the other hand, there is a prescriptive grand narrative about avante-gardism as authentic painting. Now because both these approaches challenge the existence of a status quo and point in the direction of infinite development, Lyotard assumes that both involve the same sublimicist sensibility. Hence, if we identify postmodernism with the sensibility of technoscientific culture, and if avante-garde painting shares this, then we are entitled to regard the avante-garde as postmodern too. However, Lyotard is, I think, mistaken as to the affinity between his two approaches, in so far as whilst the technoscientific culture of *Les Immatériaux* is indeed sublimicist, avante-garde painting is manifestly not. One might say that, whilst the radical innovations achieved by the avante-garde show that painting can be developed in an inexhaustible number of directions, such works do not, however, explicitly attempt to *present* this unpresentable space of infinite possibility; rather each new work simply demonstrates that the idea of totalized, 'definitive' absolute painting is nonsense – there is always something more to be done. This basic recognition involves nothing like the perceptual and imaginative struggle involved in trying to grasp all the aspects and levels of analysis offered through technoscientific approaches to (for example) the body. The sensibility highlighted by *Les Immatériaux*, in other words, is sublimicist, but the avante-garde works favoured by Lyotard are not. In effect, Lyotard refuses to follow where the deconstructive argument of *Les Immatériaux* leads. For surely, if the pseudo-autonomous surfaces of lived-reality are sustained by complex levels of immateriality, then we must expect this also to be the case with art, i.e. that its claims to authenticity are grounded on a complex interrelation of concealed social and political factors, and epistemological closures. This would mean that an art-practice which addressed itself to the deconstruction of art's supposed autonomy or authenticity would be very much in keeping with the sensibility of *Les Immatériaux*. Ironically enough, the works which do genuinely embody such a sublimicit tendency, and thus warrant the term 'postmodern', are the very ones which Lyotard excludes.

For example, whilst a great deal of recent 'neo-expressionist' painting is merely eclectic, its finest achievements are not. In the work of Malcolm Morley, George Baselitz and Anselm Kiefer, for example, convenient categories such as 'realist', 'expressionist', 'landscape', even the notion of 'good painting' itself are questioned and made strange. We experience 'art' not as a well-defined notion with definite limits and criteria, but rather as an insecure and shifting totality, where categories constantly interweave and are transformed. Previous to works such as these, 'art' has been easy to assimilate. A few paradigms of each ' -ism' give us the material for picturing to ourselves this whole domain of 'fine' art. The works of Morley, Baselitz and Kiefer, however, through their crossing of boundaries, involve us in a struggle to locate them. We compare and contrast to see how far they satisfy such and such a stylistic label (e.g. expressionist), only to find that through such analysis the label itself now seems flexible and of only relative validity. Thus the very moorings which hold our easy notion of art together are loosened and pulled apart. On these terms, whilst the avante-garde work simply demonstrates the *fact* that painting cannot be limited, the works of Morley, Baselitz and Kiefer involve us in a painful struggle that shows the very notion of art itself to be so complex as to strain our perceptual and imaginative capacities to the utmost. We thus have painting which is genuinely sublimicist and which exemplifies the postmodern sensibility of *Les Immatériaux*.

The second main line of critique which I shall take in relation to *Les Immatériaux* again involves a problem of exclusion. It is the exhibition's declared objective not to be pedagogical, demagogical or historical. However, without the politico-historical dimension, the technoscientific culture of *Les Immatériaux* appears as a self-perpetuating, self-justifying spectacle. We have a sensibility that is founded on the uncontrolled and *unquestioned* drive towards a technoscientific achievement. The questions which the exhibition explicity asks of the visitor (through the accompanying catalogue) concern only the nature of the changes taking place in contemporary life, and bypass the issue of their validity. However, just as Walter Benjamin observes that the aestheticization of politics ends in war, could we not say that the postmodern aestheticization of technoscience will tend likewise – in the direction of *nuclear* war? Against this Lyotard might assert the putative 'art' status of *Les Immatériaux* and claim that, whilst the exhibition might have political implications, these are for the particular visitor to assess on his or her own terms. *Les Immatériaux* itself attempts only the neutral task of evoking an already existent sensibility, rather than the prescriptive task of criticizing it. The problem with this response (a response which, I think, Lyotard is implicitly committed to) is twofold. First, it assumes that having the status 'art object' in itself is in conflict with explicitly raising political questions. This, of course, assumes the validity of the unjustified 'grand narrative' about authentic, autonomous painting noted earlier. However, even if we allowed Lyotard his grand narrative, there would be a further, even more glaring, problem, in so far as it is surely the case that the new sensibility which *Les Immatériaux* addresses itself to also pervades the political domain. By this, I do not simply mean the way that technoscientific methods have revolutionized patterns of political communication and determined the image of politicians, but rather the way in which new modes of political sensibility have arisen. Are not, for example, feminism, the anti-nuclear movement and Green politics all embodiments of an incredulity towards the patriarchal and alienated grand narratives of superpower politics? Are they not, thus, on Lyotard's own terms, exemplars of postmodernity? An inclusion of zones or sites alluding to these transformations of political reality, in other words, would have fitted into *Les Immatériaux* without disrupting its supposedly neutral 'art' status at all. We would thus have had a reflective dimension to counterbalance the sense of technoscience as uncontrolled spectacle. A space for asking the most *fundamental* questions would have been opened up.

The final critical issue which I wish to raise is connected with the above points. It concerns the question of what positive political implications we can draw from *Les Immatériaux* as a whole. In *The Postmodern Condition* Lyotard states that

> consensus does violence to the heterogeneity of language games. And invention is always born of dissension. Postmodern knowledge is not simply a tool of the authorities; it refines our sensitivity to differences and reinforces our ability to tolerate the incommensurable.[12]

However, this does not (as Lyotard thinks) in itself point in the direction of justice. For if specific language games and the forms of life grounded upon them have their own internal criteria of validation, and are incommensurable with each other, then participants in one game may well simply seal themselves into it, and respond with cold war or aggression to those who participate in other games.

Here the sensitivity to difference could lead, as Meaghan Morris aptly puts it, to 'a state of permanent bellicosity . . . where Might is Right'.[13] However, *Les Immatériaux* marks, I think, an important change from Lyotard's earlier position. The second volume of the catalogue, for example, extends the sublimicist approach of the exhibition to the purely linguistic level. Fifty or so concepts relevant to *Les Immatériaux* such as Body, Desire and Code, are considered by a team of theorists, and shown to have displaced and shifting meanings. This suggests that what characterizes postmodernism is not so much sensitivity to mere heterogeneity and difference, but rather a sensitivity to '*différance*' – in Derrida's sense of that term, i.e. the immaterials which are concealed by, but which sustain the pseudo-autonomous surfaces of lived-reality parallel those unstable and overlapping meanings which are concealed by, but which sustain the pseudo-autonomous discourses of the human sciences. On these terms, immaterials do not constitute absolutely heterogeneous sub-levels of reality. Rather, there are important overlaps and analogies between them, and the possibility of constant transformation. Now can a sensitivity to such *différance* point us more securely in the direction of justice? I would suggest that it can, if we rectify a difficulty in Lyotard's overall theory. The problem is this. As *Les Immatériaux* shows, our sense of reality has been defamiliarized and rendered insecure, through technoscientific immaterialization. What has not been shown, however, is why this should be found pleasurable, rather than *alienating* in the extreme. In relation to a parallel problem in his theory of avante-garde art, Lyotard invokes a Kantian notion of the sublime,[14] and it is something like this (as I suggested earlier on) which we need in order to make sense of *Les Immatériaux*. Unfortunately, Lyotard's adaptation of Kant's theory is itself problematic. For example, we are told that

> The sublime is not simple gratification, but the gratification of effort. It is impossible to represent the absolute, which is ungratifying, but one knows that one has to, that the faculty of feeling or imagining is called upon to make the perceptible represent the ineffable – and even if this fails, and even if that causes suffering, a pure gratification will emerge from the tension.[15]

But *why* should a 'pure gratification' emerge? Lyotard presents our reaching for the sublime as Sisyphean – something one has to do for no reward but the effort. But effort without pay-off is surely mere frustration. Lyotard, in other words, explains the negative side of the sublime's ambiguous pleasure, but not the positive side. Lyotard could attempt to meet this objection by saying that we enjoy the way avante-garde works and technoscientific change transform the rules of painting and sensibility, respectively. However, against this one must note that if the sublime is to be a distinct form of experience *sui generis*, it must be because there is some *intrinsic* connection between its negative and positive aspects. This is not true of Lyotard's projected response, for (on the one hand) to be overwhelmed by the infinite possibilities of painting and technoscience, and (on the other hand) to enjoy innovation in those fields, is, logically speaking, to have two *different* experiences – no matter how psychologically proximal their occurrence might be. If, therefore, we are to have a theoretically adequate notion of the sublime, we must – in a way that Lyotard does not – show some *logical* kinship between its negative and positive components. We must, in effect, argue that in our cognitive relation to certain kinds of objects, a deficiency in one aspect of cognition serves to clarify and emphasize the richness of another aspect; or (to put it in a different way) that the positive aspect *presupposes* the negative aspect in order for its scope to be fully manifest. Happily, Kant himself offers (in effect) a version of this approach. His basic position is that, whilst some phenomena may be so vast or destructive as to overwhelm our capacity to grasp it in perceptual or imaginative (i.e. sensory) terms, we can nevertheless encompass it in thought. We can even form an idea of infinity itself, despite being unable to experience a sense-perception or mental image which would fully embody that idea. Given this, Kant suggests that in such cases the very inadequacy of our sensory cognition makes the scope and superiority of our rational comprehension – the 'supersensible' side of our being – all the more striking. Our sensory pain gives way to a pleasure in reason. Now one might modify Kant's approach as follows. First, the idea of our rational being as wholly 'supersensible' (with all the difficulties that such a notion would entail) can simply be discarded, in so far as it is an outcome of Kant's broader, philosophically dubious, transcendental idealism. This would enable us to make the more modest claim that the inadequacy of sensory cognition to certain kinds of phenomena, serves to *vivify* the scope of our powers of rational comprehension. In day-to-day existence such powers are exercised more or less unnoticed. In the experience of the sublime, however, they are strikingly manifest, and this is the source of a profound satisfaction, in so far as through it we enjoy a felt transcendence of the limitations of embodiment. Now whilst Kant confines such experiences to vast or mighty objects, we can again modify his position to encompass those which are *complex*. Hence, whilst *Les Immatériaux* shows that reality is underpinned by immaterials of infinite complexity, and whilst, indeed, we cannot fully comprehend this complexity in terms of sense-perceptions or images, we can, nevertheless, conceptualize it *as* a surface sustained by infinite complexity. Reason races ahead and circumscribes that which overwhelms the senses. It is this vivification and affirmation of our rationality which overcomes the possibility of alienation.

Given this analysis, then, the sublimicist sensibility of *Les Immatériaux* emerges as the source of an *aesthetic* pleasure. We can describe it in these terms because, on the one hand, it is fundamentally a kind of vigorous 'play' between two different aspects of cognition, and, on the other hand, it is the kind of thing which can be enjoyed for its own sake – rather than for its practical or theoretical utility in relation to the life-world. This latter feature, of course, is usually labelled as 'disinterestedness'. Now the fact that such an experience is disinterested in terms of its logical grounds does not prevent it from having, in certain contexts, a further, more practical significance. (It is, indeed, a failure to realize this which accounts for the current hostility to notions of the aesthetic, felt by many contemporary theorists of postmodernism.) For example, suppose the sublimicist sensibility is brought to bear diachronically and synchronically on notions of socio-political import, such as that of 'community'. In relation to the first of these aspects, the sublimicist sensibility would regard any given community as a surface of only provisional validity. It would try (and fail) to imagine all the historical transformations which brought the community to its present stage, and all the realistic transformations which it might possibly undergo. From the synchronic viewpoint, such a sensibility would attempt (and again fail) to perceive or imagine all the individuals and groupings in the community with their different and sometimes changing experiences and interests. Now although in both cases sensory cognition is overwhelmed by the data it seeks to grasp, our possession of the *idea* of the community – our capacity to grasp it in rational terms – is made all the more vivid and thereby pleasurable. The side-effects of such sublimicizing are rather interesting. First, in even attempting to grasp the diachronic and synchronic complexities of community existence, we are sensitizing ourselves to its transformatory possibilities, and to the nature of its unstable diversities. Indeed, the fact that such a politically useful sensitization arises in the context of an aesthetic project, i.e. one that is disinterested, means that our own partiality to particular transformations and groupings will not have as much sway as it would if we had undertaken the project for the *explicit* purpose of sociopolitical understanding. It may, in other words, teach us to be fairer in our political judgements. Similarly, whilst we may attempt to view the community diachronically and synchronically in the way described as part of our ordinary political praxis, the difficulty of the task may simply frustrate us – thus leading to despair or dogmatism, or even violence. However, as part of a sublimicist experience, our sensory cognition's inadequacies lead on to a pleasure in our rationality. This means, of course, that the generation of such politically significant awareness, in a pleasurable aesthetic context rather than through the frustrating hurly-burly of politics itself, will provide an incentive for cultivating and deepening such awareness which might otherwise be lacking. Given these facts, one might hope and expect that through the sublimicization of political contexts, the aesthetic factor will help develop a political sensibility that is more deeply aware of possible transformations of existing society, yet, at the same time, is averse to solutions that violently erase the different interests of groups and individuals. Sublimicism, in other words, can point towards, and prepare us for, critical tolerance. Such tolerance, of course, is an essential feature of any notion of justice or consensus.

In conclusion, I would briefly like to relate the foregoing argument to a broader debate. Jürgen Habermas has suggested that the problems of modernity can in part be resolved through a reintegration of aesthetic experience with the life-world. As he puts it:

> as soon as such an experience is used to illustrate a life-historical situation and life problems, it enters into a language-game which is no longer that of the aesthetic critic. The aesthetic experience then not only renews the interpretation of our needs in whose light we perceive the world. It permeates as well our cognitive significations and our normative expectations and changes the manner in which all these refer to one another.[16]

Now, as Martin Jay has pointed out,[17] Habermas does not really clarify what form such a reintegrative project might take. What Habermas *is* sure of, however, is that the deconstructive postmodern approach will not help, in so far as

> Nothing remains from a de-sublimated meaning, or a destructured form; an emancipatory effect does not follow.[18]

Against this I would claim that the sublimicist sensibility highlighted by *Les Immatériaux* not only has an emancipatory effect through its affirmation of reason but that it can make a substantial contribution to precisely that reintegrative task which Habermas specifies in the passage quoted before last. For as I have shown sublimicist pleasure not only arises from the impact of technoscience, but has grounds which are distinctively aesthetic in character, and which are yet able, in the right context, to promote deeper political awareness. However, it is important as a final point to qualify this optimism, by a reiteration of the second critical issue which I raised in relation to *Les Immatériaux*. Left to itself as an unquestioned, self-justifying drive, the sublimicist aestheticization of technoscience will tend towards nuclear war. This is why it must be accompanied by a sharpened political consciousness – towards which, as I have attempted to show, a sublimicist sensibility can actively contribute. In this latter respect, of course, it has hitherto been left to fascism and the authoritarian right to aestheticize the mere means of political expression and repression, through their mass parades and glorifications of warfare. Sublimicist aestheticization, in contrast, would involve the deconstructive interrogation of socio-political reality itself, thus favouring a sensibility of critical tolerance. Aesthetics could, thereby, be returned to the life-world, but this time by, and into, the right hands.[19]

NOTES

1 Richard Rorty, 'Habermas and Lyotard on modernity', included in Richard J. Bernstein (ed.), *Habermas and Modernity*, Oxford, Blackwell 1985, pp. 161–75, at p. 174.

2 See, for example, Bernard Blistene's interview with Lyotard, in *Flash Art* 121 (March 1985).

3 'Les Immatériaux: an interview with Jean-François Lyotard' (in French), *CNAC Magazine* 26 (March–April 1985), pp. 12–16, at p. 13.

4 J.-F. Lyotard, 'Les Immatériaux', trans. Paul Smith, *Art and Text* 17 (April 1985), pp. 47–57, at p. 49.

5 Blistene's interview with Lyotard (1985), op. cit.

6 J.-F. Lyotard, 'Presenting the unpresentable: the sublime', *Artforum* (April 1982), pp. 64–9, at p. 67.

7 J.-F. Lyotard, *The Postmodern Condition: A Report on Knowledge*, trans. Geoff Bennington and Brian Massumi, Manchester, Manchester University Press 1984, p. 81.

8 Lyotard (1982), op. cit., p. 68.

9 Lyotard (1984), op. cit., p. xxiii.

10 Lyotard (1982), op. cit., p. 69.

11 ibid., p. 69.

12 Lyotard (1984), op. cit., p. xxv.

13 Meaghan Morris, 'Postmodernity and Lyotard's sublime', *Art and Text* 16 (Summer 1984), pp. 44–67, at p. 53.

14 In his paper 'The sublime and the avante-garde', *Artforum* (April 1984), pp. 36–43, Lyotard also invokes Burke's theory of the sublime in relation to avante-garde art. His basic idea is that such art is fundamentally an event – a shock which affirms the Moment, in a way that allays our fear of all moments coming to an end. Whether this existential sense can be tied to Burke's theory of the sublime or not is a question I shall explore elsewhere. In any case, given the technoscientific and epistemological orientation of *Les Immatériaux*, it is Kant's theory of the sublime which is more immediately relevant.

15 Lyotard (1982), op. cit., p. 68.

16 Jürgen Habermas, 'Modernity – an incomplete project', in *Postmodern Culture*, ed. Hal Foster, London, Pluto Press 1984, pp. 3–15, at p. 13.

17 In his essay 'Habermas and modernism', in Richard J. Bernstein (ed.), *Habermas and Modernity*, Oxford, Basil Blackwell 1985, pp. 125–39; see especially p. 133.

18 Habermas (1984), op. cit., p. 11.

19 My thanks are owed to Juliet Simpson for her advice in the writing of this paper.

INDEX

206

48, 63, 90, 116, 119, 203–4; criticized, 47; discussed 99–112; *see also* individual works

Hegel, G. W. F., 44, 63, 93, 100, 101–3, 116, 134

Heidegger, Martin, 10, 78–9, 140, 148

Herzog, Werner, film discussed, 171–3, 176–86

history, 121, 131, 140, 152, 181; universal, 171

Hobbes, Thomas, 5, 129

honour, 3

Horace (Corneille), 149–51, 149–65

Horace (from Corneille), 154–62

Horace, *see* Flaccus, Quintus Horatius

Horatius (from Livy), 147–8, 151, 154

human, 193

Human Condition, The (Arendt), 128

humanity, 174–5, 177

Hume, David, 12

Husserl, Edmund, 23

I, 20–2

Idea/s, 5, 11, 21, 23, 34, 47, 50–2, 53, 58, 65, 70, 71, 73, 74; discussed, 17–20; of freedom, 8–9, 59; general, 56; of humanity, 168; of justice, 60–1; of man, 173, 177; of nature, 138; of plurality, 61; of reason, 8, 62, 129; unitary finality, 60; of unity, 69

identity, 37, 172

Ideology of the Aesthetic, The (Eagleton), 44

ideology/ies, 89, 91

illusion, transcendental, 47, 63, 78, 104, 106, 107, 136

imagination, 16, 21, 79, 124, 131–2, 194

Industrial Revolution, 126

infinite/infinity, 51, 194, 201

injustice, 183, 184

'Introduction à une étude du politique selon Kant' (Lyotard), 45, 71

Jameson, Fredric, 97

Jay, Martin, 204

jews, 172, 188

Joyce, James, 51

judgement, 16, 18, 56, 64–6, 67–8, 71–2, 74, 76, 77, 143, 152, 155, 163, 164; aesthetic, 49, 120, 123, 124, 130, 132; analysis, 11; classical, 134; cognitive, 47; comparisons, 17, 23; concepts given to, 3–4; determinant, 123; discussed, 119–40; distinctions, 59; faculty of, 6–7, 9; implications of theory, 135–41; necessity, 48; normative basis, 144; procedure, 73; reflective, 54, 71, 123, 134, 141; teleological, 71, 130

Just Gaming (Lyotard), 110, 111, 168, 169, 185, 190; discussed, 43–4, 53, 56–62, 68–9, 71

justice, 26, 27, 33–4, 35, 56, 57, 58, 60–1, 90, 100, 107, 138, 176, 188; as abstraction, 171; conception, 31; general notion, 48; principles, 28–9; universal model, 169–70; *see also* injustice

Kant, Immanuel, 1, 3, 5, 6, 14–15, 17, 23–4, 34, 44, 50, 54, 56, 58, 59, 62, 95, 147, 163, 200, 201; discussed, 46–7, 49–51, 53, 56, 58–60, 62–77, 100–1, 113–14; and judgement, 121–5, 128, 129–30, 132–8, 140; renewed interest in, 119–20; on taste 46; *see also* individual works

Kelsen, Hans, 95

Kiefer, Anselm, 198

knowledge, 8, 12, 13, 18, 22, 43, 57, 58–9, 59, 62, 70, 87, 100, 107–9, 113, 123, 193; and pleasure, 7; postmodern, 90; space-time, 2–3

Knowledge and Human Interests (Habermas), 103

L'Economie libidinale (Lyotard), 91

L'Enthousiasme: la critique kantienne de